Juliana H. G. Ewing

Jan of the windmill;

A story of the plains - Vol. 2

Juliana H. G. Ewing

Jan of the windmill;
A story of the plains - Vol. 2

ISBN/EAN: 9783337821012

Printed in Europe, USA, Canada, Australia, Japan

Cover: Foto ©ninafisch / pixelio.de

More available books at **www.hansebooks.com**

Jan of the Windmill.

A Story of the Plains.

BY

JULIANA HORATIA EWING,
AUTHOR OF "SIX TO SIXTEEN."

BOSTON:
ROBERTS BROTHERS.
1887.

Dedicated

TO MY DEAR SISTER

MARGARET.

J. H. E.

CONTENTS.

CHAPTER I.
THE WINDMILLER'S WIFE. — STRANGERS. — TEN SHILLINGS A WEEK. — THE LITTLE JAN **1**

CHAPTER II.
THE MILLER'S CALCULATIONS. — HIS HOPES AND FEARS. — THE NURSE-BOY. — CALM **14**

CHAPTER III.
THE WINDMILLER'S WORDS COME TRUE. — THE RED SHAWL. — IN THE CLOUDS. — NURSING *v.* PIG-MINDING. — THE ROUND-HOUSE. — THE MILLER'S THUMB **20**

CHAPTER IV.
BLACK AS SLANS. — VAIR AND VOOLISH. — THE MILLER AND HIS MAN **27**

CHAPTER V.
THE POCKET-BOOK AND THE FAMILY BIBLE. — FIVE POUNDS' REWARD **33**

CHAPTER VI.
GEORGE GOES COURTING. — GEORGE AS AN ENEMY. — GEORGE AS A FRIEND. — ABEL PLAYS SCHOOLMASTER. — THE LOVE-LETTER. — MOERDYK. — THE MILLER-MOTH. — AN ANCIENT DITTY **38**

CHAPTER VII.

ABEL GOES TO SCHOOL AGAIN. — DAME DATCHETT. — A COLUMN OF SPELLING. — ABEL PLAYS MOOCHER. — THE MILLER'S MAN CANNOT MAKE UP HIS MIND 49

CHAPTER VIII.

VISITORS AT THE MILL. — A WINDMILLER OF THE THIRD GENERATION. — CURE FOR WHOOPING-COUGH. — MISS AMABEL ADELINE AMMABY. — DOCTORS DISAGREE 54

CHAPTER IX.

GENTRY BORN. — LEARNING LOST. — JAN'S BEDFELLOW. — AMABEL 63

CHAPTER X.

ABEL AT HOME. — JAN OBJECTS TO THE MILLER'S MAN. — THE ALPHABET. — THE CHEAP JACK. — "PITCHERS" . . 66

CHAPTER XI.

SCARECROWS AND MEN. — JAN REFUSES TO "MAKE GEARGE." — UNCANNY. — "JAN'S OFF." — THE MOON AND THE CLOUDS 77

CHAPTER XII.

THE WHITE HORSE. — COMROGUES. — MOERDYK. — GEORGE CONFIDES IN THE CHEAP JACK — WITH RESERVATION . 84

CHAPTER XIII.

GEORGE AS A MONEYED MAN. — SAL. — THE "WHITE HORSE." — THE WEDDING. — THE WINDMILLER'S WIFE FORGETS, AND REMEMBERS TOO LATE 91

CHAPTER XIV.

SUBLUNARY ART. — JAN GOES TO SCHOOL. — DAME DATCHETT AT HOME. — JAN'S FIRST SCHOOL SCRAPE. — JAN DEFENDS HIMSELF. 98

CHAPTER XV.

WILLUM GIVES JAN SOME ADVICE. — THE CLOCK FACE. — THE HORNET AND THE DAME. — JAN DRAWS PIGS. — JAN AND HIS PATRONS. — KITTY CHUTER. — THE FIGHT. — MASTER CHUTER'S PREDICTION 104

CHAPTER XVI.

THE MOP. — THE SHOP. — WHAT THE CHEAP JACK'S WIFE HAD TO TELL. — WHAT GEORGE WITHHELD 118

CHAPTER XVII.

THE MILLER'S MAN AT THE MOP. — A LIVELY COMPANION. — SAL LOSES HER PURSE. — THE RECRUITING SERGEANT. — THE POCKET-BOOK TWICE STOLEN. — GEORGE IN THE KING'S ARMS. — GEORGE IN THE KING'S SERVICE. — THE LETTER CHANGES HANDS, BUT KEEPS ITS SECRET . 127

CHAPTER XVIII.

MIDSUMMER HOLIDAYS. — CHILD FANCIES. — JAN AND THE PIG-MINDER. — MASTER SALTER AT HOME. — JAN HIRES HIMSELF OUT 137

CHAPTER XIX.

THE BLUE COAT. — PIG-MINDING AND TREE-STUDYING. — LEAF-PAINTINGS. — A STRANGER. — MASTER SWIFT IS DISAPPOINTED 143

CHAPTER XX.

SQUIRE AMMABY AND HIS DAUGHTER. — THE CHEAP JACK DOES BUSINESS ONCE MORE. — THE WHITE HORSE CHANGES MASTERS 154

CHAPTER XXI.

MASTER SWIFT AT HOME. — RUFUS. — THE EX-PIG-MINDER. — JAN AND THE SCHOOLMASTER 161

CHAPTER XXII.

THE PARISH CHURCH. — REMBRANDT. — THE SNOW SCENE. — MASTER SWIFT'S AUTOBIOGRAPHY 168

CHAPTER XXIII.

THE WHITE HORSE IN CLOVER. — AMABEL AND HER GUARDIANS. — AMABEL IN THE WOOD. — BOGY 179

CHAPTER XXIV.

THE PAINT-BOX. — MASTER LINSEED'S SHOP. — THE NEW SIGN-BOARD. — MASTER SWIFT AS WILL SCARLET . . . 188

CHAPTER XXV.

SANITARY INSPECTORS. — THE PESTILENCE. — THE PARSON. — THE DOCTOR. — THE SQUIRE AND THE SCHOOLMASTER. — DESOLATION AT THE WINDMILL. — THE SECOND ADVENT 195

CHAPTER XXVI.

THE BEASTS OF THE VILLAGE. — ABEL SICKENS. — THE GOOD SHEPHERD. — RUFUS PLAYS THE PHILANTHROPIST. — MASTER SWIFT SEES THE SUN RISE. — THE DEATH OF THE RIGHTEOUS 204

CHAPTER XXVII.

JAN HAS THE FEVER. — CONVALESCENCE IN MASTER SWIFT'S
COTTAGE. — THE SQUIRE ON DEMORALIZATION 211

CHAPTER XXVIII.

MR. FORD'S CLIENT. — THE HISTORY OF JAN'S FATHER. —
AMABEL AND BOGY THE SECOND 217

CHAPTER XXIX.

JAN FULFILS ABEL'S CHARGE. — SON OF THE MILL. — THE
LARGE-MOUTHED WOMAN 230

CHAPTER XXX.

JAN'S PROSPECTS, AND MASTER SWIFT'S PLANS. — TEA AND
MILTON. — NEW PARENTS. — PARTING WITH RUFUS. — JAN
IS KIDNAPPED. 238

CHAPTER XXXI.

SCREEVING. — AN OLD SONG. — MR. FORD'S CLIENT. — THE
PENNY GAFF. — JAN RUNS AWAY 246

CHAPTER XXXII.

THE BAKER. — ON AND ON. — THE CHURCH BELL. — A DI-
GRESSION. — A FAMILIAR HYMN. — THE BOYS' HOME . . 253

CHAPTER XXXIII.

THE BUSINESS MAN AND THE PAINTER. — PICTURES AND
POT BOILERS. — CIMABUE AND GIOTTO. — THE SALMON-
COLORED OMNIBUS 261

CHAPTER XXXIV.

A CHOICE OF VOCATIONS. — RECREATION HOUR. — THE BOW-
LEGGED BOY. — DRAWING BY HEART. — GIOTTO . . . 265

CHAPTER XXXV.

"WITHOUT CHARACTER?" — THE WIDOW. — THE BOW-LEGGED BOY TAKES SERVICE. — STUDIOS AND PAINTERS . 270

CHAPTER XXXVI.

THE MILLER'S LETTER. — A NEW POT BOILER SOLD . . . 277

CHAPTER XXXVII.

SUNSHINE AFTER STORM 282

CHAPTER XXXVIII.

A PAINTER'S EDUCATION. — MASTER CHUTER'S PORT. — A FAREWELL FEAST. — THE SLEEP OF THE JUST 286

CHAPTER XXXIX.

GEORGE AGAIN. — THE PAINTER'S ADVICE. — "HOME-BREWED" AT THE HEART OF OAK. — JAN CHANGES THE PAINTER'S MIND. 294

CHAPTER XL.

D'ARCY SEES BOGY. — THE ACADEMY. — THE PAINTER'S PICTURE 300

CHAPTER XLI.

THE DETECTIVE. — THE "JOOK." — JAN STANDS BY HIS MOTHER'S GRAVE. — HIS AFTER HISTORY 303

CHAPTER XLII.

CONCLUSION 308

JAN OF THE WINDMILL.

CHAPTER I.

THE WINDMILLER'S WIFE. — STRANGERS. — TEN SHIL-
LINGS A WEEK. — THE LITTLE JAN.

STORM without and within!
So the windmiller might have said, if he had been in the habit of putting his thoughts into an epigrammatic form, as a groan from his wife and a growl of thunder broke simultaneously upon his ear, whilst the rain fell scarcely faster than her tears.

It was far from mending matters that both storms were equally unexpected. For eight full years the miller's wife had been the meekest of women. If there was a firm (and yet, as he flattered himself, a just) husband in all the dreary straggling district, the miller was that man. And he always did justice to his wife's good qualities, — at least to her good quality of submission, — and would, till lately, have upheld her before any one as a model of domestic obedience. From the day when he brought home his bride, tall, pretty, and perpetually smiling, to the tall old mill and the ugly old mother who never smiled at all, there had been but one will in the household. At any rate, after the old woman's death. For during her lifetime her stern son paid her such deference that it was a moot point, perhaps, which of them really ruled. Between a mighty host of clouds had followed them; and when the wind did come, it came in no moderate measure, but brought this awful storm upon its wings, which now raged as if all the powers of mischief had got loose, and were bent on turning every thing topsy-turvy indoors and out.

What made the winds and clouds so perverse, the clerk of the weather best knows; but there was a reason for the unreasonableness of the windmiller's wife.

She had lost her child, her youngest born, and therefore, at present, her best beloved. This girl-babe was the sixth of the windmiller and his wife's children, the last that God gave them, and the first that it had pleased Him to take away.

The mother had been weak herself at the time that the baby fell ill, and unusually ill-fitted to bear a heavy blow. Then her watchful eyes had seen symptoms of ailing in the child long before the windmiller's good sense would allow a fuss to be made, and expense to be incurred about a little peevishness up or down. And it was some words muttered by the doctor when he did come, about not having been sent for soon enough, which were now doing as much as any thing to drive the poor woman frantic. They struck a blow, too, at her blind belief in the miller's invariable wisdom. If he had but listened to her in this matter, were it only for love's sake! There was something, she thought, in what that woman had said who came to help her with the last offices, — the miller discouraged "neighbors," but this was a matter of decency, — that it was as foolish for a man to have the say over babies and housework as it would be for his wife to want her word in the workshop or the mill.

Perhaps a state of subjection for grown-up people does not tend to make them reasonable, especially in their indignations. The windmiller's wife dared not, for her life, have told him in so many words that she thought it would be for their joint benefit if he would give a little more consideration to her wishes and opinions; but from this suppressed idea came many sharp and peevish words at this time, which, apart from their true source, were quite as unreasonable and perverse as the miller held them to be. Nor is being completely under the control of another, self-control. It may be doubted if it can even do much to teach it. The thread of her passive condition having been, for the time, broken by grief, the bereaved mother moaned and wailed, and rocked herself, and beat her breast, and turned fiercely upon all interference, like some poor beast in anguish.

She had clung to her children with an almost morbid tenderness, in proportion as she found her worthy husband stern and cold. A hard husband sometimes makes a soft mother, and it is perhaps upon the baby of the family that her repressed affections outpoured themselves most fully. It was so in this case, at any rate. And the little one had that unearthly beauty which is seen, or imagined, about children who die young. And the poor woman had suffered and striven so for it, to have it and to keep it. The more critical grew its illness, the intenser grew her strength and resolution by watchfulness, by every means her instinct and experience could suggest, to fight and win the battle against death. And when all was vain, the maddening thought tortured her that it might have been saved.

The miller had made a mistake, and it was a pity that he made another on the top of it, with the best intentions.

them, however, the young wife was moulded to a nicety, and her voice gained no more weight in the counsels of the windmill when the harsh tones of the mother-in-law were silenced for ever.

The miller was one of those good souls who live by the light of a few small shrewdities (often proverbial), and pique themselves on sticking to them to such a point, as if it were the greater virtue to abide by a narrow rule the less it applied. The kernel of his domestic theory was, "Never yield, and you never will have to," and to this he was proud of having stuck against all temptations from a real, though hard, affection for his own; and now, after working so smoothly for eight years, had it come to this?

The miller scratched his head, and looked at his wife, almost with amazement. She moaned, though he bade her be silent; she wept, in spite of words which had hitherto been an effectual styptic to her tears; and she met the commonplaces of his common sense with such wild, miserable laughter, that he shuddered as he heard her.

Weakness in human beings is like the strength of beasts, a power of which fortunately they are not always conscious. Unless positively brutal, you cannot well beat a sickly woman for wailing and weeping; and if she will not cease for any lesser consideration, there seems nothing for an unbending husband to do but to leave her to herself.

This the miller had to do, anyhow. For he could only spare a moment's attention to her now and then, since the mill required all his care.

In a coat and hat of painted canvas, he had been in and out ever since the storm began; now directing the two men who were working within, now struggling along the stage that ran outside the windmill, at no small risk of being fairly blown away.

He had reefed the sails twice already in the teeth of the blinding rain. But he did well to be careful. For it was in such a storm as this, five years ago "come Michaelmas," that the worst of windmill calamities had befallen him,— the sails had been torn off his mill and dashed into a hundred fragments upon the ground. And such a mishap to a seventy feet tower mill means — as windmillers well know — not only a stoppage of trade, but an expense of two hundred pounds for the new sails.

Many a sack of grist, which should have come to him, had gone down to the watermill in the valley before the new sails were at work; and the huge debt incurred to pay for them was not fairly wiped out yet. That catastrophe had kept the windmiller a poor man for five years, and it gave him a nervous dread of storms.

And talking of storms, here was another unreasonable thing. The morning sky had been (like the miller's wedded life) without a cloud. The day had been sultry, for the time of year unseasonably so. And, just when the miller most grudged an idle day, when times were hard, when he was in debt, — for some small matters, as well as the sail business, — and when, for the first time in his life, he felt almost afraid of his own hearthstone, and would fain have been busy at his trade, not a breath of wind had there been to turn the sails of the mill. Not a waft to cool his perplexed forehead, not breeze enough to stir the short grass that glared for miles over country flat enough to mock him with the fullest possible view of the cloudless sky. Then towards evening, a few gray flecks had stolen up from the horizon like thieves in the dusk, and

He hurried on the funeral, hoping that when "all was over" the mother would "settle down."

But it was this crowning insult to her agony, the shortening of the too brief time when she could watch by all that remained to her of her child, which drove her completely wild. She reproached him now plainly and bitterly enough. She would neither listen to reason nor obey; and when — with more truth than taste — he observed that other people lost children, and that they had plenty left, she laughed in his face that wild laugh which drove him back to the mill and to the storm.

How it raged! The miller's wife was an uneducated, commonplace woman enough, but, in the excited state of her nervous system, she was as sensible as any poet of a kind of comforting harmony in the wild sounds without; though at another time they would have frightened her.

They did not disturb the children, who were in bed Four in the old press-bed in the corner, and one in a battered crib, and one in the narrow bed over which the coverlet was not yet green.

The day's work was over for her, though it was only just beginning for the miller, and the mother had nothing to do but weep, and her tears fell and fell, and the rain poured and poured. That last outburst had somewhat relieved her, and she almost wished her husband would come back, as a flash of lightning dazzled her eyes, and the thunder rattled round the old mill, as if the sails had broken up again, and were falling upon the roof of the round-house. All her senses were acute to-night, and she listened for the miller's footsteps, and so, listening, in the lull after the thunder, she heard another sound. Wheels upon the road.

A pang shot through her heart. Thus had the doctor's gig sounded the night he came, — alas, too late! How long and how intensely she had listened for that! She first heard it just beyond the mile-stone. This one must be a good bit on this side of it; up the hill, in fact. She could not help listening. It was so like, so terribly like! Now it spun along the level ground. Ah, the doctor had not hurried so! Now it was at the mill, at the door, and — it stopped.

The miller's wife rose to run out, she hardly knew why. But in a moment she checked herself, and went back to her seat.

" I be crazed, surely," said the poor woman, sitting down again. " There be more gigs than one in the world, and folk often stops to ask their way of the maester."

These travellers were a long time about the putting of such a simple question, especially as the night was not a pleasant one to linger out in. The murmur of voices, too, which the woman overheard, betokened a close conversation, in which the familiar drawl of the windmiller's dialect blended audibly with that kind of clean-clipt speaking peculiar to gentlefolk.

" He 've been talking to master 's five minute an' more," muttered the miller's wife. " What can 'ee want with un?" The talking ceased as she spoke, and the windmiller appeared, followed by a woman carrying a young baby in her arms.

He was a ruddy man for his age at any time, but there was an extra flush on his cheeks just now, and some excitement in his manner, making him look as his wife was not wont to see him more than once a year, after the Foresters' dinner at the Heart of Oak. There was a diffeence, too. A little too much drink made the windmiller peevish and pompous, but just now he spoke in a kindly, almost conciliating tone.

"See, missus! Let this good lady dry herself a bit, and get warm, and the little un too."

A woman — ill-favored, though there was no positive fault to be found with her features, except that the upper lip was long and cleft, and the lower one very large — came forward with the child, and began to take off its wraps, and the miller's wife, giving her face a hasty wipe, went hospitably to help her.

"Tst! tst! little love!" she cried, gulping down a sob, due to her own sad memories, and moving the cloak more tenderly than the woman in whose arms the child lay. "What a pair of dark eyes, then! Is't a boy or girl, m'm?"

"A boy," said a voice from the door, and the miller's wife, with a suppressed shriek of timidity, became aware of a man whose entrance she had not perceived, and to whom she dropped a hasty courtesy.

He was a man slightly above the middle height, whose slenderness made him seem taller. An old cloak, intended as much to disguise as to protect him, did not quite conceal a faultlessness of costume beneath it, after the fashion of the day. Waistcoats of three kinds, one within the other, a frilled shirt, and a well-adjusted stock, were to be seen, though he held the ends of the old cloak tightly across him, as the wind would have caught them in the doorway. He wore a countryman's hat, which seemed to suit him as little as the cloak, and from beneath the brim his dark eyes glared with a restless, dissatisfied look, and were so dark and so fierce and bright that one could hardly see any other details of his face, unless it were his smooth chin, which, either from habit or from the stiffness of his stock, he carried straugely up in the air.

"Indeed, sir," said the windmiller's wife, courtesying, and setting a chair, with her eyes wandering back by a kind of fascination to those of the stranger; "be pleased to take a seat, sir."

The stranger sat down for a moment, and then stood up again. Then he seemed to remember that he still wore his hat, and removed it, holding it stiffly before him in his gloved hands. This displayed a high, narrow head, on which the natural hair was worn short and without parting, and a face which, though worn, was not old. And, for no definable reason, an impression stole over the windmiller's wife that he, like her husband, had some wish to conciliate, which in his case struggled hard with a very different kind of feeling, more natural to him.

Then he took out a watch of what would now be called the old turnip shape, and said impatiently to the miller, "Our time is short, my good man."

"To be sure, sir," said the windmiller. "Missus! a word with you here." And he led the way into the round-house, where his wife followed, wondering. Her wonder was not lessened when he laid his hand upon her shoulder, and, with flushed cheek and a tone of excitement that once more recalled the Foresters' annual meeting, said, "We've had some sore times, missus, of late, but good luck have come our way to-night."

"And how then, maester?" faltered his wife.

"That child," said the windmiller, turning his broad thumb expressively towards the inner room, "belongs to folk that want to get a home for un, and can afford to pay for un, too. And the place being healthy and out of the way, and having heard of our trouble, and you just bereaved of a little un"—

"No! no! no!" shrieked the poor mother, who now understood all. "I *couldn't*, maester, 'tis unpossible, I could *not*. Oh dear! oh dear! isn't it bad enough to lose the sweetest child that ever saw light, without taking in an outcast to fill that dear angel's place? Oh dear! oh dear!"

"And we behindhand in more quarters than one," continued the miller, prudently ignoring his wife's tears and remonstrances, "and a dear season coming on, and an uncertain trade that keeps a man idle by days together, and here's ten shillings a week dropped into our laps, so to speak. Ten shillings a week — regular and sartin. No less now, and no more hereafter, the governor said. Them were his words."

"What's ten shilling a week to me, and my child dead and gone?" moaned the mother, in reply.

"*What's ten shillings a week to you?*" cried the windmiller, who was fairly exasperated, in tones so loud that they were audible in the dwelling room, where the stranger, standing by the three-legged table, stroked his lips twice or thrice with his hand, as if to smooth out a cynical smile which strove to disturb their decorous and somewhat haughty compression. "What's ten shilling a week to you? Why, it's food to you, and drink to you, and firing to you, and boots for the children's feet. Look here, my woman. You've had a sore affliction, but that's not to say you're to throw good luck in the dirt for a whimsey. This matter's settled."

And the miller strode back into the inner room, whilst

his wife sat upon a sack of barley, wringing her hands, and moaning, " I couldn't do my duty by un, maester, I couldn't do my duty by un."

This she repeated at intervals, with her apron over her face, as before; and then, suddenly aware that her husband had left her, she hurried into the inner room to plead her own cause. It was too late. The strangers had gone. The miller was not there, and the baby lay on the end of the press bedstead, wailing as bitterly as the mother herself.

It had been placed there, with a big bundle of clothes by it, before the miller came back, and he had found it so. He found the stranger too, with his hat on his head, and his cloak fastened, glancing from time to time at the child, and then withdrawing his glance hastily, and looking forcedly round at the meagre furnishing of the miller's room, and then back at the little bundle on the bed, and away again. The woman stood with her back to the press-bed, her striped shawl drawn tightly round her, and her hands folded together as closely as her long lip pressed the heavy one below.

" Is it settled ? " asked the man.

" It is, sir," said the miller. " You'll excuse my missus being as she is, but it's fretting for the child we've a lost " —

" I understand, I understand," said the stranger, hastily. He was pulling back the rings of a silk netted purse, which he had drawn mechanically from his pocket, and which, from some sudden start of his, fell chinking on to the floor. Whatever the thought was which startled him, he thought it so sharply that he looked up in fear that he had said it aloud. But he had not spoken, and the miller had no other expression than that of an eager satisfaction on his face as the stranger counted out the gold by the flaring light of the tallow candle.

"A quarter's pay in advance," he said briefly. "It will be paid quarterly, you understand." After which, and checking himself in a look towards the child, he went out, followed by the woman.

In the round-house he paused however, and looked back into the meagre, dimly lighted room, where the little bundle upon the bed lay weeping. For a moment, a storm of irresolution seemed to seize him, and then muttering, "It can't be helped for the present, it can't be helped," he hurried towards the vehicle, in the back seat of which the woman was already seated.

The driver touched his hat to him as he approached, and turned the cushion, which he had been protecting from the rain. The stranger stumbled over the cloak as he got in, and, cursing the step, bade the man drive like something which had no connection with driving. But, as they turned, the windmiller ran out and after them.

"Stop, sir!" he cried.

"Well, what now?" said the stranger, sharply, as the horse was pulled back on his haunches.

"Is it named?" gasped the miller.

"Oh, yes, all that sort of thing," was the impatient reply.

"And what name?" asked the miller.

"Jan. J, A, N," said the stranger, shouting against the blustering wind.

"And — and — the other name?" said the windmiller, who was now standing close to the stranger's ear.

"What is yours?" he asked, with a sharp look of his dark eyes.

"Lake — Abel," said the windmiller.

"It is his also, henceforth," said the stranger, waving his hand, as if to close the subject, — "Jan Lake. Drive on, will you?"

The horse started forward, and they whirled away down the wet, gray road. And before the miller had regained his mill, the carriage was a distant speck upon the storm.

CHAPTER II.

THE MILLER'S CALCULATIONS. — HIS HOPES AND FEARS. — THE NURSE-BOY. — CALM.

THE windmiller went back to his work. He had risked something over this business in leaving the mill in the hands of others, even for so short a time.

Then the storm abated somewhat. The wind went round, and blew with less violence a fine steady breeze. The miller began to think of going into the dwelling-room for a bit of supper to carry him through his night's work. And yet he lingered about returning to his wife in her present mood.

He stuck the sharp point of his windmiller's candlestick * into a sack that stood near, and drawing up a yellow canvas "sample bag" — which served him as a purse — from the depths of his pocket, he began to count the coins by the light of the candle. He counted them over several times with increasing satisfaction, and made several slow but sure calculations as to the sum of ten shillings a week by the month, the quarter, the half, and the whole year. He then began another set of calculations of a kind less pleasant, especially to an honest man, — his debts.

* Windmiller's candlesticks are flat candlesticks made of iron, with a long handle on one side, and a sharp spike on the other, by which they can be stuck into the wall, or into a sack of grain, or anywhere that may be convenient. Each man who works in the mill has a candlestick, and one is always kept alight and stationary on the basement floor.

"There's a good bit to the doctor for both times," he murmured; "and there's the coffin, and something at the Heart of Oak for the bearers, and a couple of bottles red wine there, too, for the missus, when she were so bad. And both the boys had new shoes to follow in, — she would have it they should follow" — And so on, and so on, the windmiller ran up the list of his petty debts, and saw his way to paying them. Then he put the money back into the sample bag, and folded it very neatly, and stowed it away. And then he drew near the inner door, and peeped into the room.

His poor wife seemed to be in no better case than before. She sat on the old rocking-chair, swinging backwards and forwards, and beating her hands upon her knees in silence, and making no movement to comfort the wailing little creature on the bed.

For the first time there came upon the windmiller a sense of the fact that it is an uncertain and a rather dangerous game to drive a desperate woman into a corner. His missus was as soft-hearted a soul as ever lived, and for her to sit unmoved by the weeping of a neglected child was a proof that something was very far wrong indeed. One or two nasty stories of what tender-hearted women had done when "crazed" by grief haunted him. The gold seemed to grow hot at the bottom of his pocket. He wished he had got at the stranger's name and address, in case it should be desirable to annul the bargain. He wished the missus would cry again, that silence was worse than any thing. He wished it did not just happen to come into his head that her grandmother went "melancholy mad" when she was left a young widow, and that she had had an uncle in business who died of softening of the brain.

He wished she would move across the room and take up the child, with an intensity that almost amounted to prayer. And, in the votive spirit which generally comes with such moments, he mentally resolved that, if his missus would but "take to" the infant, he would humor her on all other points just now to the best of his power.

A strange fulfilment often treads on the heels of such vows. At this moment the wailing of the baby disturbed the miller's eldest son as he lay in the press-bed. He was only seven years old, but he had been nurse-boy to his dead sister during the brief period of her health, — the more exclusively so, that the miller's wife was then weakly, — and had watched by her sick cradle with a grief scarcely less than that of the mother. He now crept out and down the coverlet to the wailing heap of clothes, with a bright, puzzled look on his chubby face.

"Mother," he said, "mother! Is the little un come back?"

"No, no!" she cried. "That's not our'n. It's — it's another one."

"Have the Lord sent us another?" said the boy, lifting the peak of the little hood from the baby's eye, into which it was hanging, and then fairly gathering the tiny creature, by a great effort, into his arms, with the daring of a child accustomed to playing nurse to one nearly as heavy as himself. "I do be glad of that, mother. The Lord sent the other one in the night, too, mother; that night we slept in the round-house. Do 'ee mind? Whishty, whishty, love! Eh, mother, what eyes! Whishty, whishty, then! *I'm* seeing to thee, I am."

There was something like a sob in the miller's own throat, but his wife rose, and, running to the bed, fell on her knees, and with such a burst of weeping as is the thaw of bitter grief gathered her eldest child and the little outcast together to her bosom.

At this moment another head was poked up from the bedclothes, and the second child began to say its say, hoping, perhaps, thereby to get a share of attention and kisses as well as the other.

"I seed a lady and genle'm," it broke forth, "and was feared of un. They was going out of doors. The genle'm look back at us, but the lady went right on. I didn' see her face."

Matters were now in a domestic and straightforward condition, and the windmiller no longer hesitated to come in. But he was less disposed to a hard and triumphant self-satisfaction than was common with him when his will ended well. A poor and unsuccessful career had, indeed, something to do with the hardness of his nature, and in this flush of prosperity he felt softened, and resolved inwardly to "let the missus take her time," and come back to her ordinary condition without interference.

"Shall un have a bit of supper, missus?" was his cheerful greeting on coming in. "But take your time," he added, seeing her busy with the baby, "take your time."

By-and-by the nurse-boy took the child, and the woman bustled about the supper. She was still but half reconciled, and slapped the plates on to the table with a very uncommon irritability.

The windmiller ate a hearty supper and washed it well down with home-made ale, under the satisfactory feeling that he could pay for more when he wanted it. And as he began to plug his pipe with tobacco, and his wife rocked the new-comer at her breast, he said thoughtfully, —

"Do 'ee think, missus, that woman 'ud be the mother of un?"

"Mother!" cried his wife, scornfully. "She 've never been a mother, maester; of this nor any other one. To see her handle it was enough for me. The boy himself could see she never so much as looked back at un. To bring an infant out a night like this, too, and leave it with strangers. Mother, indeed, says he!"

"Take your time, missus, take your time!" murmured the miller in his head. He did not speak aloud, he only puffed his pipe.

"Do you suppose the genle'm be the father, missus?" he suggested, as he rose to go back to his work.

"Maybe," said his wife, briefly; "I can't speak one way or another to the feelings of men-folk."

This blow was hit straight out, but the windmiller forbore reply. He was not altogether ill-pleased by it, for the woman's unwonted peevishness broke down in new tears over the child, whom she bore away to bed, pouring forth over it half inarticulate indignation against its unnatural parents.

"She 've a soft heart, have the missus," said the windmiller, thoughtfully, as he went to the outer door. "I 'm in doubts if she won't take to it more than her own yet. But she shall have her own time."

The storm had passed. The wolds lay glistening and dreary under a watery sky, but all was still. The windmiller looked upwards mechanically. To be weatherwise was part of his trade. But his thoughts were not in the clouds to-night. He brought the sample bag, without thinking of it, to the surface of his pocket, and dropped it slowly back again, murmuring, "Ten shilling a week."

And as he turned again to his night's work he added, with a nod of complete conviction, "It'll more'n keep *he.*"

CHAPTER III.

THE WINDMILLER'S WORDS COME TRUE. — THE RED SHAWL. — IN THE CLOUDS. — NURSING *v.* PIG-MINDING. — THE ROUND-HOUSE. — THE MILLER'S THUMB.

STRANGE to say, the windmiller's idea came true in time, — the foster-child was the favorite.

He was the youngest of the family, for the mother had no more children. This goes for something.

Then, when she had once got over her repugnance to adopting him, he did do much to heal the old grief, and to fill the empty place in her heart as well as in the cradle.

He was a frail, fretful little creature, with a very red face just fading into yellow, about as much golden down on his little pate as would furnish a moth with plumage, and eyes like sloe-berries. It was fortunate rather than otherwise that he was so ailing for some weeks that the good wife's anxieties came over again, and, in the triumph of being this time successful, much of the bitterness of the old loss passed away.

In a month's time he looked healthy, if not absolutely handsome. The windmiller's wife, indeed, protested that he was lovely, and she never wearied of marvelling at the unnatural conduct of those who had found it in their hearts to intrust so sweet a child to the care of strangers;

though it must be confessed that nothing would have pleased her less than the arrival of two doting and conscientious parents to reclaim him.

Indeed, pity had much to do with the large measure of love that she gave to the deserted child. A meaner sentiment, too, was not quite without its influence in the predominance which he gradually gained over his foster brothers and sisters. There was little enough to be proud of in all that could be guessed as to his parentage (the windmiller knew nothing), but there was scope for any amount of fancy; and if the child displayed any better manners or talents than the other children, Mrs. Lake would purse her lips, and say, with a somewhat shabby pride, —

"Anybody may see 'tis gentry born."

"I've been thinking," said the windmiller, one day, "that if that there woman weren't the mother, 'tis likely the mother's dead."

"'Tis likely, too," said his wife; and her kindness abounded the more towards the motherless child.

Little Abel was nurse-boy to it, as he had been to his sister. Not much more than a baby himself, he would wrap an old shawl round the baby who was quite a baby, stagger carefully out at the door, and drop dexterously — baby uppermost — on to the short, dry grass that lay for miles about the mill.

The shawl was a special shawl, though old. It was red, and the bright color seemed to take the child's fancy; he was never so good as when playing upon the gay old rag. His black eyes would sparkle, and his tiny fingers clutch at it, when the mother put it about him as he swayed in Abel's courageous grasp. And then Abel would spread it for him, like an eastern prayer carpet, under the shadow of the old mill.

Little need had he of any medicine, when the fresh strong air that blew about the downs was filling his little lungs for most of the day. Little did he want toys, as he lay on his red shawl gazing upwards hour by hour, with Abel to point out every change in their vast field of view.

It is a part of a windmiller's trade to study the heavens, and Abel may have inherited a taste for looking skywards. Then, on these great open downs there is so much sky to be seen, you can hardly help seeing it, and there is not much else to look at. Had they lived in a village street, or even a lane, Abel and his charge might have taken to other amusements, — to games, to grubbing in hedges, or amid the endless treasures of ditches. But as it was, they lay hour after hour and looked at the sky, as at an open picture-book with ever-changing leaves.

"Look 'ee here!" the nurse-boy would cry. "See to the crows, the pretty black crows! Eh, there be a lap-wing! Lap-py, lap-py, lap-py, there he go! Janny catch un!"

And the baby would stretch his arms responsive to Abel's expressive signs, and cry aloud for the vanishing bird.

If no living creature crossed the ether, there were the clouds. Sometimes a long triangular mass of small white fleecy clouds would stretch across half the heavens, having its shortest side upon the horizon, and its point at the zenith, where one white fleece seemed to be leading a gradually widening flock across the sky.

"See then!" the nurse-boy would cry. "See to the pretty sheep up yonder! Janny mind un! So! so!"

And if some small gray scud, floating lower, ran past the far-away cirrus, Abel would add with a quaint seriousness, " 'Tis the sheep-dog. How he runs then! Bow-wow!"

At sunset such a flock wore golden fleeces, and to them, and to the crimson hues about them, the little Jan stretched his fingers, and crowed, as if he would have clutched the western sky as he clutched his own red shawl.

But Abel was better pleased when, in the dusk, the flock became dark gray.

" 'They be Master Salter's pigs now," said he. For pigs in Abel's native place were both plentiful and black; and he had herded Master Salter's flock (five and twenty black, and three spotted) for a whole month before his services were required as nurse-boy to his sister.

But for the coming of the new baby, he would probably have gone back to the pigs. And he preferred babies. A baby demands attention as well as a herd of pigs, but you can get it home. It does not run off in twenty-eight different directions, just when you think you have safely turned the corner into the village.

Master Salter's swine suffered neglect at the hands of several successors to the office Abel had held, and Master Salter — whilst alluding to these in indignant terms as "young varments," "gallus birds," and so forth — was pleased to express his regret that the gentle and trustworthy Abel had given up pig-minding for nursing.

The pigs' loss was the baby's gain. No tenderer or more careful nurse could the little Jan have had. And he throve apace.

The windmiller took more notice of him than he had been wont to do of his own children in their babyhood.

He had never been a playful or indulgent father, but he now watched with considerable interest the child who, all unconsciously, was bringing in so much "grist to the mill."

When the weather was not fine enough for them to be out of doors, Abel would play with his charge in the round-house, and the windmiller never drove him out of the mill, as at one time he would have done. Now and then, too, he would pat the little Jan's head, and bestow a word of praise on his careful guardian.

It may be well, by-the-by, to explain what a round-house is. Some of the brick or tower mills widen gradually and evenly to the base. Others widen abruptly at the lowest story, which stands out all round at the bottom of the mill, and has a roof running all round too. The projection is, in fact, an additional passage, encircling the bottom story of the windmill. It is the round-house. If you take a pill-box to represent the basement floor of a tower-mill, and then put another pill-box two or three sizes larger over it, you have got the circular passage between the two boxes, and have added a round-house to the mill. The round-house is commonly used as a kind of store-room.

Abel Lake's windmill had no separate dwelling-house. His grandfather had built the windmill, and even his father had left it to the son to add a dwelling-house, when he should perhaps have extended his resources by a bit of farming or some other business, such as windmillers often add to their trade proper. But that calamity of the broken sails had left Abel Lake no power for further outlay for many years, and he had to be content to live in the mill.

The dwelling-room was the inner part of the basement floor. Near the door which led from this into the round house was the ladder leading to the next story, and close by that the opening through which the sacks of grain were drawn up above. The story above the basement held the millstones and the "smutting" machine, for cleaning dirty wheat. The next above that held the dressing machine, in which the bran was separated from the flour. In the next above that were the corn-bins. To the next above that the grain was drawn up from the basement in the first instance. The top story of all held the machinery connected with the turning of the sails. Ladders led from story to story, and each room had two windows on opposite sides of the mill.

Use is second nature, and all the sounds which haunt a windmill were soon as familiar and as pleasant to the little Jan as if he had been born a windmiller's son. Through many a windy night he slept as soundly as a sailor in a breeze which might disturb the nerves of a land-lubber. And when the north wind blew keen and steadily, and the chains jangled as the sacks of grist went upwards, and the millstones ground their monotonous music above his head, these sounds were only as a lullaby to his slumbers, and disturbed him no more than they troubled his foster-mother, to whom the revolving stones ground out a homely and welcome measure: "Dai-ly bread, dai-ly bread, dai-ly bread."

For another sign of his being a true child of the mill, his nurse Abel anxiously watched.

Though Abel preferred nursing to pig-minding, he had a higher ambition yet, which was to begin his career as a windmiller. It was not likely that he could be of use to his father for a year or two, and the fact that he was of very great use to his mother naturally tended to delay his promotion to the mill.

Mrs. Lake was never allowed to say no to her husband, and she seemed to be unable, and was certainly unwilling, to say it to her children. Happily, her eldest child was of so sweet and docile a temper that spoiling did him little harm; but even with him her inability to say no got the mother into difficulties. She was obliged to invent excuses to "fub off," when she could neither consent nor refuse.

So, when Abel used to cling about her, crying, " Mother dear, when 'll I be put t' help father in the mill? Do 'ee ask un to let me come in now! I be able to sweep 's well as Gearge. I sweeps the room for thee," — she had not the heart or the courage to say, "I want thee, and thy father doesn't," but she would take the boy's hand tenderly in hers, and making believe to examine his thumbs with a purpose, would reply, " Wait a bit, love. Thee's a sprack boy, and a good un, but thee's not rightly got the miller's thumb."

And thus it came about that Abel was for ever sifting bits of flour through his finger and thumb, to obtain the required flatness and delicacy which marks the latter in a miller born; and playing lovingly with little Jan on the floor of the round-house, he would pass some through the baby's fingers also, crying, —

" Sift un, Janny! sift un! Thee's a miller's lad, and thee must have a miller's thumb."

CHAPTER IV.

BLACK AS SLANS. — VAIR AND VOOLISH. — THE MILLER AND HIS MAN.

IT was a great and important time to Abel when Jan learned to walk; but, as he was neither precocious nor behindhand in this respect, his biographer may be pardoned for not dwelling on it at any length.

He had a charming demure little face, chiefly differing from the faces of the other children of the district by an overwhelming superiority in the matter of forehead.

Mrs. Lake had had great hopes that he would differ in another respect also.

Most of the children of the neighborhood were fair. Not fair as so many North-country children are, with locks of differing, but equally brilliant, shades of gold, auburn, red, and bronze; but white-headed, and often white-faced, with white-lashed inexpressive eyes, as if they had been bleaching through several generations.

Now, when the dark bright eyes of the little Jan first came to be of tender interest with Mrs. Lake, she fully hoped, and constantly prophesied, that he would be "as black as a rook;" a style of complexion to which she gave a distinct preference, though the miller was fair by nature as well as white by trade. Jan's eyes seemed conclusive.

"Black as slans they be," said his foster-mother. And slans meant sloe-berries where Mrs. Lake was born.

An old local saying had something perhaps to do with her views: —

> "Lang and lazy,
>   Black and proud;
> Vair and voolish,
>   Little and loud."

"Fair and foolish" youngsters certainly abounded in the neighborhood to an extent which justified a wish for a change.

As to pride, meek Mrs. Lake was far from regarding it as a failing in those who had any thing to be proud of, such as black hair and a possible connection with the gentry. And fate having denied to her any chance of being proud or aggressive on her own account, she derived a curious sort of second-hand satisfaction from seeing these qualities in those who belonged to her. It did to some extent console her for the miller's roughness to herself, to hear him rating George. And she got a sort of reflected dignity out of being able to say, "My maester's a man as will have his way."

But her hopes were not realized. That yellow into which the beefsteak stage of Jan's infant complexion had faded was not destined to deepen into gipsy hues. It gave place to the tints of the China rose, and all the wind and sunshine on the downs could not tan, though they sometimes burnt, his cheeks. The hair on his little head became more abundant, but it kept its golden hue. His eyes remained dark, — a curious mixture; for as to hair and complexion he was irredeemably fair.

The mill had at least one "vair and voolish" inmate, by common account, though by his own (given in confidence to intimate friends) he was "not zuch a vool as he looked."

This was George Sannel, the miller's man.

Master Lake had had a second hand in to help on that stormy night when Jan made his first appearance at the mill; but as a rule he only kept one man, whom he hired for a year at a time, at the mop or hiring fair held yearly in the next town.

George, or Gearge as he was commonly called, had been more than two years in the windmill, and was looked upon in all respects as "one of the family." He slept on a truckle-bed in the round-house, which, though of average size, would not permit him to stretch his legs too recklessly without exposing his feet to the cold.

For "Gearge" was six feet one and three-quarters in his stockings.

He had a face in some respects like a big baby's. He had a turn-up nose, large smooth cheeks, a particularly innocent expression, a forehead hardly worth naming, small dull eyes, with a tendency to inflammation of the lids which may possibly have hindered the lashes from growing, and a mouth which was generally open, if he were neither eating nor sucking a "bennet." When this countenance was bathed in flour, it might be an open question whether it were improved or no. It certainly looked both "vairer" and more "voolish!"

There is some evidence to show that he was "lazy," as well as "lang," and yet he and Master Lake contrived to pull on together.

Either because his character was as childlike as his face, and because — if stupid and slothful by nature — he was also of so submissive, susceptible, and willing a temper that he disarmed the justest wrath; or because he was, as he said, not such a fool as he looked, and had in his own lubberly way taken the measure of the masterful windmiller to a nicety, George's most flagrant acts of neglect had never yet secured his dismissal.

Indeed, it really is difficult to realize that any one who is lavish of willingness by word can wilfully and culpably fail in deed.

"I be a uncommon vool, maester, sartinly," blubbered George on one occasion when the miller was on the point of turning him off, as a preliminary step on the road to the "gallus," which Master Lake expressed his belief that he was "sartin sure to come to." And, as he spoke, George made dismal daubs on his befloured face with his sleeve, as he rubbed his eyes with his arm from elbow to wrist.

"Sech a governor as you be, too!" he continued. "Poor mother! she allus said I should come to no good, such a gawney as I be! No more I shouldn't but for you, Master Lake, a-keeping of me on. Give un another chance, sir, do 'ee! I be mortal stoopid, sir, but I'd work my fingers to the bwoan for the likes of you, Master Lake!"

George stayed on, and though the very next time the windmiller was absent his "voolish" assistant did not get so much as a toll-dish of corn ground to flour, he was so full of penitence and promises that he weathered that tempest and many a succeeding one.

On that very eventful night of the storm, and of Jan's arrival, George's neglect had risked a recurrence of the sail catastrophe. At least if the second man's report was to be trusted.

This man had complained to the windmiller that, during his absence with the strangers, George, instead of doubling his vigilance now that the men were left short-handed, had taken himself off under pretext of attending to the direction of the wind and the position of the sails outside, a most important matter, to which he had not, after all, paid the slightest heed; and what he did with himself, whilst leaving the mill to its fate and the fury of the storm, his indignant fellow-servant professed himself "blessed if he knew."

But few people are as grateful as they should be when informed of misconduct in their own servants. It is a reflection on one's judgment.

And unpardonable as George's conduct was, if the tale were true, the words in which he couched his self-defence were so much more grateful to the ears of the windmiller than the somewhat free and independent style in which the other man expressed his opinion of George's conduct and qualities, that the master took his servant's part, and snubbed the informer for his pains.

In justice to George, too, it should be said that he stoutly and repeatedly denied the whole story, with many oaths and imprecations of horrible calamities upon himself if he were lying in the smallest particular. And this with reiteration so steady, and a countenance so guileless and unmoved, as to contrast favorably with the face of the other man, whose voice trembled and whose forehead flushed, either with overwhelming indignation or with a guilty consciousness that he was bearing false witness.

Master Lake employed him no more, and George stayed on.

But, for that matter, Master Lake's disposition was not one which permitted him to profit by the best qualities of those connected with him. He was a bit of a tyrant, and more than one man, six times as clever, and ten times as hard-working as George, had gone when George would

have stayed, from crossing words with the windmiller
The safety of the priceless sails, if all were true, had been
risked by the man he kept, and secured by the man he
sent away, but Master Lake was quite satisfied with his
own decision.

"I bean't so fond myself of men as is so mortal sprack
and fussy in a strange place," the miller observed to Mrs.
Lake in reference to this matter.

Mrs. Lake had picked up several of her husband's bits
of proverbial wisdom, which she often flattered him by
retailing to his face.

"Too hot to hold, mostly," was her reply, in knowing
tones.

"Ay, ay, missus, so a be," said the windmiller. And
after a while he added, "Gearge is slow, sartinly, mortal
slow; but Gearge is sure."

CHAPTER V.

THE POCKET-BOOK AND THE FAMILY BIBLE. — FIVE POUNDS' REWARD.

OF the strange gentleman who brought Jan to the windmill, the Lakes heard no more, but the money was paid regularly through a lawyer in London.

From this lawyer, indeed, Master Lake had heard immediately after the arrival of his foster-son.

The man of business wrote to say that the gentleman who had visited the mill on a certain night had, at that date, lost a pocket-book, which he thought might have been picked up at the mill. It contained papers only valuable to the owner, and also a five-pound note, which was liberally offered to the windmiller if he could find the book, and forward it at once.

Master Lake began to have a kind of reckless, gambling sort of feeling about luck. Here would be an easily earned five pounds, if he could but have the luck to find the missing property! That ten shillings a week had come pretty easily to him. When all is said, there *are* people into whose mouths the larks fall ready cooked!

The windmiller looked inside the mill and outside the mill, and wandered a long way along the chalky road with his eyes downwards, but he was no nearer to the five-pound note for his pains. Then he went to his wife, but she had seen nothing of the pocket-book; on which her husband somewhat unreasonably observed that, "A might a been zartin *thee* couldn't help un!"

He next betook himself to George, who was slowly, and it is to be hoped surely, sweeping out the round-house.

"Gearge, my boy," said the windmiller, in not too anxious tones, "have 'ee seen a pocket-book lying about anywheres?"

George leaned upon his broom with one hand, and with the other scratched his white head.

"What be a pocket-book, then, Master Lake?" said he, grinning, as if at his own ignorance.

"Thee's eerd of a pocket-book before now, thee vool, sure-ly!" said the impatient windmiller.

"I'se eerd of a pocket of hops, Master Lake," said George, after an irritating pause, during which he still smiled, and scratched his poll as if to stimulate recollection.

"Book — book — book! pocket-*book!*" shouted the miller. "If thee can't read, thee knows what a book is, thee gawney!"

"What a vool I be, to be sure!" said George, his simple countenance lighted up with a broader smile than before. "I knows a book, sartinly, Master Lake, I knows a book. There's one," George continued, speaking even slower than before, — "there's one inzide, sir, — a big un. On the shelf it be. A Vamly Bible they calls un. And I'm sartin sure it be there," he concluded, "for a hasn't been moved since the last time you christened, Master Lake."

The miller turned away, biting his lip hard, to repress a useless outburst of rage, and George, still smiling sweetly, spun the broom dexterously between his hands, as a man spins the water out of a stable mop. Just before Master Lake had got beyond earshot, George lowered the broom, and began to scratch his head once more. "I be a proper vool, sartinly," said he; and when the miller heard this, he turned back. "Mother allus said I'd no more sense in my yead than a dumbledore," George candidly confessed. And by a dumbledore he meant a humble-bee. "It do take me such a time to mind any thing, sir."

"Well, never mind, Gearge," said the miller; "if thee's slow, thee's sure. What do 'ee remember about the book, now, Gearge? A don't mind giving thee five shilling, if thee finds un, Gearge."

"A had un down at the burying, I 'member quite well now, sir. To put the little un's name in 'twas. I thowt a hadn't been down zince christening, I be so stoopid sartinly."

"What are you talking about, ye vool?" roared the miller.

"The book, sir, sartinly," said George, his honest face beaming with good-humor. "The Vamly Bible, Master Lake."

And as the windmiller went off muttering something which the Family Bible would by no means have sanctioned, George returned chuckling to a leisurely use of his broom on the round-house floor.

Master Lake did not find the pocket-book, and after a day or two it was advertised in a local paper, and a reward of five pounds offered for it.

George Sannel was seated one evening in the "Heart of Oak" inn, sipping some excellent home-brewed ale, which had been warmed up for his consumption in a curious funnel-shaped pipkin when his long lop-ears caught a remark made by the inn-keeper, who was reading out bits from the local paper to a small audience, unable to read it for themselves.

"Five pound reward!" he read. "Lor massy! There be a sum to be easily earned by a sharp-eyed chap with good luck on 's side."

"And how then, Master Chuter?" said George, pausing, with the steaming mug half-way to his lips.

"Haw, haw!" roared the inn-keeper: "you be a sharp-eyed chap, too! Do 'ee think 'twould suit thee, Gearge? Thee 's a sprack chap, sartinly, Gearge!"

"Haw, haw, haw!" roared the other members of the company, as they slowly realized Master Chuter's irony at the expense of the "voolish" Gearge.

George took their rough banter in excellent part. He sipped his beer, and grinned like a cat at his own expense. But after the guffaws had subsided, he said, "Thee 's not told un about that five pound yet, Master Chuter."

The curiosity of the company was by this time aroused, and Master Chuter explained: "'Tis a gentleman by the name of Ford as is advertising for a pocket-book, a seems to have lost on the downs, near to Master Lake's windmill. 'Tis thy way, too, Gearge, after all. Thee must get up yarly, Gearge. 'Tis the yarly bird catches the worm. And tell Master Lake from me, 'll have all the young varments in the place a driving their pigs up to his mill, to look for the pocket-book, while they makes believe to be minding their pigs."

"'Tis likely, too," said George. And the two or three very aged laborers in smocks, and one other lubberly boy, who composed the rest of the circle, added, severally and collectively, "'Tis likely, too."

But, as George beat his way home over the downs in the dusk, he said aloud, under cover of the roaring wind, and in all the security of the open country, —

"Vive pound! vive pound! And a offered me vive shilling for un. Master Lake, you be dog-ged cute; but Gearge bean't quite such a vool as a looks."

After a short time the advertisement was withdrawn.

CHAPTER VI.

GEORGE GOES COURTING. — GEORGE AS AN ENEMY. — GEORGE AS A FRIEND. — ABEL PLAYS SCHOOL-MASTER. — THE LOVE-LETTER. — MOERDYK. — THE MILLER-MOTH. — AN ANCIENT DITTY.

ONE day George Sannel asked and obtained leave for a holiday.

On the morning in question, he dressed himself in the cleanest of smocks, greased his boots, stuck a bloody warrior, or dark-colored wallflower, in his bosom, put a neatly folded, clean cotton handkerchief into his pocket, — which, even if he did not use it, was a piece of striking dandyism, — and scrubbed his honest face to such a point of cleanliness that Mrs. Lake was almost constrained to remark that she thought he must be going courting.

George did not blush, — he never blushed, — but he looked "voolish" enough to warrant the suspicion that his errand was a tender one, and he had no other reason to give for his spruce appearance.

It was, perhaps, in his confusion that he managed to convey a mistaken notion of the place to which he was going to Mrs. Lake. She was under the impression that he went to the neighboring town, whereas he went to one in an exactly opposite direction, and some miles farther away.

He went to the bank, too, which seems an unlikely place

for tender tryst; but George's proceedings were apt to be less direct than the simplicity of his looks and speech would have led a stranger to suppose. When he reached home, the windmiller and his family were going to bed, for the night was still, and the mill idle. George betook himself at once to where his truckle-bed stood in the round-house, and proceeded to light his mill-candlestick, which was stuck into the wall.

From the chink into which it was stuck he then counted seven bricks downwards, and the seventh yielded to a slight effort and came out. It was the door, so to speak, of a hole in the wall of the mill, from which he drew a morocco-bound pocket-book. After an uneasy glance over his shoulder, to make sure that the long dark shadow which stretched from his own heels, and shifted with the draught in which the candle flared, was not the windmiller creeping up behind him, he took a letter out of the book and held it to the light as if to read it. But he never turned the page, and at last replaced it with a sigh. Then he put the pocket-book back into the hole, and pushed in after it his handkerchief, which was tied round something which chinked as he pressed it in. Then he replaced the brick, and went to bed. He said nothing about the bank in the morning nor about the hole in the mill-wall; and he parried Mrs. Lake's questions with gawky grins and well-assumed bashfulness.

Abel overheard his mother's jokes on the subject of "Gearge's young 'ooman," and they recurred to him when he and George formed a curious alliance, which demands explanation.

It was not solely because the windmiller looked favorably upon the little Jan that he and Abel were now allowed to wander in the business parts of the windmill, when they could not be out of doors, to an extent never before permitted to the children. Part of the change was due to a change in the miller's man.

However childlike in some respects himself, George was not fond of children, and he had hitherto seemed to have a particular spite against Abel. He, quite as often as the miller, would drive the boy from the round-house, and thwart his fancy for climbing the ladders to see the processes of the different floors.

Abel would have been happy for hours together watching the great stones grind, or the corn poured by golden showers into the hopper on its way to the stones below. Many a time had he crept up and hidden himself behind a sack; but George seemed to have an impish ingenuity in discovering his hiding-places, and would drive him out as a dog worries a cat, crying, "Come out, thee little varment! Master Lake he don't allow thee hereabouts."

The cleverness of the miller's man in discovering poor Abel's retreats probably arose from the fact that he had so rooted a dislike for the routine work of his daily duties that he would rather employ himself about the mill in any way than by attending to the mill-business, and that his idleness and stupidity over work were only equalled by his industry and shrewdness in mischief.

Poor Abel had a dread of the great, gawky, mischievous-looking man, which probably prevented his complaining to his mother of many a sly pinch and buffet which he endured from him. And George took some pains to keep up this wholesome awe of himself, by vague and terrifying speeches, and by a trick of what he called "dropping on" poor Abel in the dusk, with hideous grimaces and uncouth sounds.

He once came thus upon Abel in an upper floor, and the

boy fled from him so hastily that he caught his foot in the ladder and fell headlong. Though it must have been quite uncertain for some moments whether Abel had not broken his neck, the miller's man displayed no anxiety. He only clapped his hands upon his knees, in a sort of uncouth ecstasy of spite, saying, " Down a comes vlump, like a twoad from roost. Haw, haw, haw!"

Happily, Abel fell with little more damage to himself than the mill-cats experienced in many such a tumble, as they fled before the tormenting George.

But, after all this, it was with no small surprise that Abel found himself the object of attentions from the miller's man, which bore the look of friendliness.

At first, when George made civil speeches, and invited Abel to " see the stwones a-grinding," he only felt an additional terror, being convinced that mischief was meant in reality. But, when days and weeks went by, and he wandered unmolested from floor to floor, with many a kindly word from George, and not a single cuff or nip, the sweet-tempered Abel began to feel gratitude, and almost an affection, for his quondam tormentor.

George, for his part, had hitherto done some violence to his own feelings by his constant refusal to allow Abel to help him to sweep the mill or couple the sacks for lifting. He would have been only too glad to put some of his own work on the shoulders of another, had it not been for the vexatious thought that he would be giving pleasure by so doing where he only wanted to annoy. And in his very unamiable disposition malice was a stronger quality even than idleness.

But now, when for some reason best known to himself, he wished to win Abel's regard, it was a slight recompense to him for restraining his love of tormenting that he got a good deal of work out of Abel at odd moments when the miller was away. So well did he manage this, that a marked improvement in the tidiness of the round-house drew some praise from his master.

"Thee'll be a sprack man yet, Gearge," said the windmiller, encouragingly. "Thee takes the broom into the corners now."

"So I do," said George, unblushingly, "so I do. But lor, Master Lake, what a man you be to notice un!"

George's kinder demeanor towards Abel began shortly after the coming of the little Jan, and George himself accounted for it in the following manner: —

"You do be kind to me now, Gearge," said Abel, gratefully, as he stood one day, with the baby in his arms, watching the miller's man emptying a sack of grain into the hopper.

"I likes to see thee with that babby, Abel," said George, pausing in his work. "Thee's a good boy, Abel, and careful. I likes to do any thing for thee, Abel."

"I wish I could do any thing for thee, Gearge," said Abel; "but I be too small to help the likes of you, Gearge."

"If you're small, you're sprack," said the miller's man. "Thee's a good scholar, too, Abel. I'll be bound thee can read, now? And a poor gawney like I doesn't know's letters."

"I can read a bit, Gearge," said Abel, with pride; "but I've been at home a goodish while; but mother says she'll send I to school again in spring, if the little un gets on well and walks."

"I wish I could read," said George, mournfully; "but time's past for me to go to school, Abel; and who'd teach a great lummakin vool like I his letters?"

"I would, Gearge, I would!" cried Abel, his eyes sparkling with earnestness. "I can teach thee thy letters, and by the time thee's learned all I know, maybe I'll have been to school again, and learned some more."

This was the foundation of a curious kind of friendship between Abel and the miller's man.

On the same shelf with the "Vamly Bible," before alluded to, was a real old horn-book, which had belonged to the windmiller's grandmother. It was simply a sheet on which the letters of the alphabet, and some few words of one syllable, were printed, and it was protected in its frame by a transparent front of thin horn, through which the letters could be read, just as one sees the prints through the ground-glass of "drawing slates."

From this horn-book Abel labored patiently in teaching George his letters. It was no light task. George had all the cunning and shrewdness with which he credited himself; but a denser head for any intellectual effort could hardly have been found for the seeking. Still they struggled on, and as George went about the mill he might have been heard muttering, —

"A B C G. No! Cuss me for a vool! A B C *D*. Why didn't they whop my letters into I when a was a boy? A B C" — and so persevering with an industry which he commonly kept for works of mischief.

One evening he brought home a newspaper from the Heart of Oak, and when Mrs. Lake had taken the baby, he persuaded Abel to come into the round-house and give him a lesson. Abel could read so much of it that George was quite overwhelmed by his learning.

"Thee be's mortal larned, Abel, sartinly. But I'll never read like thee," he added, despairingly. "Drattle th' old witch, why didn't she give I some schooling?" He spoke with spiteful emphasis, and Abel, too well used to his rough language to notice the uncivil reference to his mother, said with some compassion, —

"Were you never sent to school then, Gearge?"

"They should ha' kept me there," said George, self-defensively. "I played moocher," he continued, — by which he meant truant, — "and then they whopped I, and a went home to mother, and she kept un at home, the old vool!"

"Well, Gearge, thee must work hard, and I'll teach thee, Gearge, I'll teach thee!" said little Abel, proudly. "And by-and-by, Gearge, we'll get a slate, and I'll teach thee to write too, Gearge, that I will!"

George's small eyes gave a slight squint, as they were apt to do when he was thinking profoundly.

"Abel," said he, "can thee read writing, my boy?"

"I think I could, Gearge," said Abel, "if 'twas pretty plain."

"Abel, my boy," said George, after a pause, with a broad sweet smile upon his "voolish" face, "go to the door and see if the wind be rising at all; us mustn't forget th' old mill, Abel, with us larning. Sartinly not, Abel, mun."

Proud of the implied partnership in the care of the mill, Abel hastened to the outer door. As he passed the inner one, leading into the dwelling-room, he could hear his mother crooning a strange, drony, old local ditty, as she put the little Jan to sleep. As Abel went out, she was singing the first verse: —

> "The swallow twitters on the barn,
> The rook is cawing on the tree,
> And in the wood the ringdove coos,
> But my false love hath fled from me."

Abel opened the door, and looked out. One of those small white moths known as "millers" went past him. The night was still, — so utterly still that no sound of any sort whatever broke upon the ear. In dead silence and loneliness stood the mill. Even the miller-moth had gone; and a cat ran in by Abel's legs, as if the loneliness without were too much for her. The sky was gray.

Abel went back to the round-house, where George was struggling to fix the candlestick securely in the wall.

"Cuss the thing!" he exclaimed, whilst the skin of his face took a mottled hue that was the nearest approach he ever made to a blush. "The tallow've been a dropping, Abel, my boy. I think 'twas the wind when you opened the door, maybe. And I've been a trying to fix un more firmly. That's all, Abel; that's all."

"There ain't no signs of wind," said Abel. "It's main quiet and unked too outside, Gearge. And I do think it be like rain. There was a miller-moth, Gearge; do that mean any thing?"

"I can't say," said George. "I bean't weatherwise myself, Abel. But if there be no wind, there be no work, Abel; so us may go back to our larning. Look here, my boy," he added, as Abel reseated himself on the grain-sack which did duty as chair of instruction, and drawing, as he spoke, a letter forth to the light; "come to the candle, Abel, and see if so be thee can read this, but don't tell any one I showed it thee, Abel."

"Not me, Gearge," said Abel, warmly; and he added, — "Be it from thy young 'ooman, Gearge?"

No rustic swain ever simpered more consciously or looked more foolish than George under this accusation, as he said, " Be quiet, Abel, do 'ee."

"She be a good scholar, too!" said Abel, looking admiringly at the closely written sheet.

George could hardly disguise the sudden look of fury in his face, but he hastily covered up the letter with his hands in such a manner as only to leave the first word on the page visible. There was a deeply cunning reason for this clever manœuvre. George held himself to be pretty "cute," and he reckoned that, by only showing one word at a time, he could effectually prevent any attempt on Abel's part to read the letter himself without giving its contents to George. Like many other cunning people, George overreached himself. The first word was beyond Abel's powers, though he might possibly have satisfied George's curiosity on one essential point, by deciphering a name or two farther on. But the clever George concluded that he had boasted beyond his ability, so he put the letter away.

Abel tried hard at the one word which George exhibited, and gazed silently at it for some time with a puzzled face.

"Spell it, mun, spell it!" cried the miller's man, impatiently. It was a process which he had seen to succeed, when a long word had puzzled his teacher in the newspaper, before now.

"M O E R, mower; D Y K, dik," said Abel. But he looked none the wiser for the effort.

"Mower dik! What be that?" said George, peering at the word. "Do 'ee think it be Mower dik, Abel?"

"I be sure," said Abel.

"Or do 'ee think 'tis '*My dear Dick*'?" suggested George, anxiously, and with a sort of triumph in his tone, as if that were quite what he expected.

"No, no. 'Tis an O, Gearge, that second letter. Beside, 'twould have been *My dear Gearge* to thee, thou knows."

Again the look with which the miller's man favored Abel was far from pleasant. But he controlled his voice to its ordinary drawl (always a little slower and more simple sounding, when he specially meant mischief).

"So 'twould, Abel. So 'twould. What a vool I be, to be sure! But give it to I now. We'll look at it another time, Abel."

"I be very sorry, Gearge," said Abel, who had a consciousness that the miller's man was ill-pleased in spite of his civility. "It be so long since I was at school, and it be such a queer word. Do 'ee think she can have spelt un wrong, Gearge?"

"'Tis likely she have," said George, regaining his composure.

"Abel! Abel! Abel!" cried the mother from the dwelling-room. "Come to thee bed, child!"

"Good-night, Gearge. I'm main sorry to be so stupid, Gearge," said Abel, and off he ran.

Mrs. Lake was walking up and down, rocking the little Jan in her arms, who was wailing fretfully.

"I be puzzled to know what ails un," said Mrs. Lake, in answer to Abel's questions. "He be quite in a way tonight. But get thee to bed, Abel."

And though Abel begged hard to be allowed to try his powers of soothing with the little Jan, Mrs. Lake insisted upon keeping the baby herself; and Abel undressed, and crept into the press-bed. He fell asleep in spite of a somewhat disturbed mind. That mysterious word and George's evident displeasure worried him, and he was troubled also by the unusual fretfulness of the little Jan, and the sound of sorrow in his baby wail. His last waking thoughts were a strange mixture, passing into stranger dreams.

The word Moerdyk danced before his eyes, but brought no meaning with it. Jan's cries troubled him, and with both there blended the droning of the ancient plaintive ditty, which the foster-mother sang over and over again as she rocked the child in her arms. That wail of the baby's must have in some strange manner recalled the first night of his arrival, when Abel found him wailing on the bed. For the fierce eyes of the strange gentleman haunted Abel's dreams, but in the face of the miller's man.

The poor boy dreamed horribly of being " dropped on " by George, with fierce back eyes added to the terrors of his uncouth grimaces. He seemed to himself to fly blindly and vainly through the mill from his tormentor, till George was driven from his thoughts by his coming suddenly upon the little Jan, wailing as he really did wail, round whose head a miller-moth was sailing slowly, and singing in a human voice:—

"The swallow twitters on the barn,
The rook is cawing on the tree,
And in the wood the ringdove coos,
But my false love hath fled from me.

Like tiny pipe of wheaten straw,
The wren his little note doth swell,
And every living thing that flies,
Of his true love doth fondly tell.

But I alone am left to pine,
And sit beneath the withy tree;
For truth and honesty be gone,
And my false love hath fled from me."

CHAPTER VII.

ABEL GOES TO SCHOOL AGAIN. — DAME DATCHETT. — A COLUMN OF SPELLING. — ABEL PLAYS MOOCHER. — THE MILLER'S MAN CANNOT MAKE UP HIS MIND.

ABEL went to school again in the spring, and, though George would have been better pleased had he forgotten the whole affair, he remembered the word in George's young woman's love-letter which had puzzled him; and never was a spelling-lesson set him among the M's that he did not hope to come across it and to be able to demand the meaning of Moerdyk from his Dame.

Without the excuse of its coming in the column of spelling set by herself, Abel dared not ask her to solve his puzzle; for never did teacher more warmly resent questions which she was unable to answer than Dame Datchett.

Abel could not fully make up his mind whether it should be looked up among two-syllabled or three-syllabled words. He decided for the former, and one day brought his spelling-book to George in the round-house.

"I've been a looking for that yere word, Gearge," said he. "There's lots of Mo's, but it bean't among 'em. Here they be. Words of two syllables; M, Ma, Me, Mi; here they be, Mo." And Abel began to rattle off the familiar column at a good rate, George looking earnestly over his shoulder, and following the boy's finger as it moved rapidly down the page. "'Mocking, Modern, Mohawk, Molar, Molly, Moment, Money, Moping, Moral, Mortal, Moses, Motive, Movement."

"Stop a bit, mun," cried George; "what do all they words mean? They bothers me."

"I knows some of 'em," said Abel, "and I asked Dame Datchett about the others, but she do be so cross; and I thinks some of 'em bothered she too. There's mocking. I knows that. 'What's a modern, Dame?' says I. 'A muddle-headed fellow the likes of you,' says she. 'What's a mohawk, Dame?' says I. 'It's what you'll come to before long, ye young hang-gallus,' says she. I was feared on her, Gearge, I can tell 'ee; but I tried my luck again. 'What's a molar, Dame?' says I. ''Tis a wus word than t'other,' says she; 'and, if 'ee axes me any more voolish questions, I'll break thee yead for 'ee.' Do 'ee think 'tis a very bad word, Gearge?" added Abel, with a rather indefensible curiosity.

"I never heard un," said George. And this was perhaps decisive against the Dame's statement. "And I don't believe un neither. I think it bothered she. I believe 'tis a genteel word for a man as catches oonts. They call oonts *moles* in some parts, so p'r'aps they calls a man as catches moles a molar, as they calls a man as drives a mill a miller."

"'Tis likely too, Gearge," said Abel.

"Well! Molly we knows. And moment, and moping, and moral."

"What's moral?" inquired George.

"'Tis what they put at the end of Vables, Gearge. There's Vables at the end of the spelling-book, and I've read un all. There's the Wolf and the Lamb, and"—

"I knows now," said George. "'Tis like the last verse of that song about the Harnet and the Bittle. Go on, Abel."

"Mortal. That's swearing. Moses. That's in the Bible, Gearge. Motive. I thought I'd try un just once more. 'What's a motive, Dame?' says I. 'I've got un here, says she, quite quiet-like. But I seed her feeling under 's chair, and I know'd 'twas for the strap, and I ran straight off, spelling-book and all, Gearge."

"So thee've been playing moocher, eh?" said George, with an unpleasant twinkle in his eyes. "What'll Master Lake say to that?"

"Don't 'ee tell un, Gearge!" Abel implored; "and, O Gearge! let I tell mother about the word. Maybe she've heard tell of it. Let I show her the letter, Gearge. She'll read it for 'ee. She's a scholar, is mother."

There was no mistaking now the wrath in George's face. The fury that is fed by fear blazes pretty strongly at all times.

"Look 'ee, Abel, my boy," said he, pinching Abel's shoulder till he turned red and white with pain. "If thee ever speaks of that letter and that word to any mortal soul, I'll tell Master Lake thee plays moocher, and I'll half kill thee myself. Thee shall rue the day ever thee was born!" he added, almost beside himself with rage and terror. And as, after a few propitiating words, Abel fled from the mill, George ground his hands together and muttered, "Motive! I wish the old witch had motived every bone in thee body, or let me do 't!"

Master George Sannel was indeed a little irritable at this stage of his career. Like the miller, he had had one stroke of good luck, but capricious fortune would not follow up the blow.

He had made five pounds pretty easily. But how to turn some other property of which he had become possessed to profit for himself was, after months of waiting, a puzzle still.

He was well aware that his own want of education was the great hindrance to his discovering for himself the exact worth of what he had got. And to his suspicious nature the idea of letting any one else into his secret, even to gain help, was quite intolerable.

Abel seemed to be no nearer even to the one word that George had showed him, after weeks of "schooling," and George himself progressed so slowly in learning to read that he was at times tempted to give up the effort in despair.

Of his late outburst against Abel he afterwards repented, as impolitic, and was soon good friends again with his very placable teacher.

Much of the time when he should have been at work did George spend in "puzzling" over his position. Sometimes, as from an upper window of the mill he saw the little Jan in Abel's arms, he would mutter, —

"If a body were to kidnap un, would they advertise *he*, I wonders?" and after some consideration would shake his white head doubtfully, saying, "No, they wants to get rid of un, or they wouldn't have brought un here."

Happily for poor little Jan, the unscrupulous rustic rejected the next idea which came to him as too doubtful of success.

"I wonder if they'd come down something handsome to them as could tell 'em the young varmint was off their hands for good and all. 'Twould save un ten shilling a week. Ten shilling a week! I heard un with my own ears.

I'd a kep' un for five, if they'd asked me. I wonders now. Little uns like that does get stole by gipsies sometimes. Varmer Smith's son were, and never heard on again. They falls into a mill-race too sometimes. They be so venturesome. But I doubt 'twouldn't do. Them as it belongs to might be glad enough to get rid of un, and save their credit and their money too by turning upon I after all."

The miller's man puzzled himself in vain. He could think of no mode of action at once safe and certain of success. He did not even know whether what he possessed had any value, or how or where to make use of it. But a sort of dim hope of seeing his way yet kept him about the mill, and he persevered in the effort to learn to read, and kept his big ears open for any thing that might drop from the miller or his wife to throw light on the history of Jan, with whom his hopes were bound up.

Meanwhile, with a dogged patience, he bided his time.

CHAPTER VIII.

VISITORS AT THE MILL. — A WINDMILLER OF THE THIRD GENERATION. — CURE FOR WHOOPING-COUGH. — MISS AMABEL ADELINE AMMABY. — DOCTORS DISAGREE.

ONE of the earliest of Jan's remembrances — of those remembrances, I mean, which remained with him when childhood was past — was of little Miss Amabel, from the Grange, being held in the hopper of the windmill for whooping-cough.

Jan was between three and four years old at this time, the idol of his foster-mother, and a great favorite with his adopted brothers and sisters. A quaint little fellow he was, with a broad, intellectual-looking face, serious to old-fashionedness, very fair, and with eyes "like slans."

He was standing one morning at Mrs. Lake's apron-string, his arms clasped lovingly, but somewhat too tightly, round the waist of a sandy kitten, who submitted with wonderful good-humor to the well-meant strangulation, his black eyes intently fixed upon the dumplings which his foster-mother was dexterously rolling together, when a strange footstep was heard shuffling uncertainly about on the floor of the round-house just outside the dwelling-room door. Mrs. Lake did not disturb herself. Country folk were constantly coming with their bags of grist, and both George and the miller were at hand, for a nice breeze was blowing, and the mill ground merrily.

After a few seconds, however, came a modest knock on the room-door, and Mrs. Lake, wiping her hands, proceeded to admit the knocker. She was a smartly dressed woman, who bore such a mass of laces and finery, with a white woollen shawl spread over it, apparently with the purpose of smothering any living thing there might chance to be beneath, as, in Mrs. Lake's experienced eyes, could be nothing less than a baby of the most genteel order.

The manners of the nurse were most genteel also, and might have quite overpowered Mrs. Lake, but that the windmiller's wife had in her youth been in good service herself, and, though an early marriage had prevented her from rising beyond the post of nursemaid, she was fairly familiar with the etiquette of the nursery and of the servants' hall.

"Good morning, ma'am," said the nurse, who no sooner ceased to walk than she began a kind of diagonal movement without progression, in which one heel clacked, and all her petticoats swung, and the baby who, head downwards, was snorting with gaping mouth under the woollen coverlet, was supposed to be soothed. "Good morning, ma'am. You'll excuse my intruding"—

"Not at all, mum," said Mrs. Lake. By which she did not mean to reject the excuse, but to disclaim the intrusion.

When the nurse was not speaking, she kept time to her own rocking by a peculiar click of her tongue against the roof of her mouth; and indeed it sometimes mingled, almost confusingly, with her conversation. "You're very obliging, ma'am, I'm sure," said she, and, persuaded by Mrs. Lake, she took a seat. "You'll excuse me for asking a singular question, ma'am, but *was your husband's father and grandfather both millers?*"

"They was, mum," said Mrs. Lake. "My husband's father's father built this mill where we now stands. It cost him a deal of money, and he died with a debt upon it. My husband's father paid un off; and he meant to have built a house, mum, but he never did, worse luck for us. He allus says, says he, — that's my husband's father, mum, — 'I'll leave that to Abel,' — that's my maester, mum. But nine year ago come Michaelmas" —

Mrs. Lake's story was here interrupted by a frightful outburst of coughing from the unfortunate baby, who on the removal of the woollen shawl presented an appearance which would have been comical but for the sympathy its condition demanded.

A very red and utterly shapeless little face lay, like a crushed beet-root, in a mass of dainty laces almost voluminous enough to have dressed out a bride. As a sort of crowning satire, the face in particular was surrounded by a broad frill, spotted with bunches of pink satin ribbon, and farther encased in a white satin hood of elaborate workmanship and fringes.

The contrast between the natural red of the baby's complexion and its snowy finery was ludicrously suggestive of an over-dressed nigger, to begin with; but when, in the paroxysms of its cough, the tiny creature's face passed by shades of plum-color to a bluish black, the result was appalling to behold.

Mrs. Lake's experienced ears were not slow to discover that the child had got whooping-cough, which the nurse confessed was the case. She also apologized for bringing in the baby among Mrs. Lake's children, saying that she had "thought of nothing but the poor little chirrub herself."

"Don't name it, mum," replied the windmiller's wife. "I always say if children be to have things, they'll have 'em; and if not, why they won't." A theory which seems to sum up the views of the majority of people in Mrs. Lake's class of life upon the spread of disease.

"I'm sure I don't know what's coming to my poor head," the nurse continued: "I've not so much as told you who I am, ma'am. I'm nurse at the Grange, ma'am, with Mr. Ammaby and Lady Louisa. They've been in town, and her ladyship's had the very best advice, and now we've come to the country for three months, but the dear child don't seem a bit the better. And we've been trying every thing, I'm sure. For any thing I heard of I've tried, as well as what the doctor ordered, and rubbing it with some stuff Lady Louisa's mamma insisted upon, too, — even to a frog put into the dear child's mouth, and drawed back by its legs, that's supposed to be a certain cure, but only frightened it into a fit I thought it never would have come out of, as well as fetching her ladyship all the way from her boudoir to know what was the matter — which I no more dared tell her than fly."

"Dear, dear!" said the miller's wife; "have you tried goose-grease, mum? 'Tis an excellent thing."

"Goose-grease, ma'am, and an excellent ointment from the bone-setter's at the toll-bar, which the butler paid for out of his own pocket, knowing it to have done a world of good to his sister that had a bad leg, besides being a certain cure for coughs, and cancer, and consumption as well. And *then* the doctor's *imprecation* on its little chest, night and morning, besides; but nothing don't seem to do no good," said the poor nurse. "And so, ma'am,— her ladyship being gone to the town,— thinks I, I'll take the dear child to the windmill. For they do say,— where I came from, ma'am, — that if a miller, that's the son of a miller, and the grandson of a miller, holds a child that's got the whooping-cough in the hopper of the mill whilst the mill's going, it cures them, however bad they be."

The reason of the nurse's visit being now made known, Mrs. Lake called her husband, and explained to him what he was asked to do for "her ladyship's baby." The miller scratched his head.

"I've heard my father say that his brother that drove a mill in Cheshire had had it to do," said he, "but I never did it myself, ma'am, nor ever see un done. And a hopper be an ackerd place, ma'am. We've ground many a cat in this mill, from getting in the hopper at nights for warmth. However," he added, "I suppose I can hold the little lady pretty tight." And finally, though with some unwillingness, the miller consented to try the charm; being chiefly influenced by the wish not to disoblige the gentlefolk at the Grange.

The little Jan had watched the proceedings of the visitors with great attention. During the poor baby's fit of coughing, he was so absorbed that the sandy kitten slipped through his arms and made off, with her tail as stiff as a sentry's musket; and now that the miller took the baby into his arms, Jan became excited, and asked, "What daddy do with un?"

"The old-fashioned little piece!" exclaimed the nurse, admiringly. And Mrs. Lake added, "Let un see the little lady, maester."

The miller held out the baby, and the nurse, removing a

dainty handkerchief edged with Valenciennes lace from its face, introduced it as "Miss Amabel Adeline Ammaby;" and Mrs. Lake murmured, "What a lovely little thing!" By which, for truth's sake, it is to be hoped she meant the lace-edged handkerchief.

In the exchange of civilities between the two women the respective children in their charge were admonished to kiss each other, — a feat which was accomplished by Jan's kissing the baby very tenderly, and with all his usual gravity.

As this partly awoke the baby from a doze, its red face began to crease, and pucker, and twist into various contortions, at which Jan gazed with a sort of solemn curiosity in his black eyes.

"Stroke the little lady's cheeks, love," said Mrs. Lake, irrepressibly proud of the winning ways and quaint grace which certainly did distinguish her foster-child.

Jan leaned forward once more, and passed his little hand softly down the baby's face twice or thrice, as he was wont to stroke the sandy kitten, as it slept with him, saying, "Poor itta pussy!"

"It's not a puss-cat, bless his little heart!" said the matter-of-fact nurse. "It's little Miss Amabel Adeline Ammaby."

"Say it, love!" said Mrs. Lake, adding, to the nurse, "he can say any thing, mum."

"Miss *Am — abel Ad — e — line Am — ma — by*," prompted the nurse.

"Amabel!" said the little Jan, softly. But, after this feat, he took a fit of childish reticence, and would say no more; whilst, deeply resentful of the liberties Jan had taken, Miss Amabel Adeline Ammaby twisted her features till she looked like a gutta-percha gargoyle, and squalled as only a fretful baby can squall.

She was calmed at last, however, and the windmiller took her once more into his arms, and Mrs. Lake carrying Jan, they all climbed up the narrow ladder to the next floor.

Heavily ground the huge stones with a hundred and twenty revolutions a minute, making the chamber shake as they went round.

They made the nurse giddy. The simplest machinery has a bewildering effect upon an unaccustomed person. So has going up a ladder; which makes you feel much less safe in the place to which it leads you than if you had got there by a proper flight of stairs. So — very often — has finding yourself face to face with the accomplishment of what you have been striving for, if you happen to be weak-minded.

Under the combined influences of all these causes, the nurse listened nervously to Master Lake, as he did the honors of the mill.

"Those be the mill-stones, ma'am. Pretty fastish they grinds, and they goes faster when the wind's gusty. Many a good cat they've ground as flat as a pancake from the poor gawney beasts getting into the hopper."

"Oh, sir!" cried the nurse, now thoroughly alarmed, "give me the young lady back again. Deary, deary me! I'd no notion it was so dangerous. Oh, don't, sir! don't!"

"Tut, tut! I'll hold un safe, ma'am," said the windmiller, who had all a man's dislike for shirking at the last moment what had once been decided upon; and, as the nurse afterwards expressed it, before she had time to scream, he had tucked Miss Amabel Adeline Ammaby's finery well round her, and had dipped her into the hopper and out again.

In that moment of suspense both the women had been silent, and the little Jan had gazed steadily at the operation. As it safely ended, they both broke simultaneously into words.

"You might have knocked me down with a feather, mum!" gasped Mrs. Lake. "I couldn't look, mum. I couldn't have looked to save my life. I turned my back."

"I'd back 'ee allus to do the silliest thing as could be done, missus," said the miller, who had a pleasant husbandly way of commenting upon his wife's conversation to her disparagement, when she talked before him.

"As for me, ma'am," the nurse said, "I couldn't take my eyes off the dear child's hood. But move, — no thank you, ma'am, — I couldn't have moved hand or foot for a five-pound note, paid upon the spot."

The baby got well. Whether the mill charm worked the cure, or whether the fine fresh breezes of that healthy district made a change for the better in the child's state, could not be proved.

Nor were these the only possible causes of the recovery.

The kind-hearted butler blessed the day when he laid out three and eightpence in a box of the bone-setter's ointment, to such good purpose.

Lady Louisa's mamma triumphantly hoped that it would be a lesson to her dear daughter never again to set a London doctor's advice (however expensive) above a mother's (she meant a grandmother's) experience.

The cook said, "Goose-grease and kitchen physic for her!"

And of course the doctor very properly, as well as

modestly, observed that "he had confidently anticipated permanent beneficial results from a persevering use of the embrocation."

And only to the nurse and the windmiller's family was it known that Miss Amabel Adeline Ammaby had been dipped in the mill-hopper.

CHAPTER IX.

GENTRY BORN. — LEARNING LOST. — JAN'S BEDFELLOW. — AMABEL.

AFTER the nurse and baby had left the mill, Mrs. Lake showered extra caresses upon the little Jan. It had given her a strange pleasure to see him in contact with the Squire's child. She knew enough of the manners and customs, the looks and the intelligence of the children of educated parents, to be aware that there were "makings" in those who were born heirs to developed intellects, and the grace that comes of discipline, very different from the "makings" to be found in the "voolish" descendants of ill-nurtured and uneducated generations.

She had no philosophical — hardly any reasonable or commendable — thoughts about it. But she felt that Jan's countenance and his "ways" justified her first belief that he was "gentry born."

She was proud of his pretty manners. Indeed, curiously enough, she had recalled her old memories of nursery etiquette under a first-rate upper nurse in "her young days," to apply them to the little Jan's training.

Why she had not done this with her own children is a question that cannot perhaps be solved till we know why so many soldiers, used for, it may be, a quarter of a century to personal cleanliness as scrupulous as a gentleman's, and to enforced neatness of clothes, rooms, and general habits, take back to dirt and slovenliness with greediness when they leave the service; and why many a nurse, whose voice and manners were beyond reproach in her mistress's nursery, brings up her own children in after life on the village system of bawling, banging, threatening, cuddling, stuffing, smacking, and coarse language, just as if she had never experienced the better discipline attainable by gentle firmness and regular habits.

Mrs. Lake had a small satisfaction in Jan's brief and limited intercourse with so genteel a baby, and after it was all over she amused herself with making him repeat the baby's very genteel (and as she justly said "uncommon") name.

When Abel came back from school, he resumed his charge, and Mrs. Lake went about other work. She was busy, and the nurse-boy put Jan to bed himself. The sandy kitten waited till Jan was fairly established, so as to receive her comfortably, and then she dropped from the roof of the press-bed, and he cuddled her into his arms, where she purred like a kettle just beginning to sing.

Outside, the wind was rising, and, passing more or less through the outer door, it roared in the round-house; but they were well sheltered in the dwelling-room, and could listen complacently to the gusts that whirled the sails, and made the heavy stones fly round till they shook the roof. Just above the press-bed a candle was stuck in the wall, and the dim light falling through the gloom upon the children made a scene worthy of the pencil of Rembrandt, that great son of a windmiller.

When Mrs. Lake found time to come to the corner where the old press-bed stood, the kitten was asleep, and Jan very nearly so; and by them sat Abel, watching every breath that his foster-brother drew. And, as he watched, his trustworthy eyes and most sweet smile lighting up a face to which his forefathers had bequeathed little beauty or intellect, he might have been the guardian angel of the nameless Jan, scarcely veiled under the likeness of a child.

His mother smiled tenderly back upon him. He was very dear to her, and not the less so for his tenderness to Jan.

Then she stooped to kiss her foster-child, who opened his black eyes very wide, and caught the sleeping kitten round the head, in the fear that it might be taken from him.

"Tell Abel the name of pretty young lady you see to-day, love," said Mrs. Lake.

But Jan was well aware of his power over the miller's wife, and was apt to indulge in caprice. So he only shook his head, and cuddled the kitten more tightly than before.

"Tell un, Janny dear. Tell un, there's a lovey!" said Mrs. Lake. "Who did daddy put in the hopper?"

But still Jan gazed at nothing in particular with a sly twinkle in his black eyes, and continued to squeeze poor Sandy to a degree that can have been little less agonizing than the millstone torture; and obdurate he would probably have remained, but that Abel, bending over him, said, "Do 'ee tell poor Abel, Jan."

The child fixed his bright eyes steadily on Abel's well-loved face for a few seconds, and then said quite clearly, in soft, evenly accented syllables, —

"Amabel."

And the sandy kitten, having escaped with its life, crept back into Jan's bosom and purred itself to rest.

CHAPTER X.

ABEL AT HOME. — JAN OBJECTS TO THE MILLER'S MAN. — THE ALPHABET. — THE CHEAP JACK. — "PITCHERS."

POOR Abel was not fated to get much regular schooling. He particularly liked learning, but the interval was all too brief between the time when his mother was able to spare him from housework and the time when his father began to employ him in the mill.

George got more lazy and stupid, instead of less so, and though in some strange manner he kept his place, yet when Master Lake had once begun to employ his son, he found that he would get along but ill without him.

To Jan, Abel's being about the windmill gave the utmost satisfaction. He played with his younger foster brothers and sisters contentedly enough, but his love for Abel, and for being with Abel, was quite another thing.

Mrs. Lake, too, had no confidence in any one but Abel as a nurse for her darling; the consequence of which was, that the little Jan was constantly trotting at his foster-brother's heels through the round-house, attempting valiant escalades on the ladders, and covering himself from head to foot with flour in the effort to cultivate a miller's thumb.

One day Mrs. Lake, having sent the other children off

to school, was bent upon having a thorough cleaning-out of the dwelling-room, during which process Jan was likely to be in her way; so she caught him up in her arms and went to seek Abel in the round-house.

She had the less scruple in availing herself of his services, that there was no wind, and business was not brisk in the windmill.

"Maester!" she cried, "can Abel mind Jan a bit? I be going to clean the house."

"Ay, ay," said the windmiller, "Abel can mind un. I be going to the village myself, but there's Gearge to start, if so be the wind rises. And then if he want Abel, thee must take the little un again."

"Sartinly I will," said his wife; and Abel willingly received his charge and carried him off to play among the sacks.

George joined them once, but Jan had a rooted and unconquerable dislike to the miller's man, and never replied to his advances with any thing more friendly than anger or tears. This day was no exception to others in this respect; and after a few fruitless attempts to make himself acceptable, in the course of which he trod on the sandy kitten's tail, who ran up Jan's back and spat at her enemy from that vantage-ground, George went off muttering in terms by no means complimentary to the little Jan. Abel did his best to excuse the capricious child to George, besides chiding him for his rudeness — with very little effect. Jan dried his black eyes as the miller's man made off, but he looked no more ashamed of himself than a good dog looks who has growled or refused the paw of friendship to some one for excellent reasons of his own.

After George had gone, they played about happily

enough, Jan riding on Abel's back, and the sandy kitten on Jan's, in and out among the corn-sacks, full canter as far as the old carved meal-chest, and back to the door again.

Poor Abel, with his double burden, got tired at last, and they sat down and sifted flour for the education of their thumbs. Jan was pinching and flattening his with a very solemn face, in the hope of attaining to a miller's thumb by a shorter process than the common one, when Abel suddenly said, —

"I tell thee what, then, Jan: 'tis time thee learned thy letters. And I'll teach thee. Come hither."

Jan jumped up, thereby pitching the kitten headlong from his shoulders, and ran to Abel, who was squatting by some spilled flour near a sack, and was smoothing it upon the floor with his hands. Then very slowly and carefully he traced the letter A in the flour, keenly watched by Jan.

"That's A," said he. "Say it, Jan. A."

"A," replied Jan, obediently. But he had no sooner said it, than, adding hastily, "Let Jan do it," he traced a second A, slightly larger than Abel's, in three firm and perfectly proportioned strokes.

His moving finger was too much for the kitten's feelings, and she sprang into the flour and pawed both the A's out of existence.

Jan slapped her vigorously, and having smoothed the surface once more, he drew A after A with the greatest rapidity, scrambling along sideways like a crab, and using both hands indifferently, till the row stretched as far as the flour would permit.

Abel's pride in his pupil was great, and he was fain to

run off to call his mother to see the performances of their prodigy, but Jan was too impatient to spare him.

"Let Jan do more!" he cried.

Abel traced a B in the flour. "That's B, Jan," said he.

"Jan do it," replied Jan, confidently.

"But say it," said his teacher, restraining him. "Say B, Jan."

"B," said Jan, impatiently; and adding, "Jan do it," he began a row of B's. He hesitated slightly before making the second curve, and looked at his model, after which he went down the line as before, and quite as successfully. And the kitten went down also, pawing out each letter as it was made, under the impression that the whole affair was a game of play with herself.

"There bean't a letter that bothers him," cried Abel, triumphantly, to the no less triumphant foster-mother.

Jan had, indeed, gone through the whole alphabet, with the utmost ease and self-confidence; but his remembrance of the names of the letters he drew so readily proved to be far less perfect than his representations of them on the floor of the round-house.

Abel found his pupil's progress hindered by the very talent that he had displayed. He was so anxious to draw the letters that he would not learn them, and Abel was at last obliged to make one thing a condition of the other.

"Say it then, Jan," he would cry, "and then thee shall make 'em."

Mrs. Lake commissioned Abel to buy a small slate and pencil for Jan at the village shop, and these were now the child's favorite toys. He would sit quiet for any length of time with them. Even the sandy kitten was neglected, or got a rap on its nose with the slate-pencil, when to toy with the moving point had been too great a temptation to be resisted. For a while Jan's taste for wielding the pencil was solely devoted to furthering his learning to read. He drew letters only till the day that the Cheap Jack called.

The Cheap Jack was a travelling pedler, who did a good deal of business in that neighborhood. He was not a pedler pure, for he had a little shop in the next town. Nature had not favored him. He was a hunchback. He was, or pretended to be, deaf. He had a very ugly face, made uglier by dirt, above which he wore a mangy hair cap.

He sold rough pottery, cheap crockery and glass, mock jewelry, low song-books, framed pictures, mirrors, and quack medicines. He bought old bottles, bones, and rags. And what else he bought or sold, or dealt with, was dimly guessed at by a few, but fully known to none.

Where he was born, what was his true name or age, whether on any given occasion he was speaking less than lies, and what was the ultimate object of his words and deeds, — at these things no one even guessed. That his conscience was ever clean, that his dirty face once masked no vile or petty plots for evil in the brain behind, that at some past period he was a child, — these things it would have tasked the strongest faith to realize.

He was not so unpopular with children as the miller's man.

The instinct of children is like the instinct of dogs, very true and delicate as a rule. But dogs, from Cerberus downwards, are liable to be biassed by sops. And four paper-covered sails, that twirl upon the end of a stick as the wind blows, would warp the better judgment of most little boys. especially (for a bargain is more precious than a gift) when the thing is to be bought for a few old bones.

Jan was a little afraid of the Cheap Jack, but he liked his whirligigs. They went when the mill was going, and sometimes when the mill wouldn't go, if you ran hard to make a breeze.

But it so happened that the first day on which the Cheap Jack came round after Jan had begun to learn his letters, he brought forth some wares which moved Jan's feelings more than the whirligigs did.

"Buy a nice picter, marm?" said the Cheap Jack to Mrs. Lake, who, with the best intentions not to purchase, felt that there could be no harm in seeing what the man had got.

"You shall have 'Joseph and his Bretheren' cheap," roared the hunchback, becoming more pressing as the windmiller's wife seemed slow to be fascinated, and shaking "Joseph and his Brethren," framed in satin-wood, in her face, as he advanced upon her with an almost threatening air. "Don't want 'em? Take 'Antony and Cleopatterer.' It's a sweet picter. Too dear? Do you know what sech picters costs to paint? Look at Cleopatterer's dress and the jewels she has on. I don't make a farthing on 'em. I gets daily bread out of the other things, and only keeps the picters to oblige one or two ladies of taste that likes to give their rooms a genteel appearance."

The long disuse of such powers of judgment as she had, and long habit of always giving way, had helped to convert Mrs. Lake's naturally weak will and unselfish disposition into a sort of mental pulp, plastic to any pressure from without. To men she invariably yielded; and, poor specimen of a man as the Cheap Jack was, she had no fibre of personal judgment or decision in the strength of which to oppose his assertions, and every instant she became more and more convinced that wares she neither wanted nor approved of were necessary to her, and good bargains, because the man who sold them said so.

The Cheap Jack was a knave, but he was no fool. In a crowded market-place, or at a street door, no oilier tongue wagged than his. But he knew exactly the moment when a doubtful bargain might be clinched by a bullying tone and a fierce look on his dirty face, at cottage doors, on heaths or downs, when the good wife was alone with her children, and the nearest neighbor was half a mile away.

No length of experience taught Mrs. Lake wisdom in reference to the Cheap Jack.

Each time that his cart appeared in sight she resolved to have nothing to do with him, warned by the latest cracked jug, or the sugar-basin which, after three-quarters of an hour wasted in chaffering, she had beaten down to three-halfpence dearer than what she afterwards found to be the shop price in the town. But proof to the untrained mind is "as water spilled upon the ground." And when the Cheap Jack declared that she was quite free to look without buying, and that he did not want her to buy, Mrs. Lake allowed him to pull down his goods as before, and listened to his statements as if she had never proved them to be lies, and was thrown into confusion and fluster when he began to bully, and bought in haste to be rid of him, and repented at leisure — to no purpose as far as the future was concerned.

"Look here!" yelled the hunchback, as he waddled with horrible swiftness after the miller's wife, as she withdrew into the mill; "which do you mean to have? *I* gets nothing on 'em, whichever you takes, so please yourself. Take 'Joseph and his Bretheren.' The frame's worth twice the money. Take the other, too, and I'll take sixpence off the pair, and be out of pocket to please you."

"Nothing to-day, thank you!" said Mrs. Lake, as loudly as she could.

"Got any other sort, you say?" said the Cheap Jack. "I've got all sorts, but some parties is so difficult to please.

"Wait a bit, wait a bit," he continued, as Mrs. Lake again tried to make him (willing to) hear that she wanted none of his wares; and, vanishing with the uncanny quickness common to him, he waddled swiftly back again to his cart, and returned, before Mrs. Lake could secure herself from intrusion, laden with a fresh supply of pictures, the weight of which it seemed marvellous that he could support.

"Now you've got your choice, marm," he said. "It's no trouble to me to oblige a good customer. There's picters for you!"

"*Pitchers!*" said Jan, admiringly, as he crept up to them.

"So they are, my little man. Now then, help your mammy to choose. Most of these is things you can't get now, for love nor money. Here you are,—'Love and Beauty.' That's a sweet thing. 'St Joseph,' 'The Robber's Bride,' 'Child and Lamb,' 'Melan-choly.' Here's an old"—

"Pitcher!" exclaimed Jan once more, gazing at an old etching in a dirty frame, which the Cheap Jack was holding in his hand. "Pitcher, pitcher! let Jan look!" he cried.

It was of a water-mill, old, thatched, and with an unprotected wheel, like the one in the valley below. Some gnarled willows stretched across the water, whose trunks seemed hardly less time-worn and rotten than the wheel below. This foreground subject was in shadow, and strongly drawn, but beyond it, in the sunlight, lay a bit of delicate distance, on the rising ground of which stood one of those small wooden windmills known as Post-mills. An old woman and a child were just coming into the shade, and passing beneath a wayside shrine. What in the picture took Jan's fancy it is impossible to say, but he gazed at it with exclamations of delight.

The Cheap Jack saw that it was certain to be bought, and he raised the price accordingly.

Mrs. Lake felt the same conviction, and began to try at least to get a good bargain.

"'Tis a terr'ble old frame," said she. "There be no gold left on 't." And no more there was.

"What do you say?" screamed the Cheap Jack, with his hand to his ear, and both a great deal too close to Mrs. Lake's face to be pleasant.

"'Tis such an old frame," she shouted, "and the gold be all gone."

"Old!" cried the hunchback, scowling; "who says I sell old things? Every picter in that lot's brand new and dirt cheap."

"The gold be rubbed off," screamed Mrs. Lake in his ear.

"Brighten it up, then," said the Cheap Jack.

"Gold ain't paint; gold ain't paper; rub it up!" and, suiting the action to the word, he rubbed the dirty old frame vigorously with the dirty sleeve of his smock.

"It don't seem to brighten it, nohow," said Mrs. Lake, looking nervously round; but neither the miller nor George was to be seen.

"Real gold allus looks like this in damp weather," said the Cheap Jack. "Hang it up in a warm room, dust it lightly every morning with a dry handkerchief, an' it'll come out that shining you'll see your face in it. And when summer comes, cover it up in yaller gauze to keep off the flies."

Mrs. Lake looked wistfully at the place the Cheap Jack had rubbed, but she had no redress, and saw no way out of her hobble but to buy the picture.

When the bargain was completed, the Cheap Jack fell back into his oiliest manner; it being part of his system not only to bully at the critical moment, but to be very civil afterwards, so as to leave an impression so pleasant on the minds of his lady customers that they could hardly do other than thank him for his promise to call again shortly with "bargains as good as ever."

The Cheap Jack was a man of many voices. The softness of his parting words to Mrs. Lake, "I'd go three mile out of my road, ma'am, to call on a lady like you," had hardly died away, when he woke the echoes of the plains by addressing his horse in a very different tone.

The Wiltshire carters and horses have a language between them which falls darkly upon the ear of the unlearned therein; but the uncouth yell which the Cheap Jack addressed to his beast was not of that dialect. The sound he made on this occasion was not, Gā oot! Coom hedder! or, There right! but the horse understood it.

It is probable that it never heard the Cheap Jack's softer intonations, for its protuberant bones gave a quiver beneath the scarred skin as he yelled. Then its drooping ears pricked faintly, the quavering forelegs were braced, one desperate jog of the tottering load of oddities, and it set slowly and silently forward.

The Cheap Jack did not follow his wares; he scrambled softly round the mill, like a deformed cat, looking about him on all sides. Then he made use of another sound, — a sharp, suggestive sound, whistled between two of his fingers.

Then he looked round again.

No one appeared. The wheels of the distant cart scraped slowly along the road, but this was the only sound the Cheap Jack heard.

He whistled softly again.

And as the cart took the sharp turn of the road, and was lost to sight, the miller's man appeared, and the Cheap Jack greeted him in the softest tone he had yet employed.

"Ah, there you are, my dear!"

Meanwhile, Mrs. Lake sat within, and looked ruefully at the damaged frame, and wished that the master, or at least the man, had happened to be at home.

It is to be feared that our self-reproach for having done wrong is not always so certain, or so keen, as our self-reproach for having allowed ourselves to suffer wrong — in a bad bargain.

Whether this particular picture was a bad bargain it is not easy to decide.

It was scandalously dear for its condition, and for what it had cost the hunchback, but it was cheap for the pleasure it gave to the little Jan.

CHAPTER XI.

SCARECROWS AND MEN. — JAN REFUSES TO "MAKE GEARGE." — UNCANNY. — "JAN'S OFF." — THE MOON AND THE CLOUDS.

THE picture gave Jan great pleasure, but it proved a stumbling-block on the road to learning.

To "make letters" on his slate had been the utmost of his ambition, and as he made them he learned them. But after the Cheap Jack's visit his constant cry was, "Jan make pitchers." And when Abel tried to confine his attention to the alphabet, he would, after a most perfunctory repetition of a few letters that he knew, and hap-hazard blunders over fresh ones, fling his arms round Abel's neck and say coaxingly, "Abel dear, make Janny *pitchers* on his slate."

Abel's pictures, at the best, were of that style of wall decoration dear to street boys.

"Make a pitcher of a man," Jan would cry. And Abel did so, bit by bit, to Jan's dictation. Thus:

"Make 's head. Make un round. Make two eyes. Make a nose. Make a mouth. Make 's arms. Make 's fingers," &c. And, with some "free-handling," Abel would strike the five fingers off, one by one, in five screeching strokes of the slate-pencil. But his art was conventional, and when Jan said, "Make un a miller's thumb," he was puzzled, and could only bend the shortest of the five strokes slightly backwards to represent the trade-mark of his forefathers.

And when a little later Jan said one day, " 'Tis a galley crow, that is. *Now* make a pitcher of a MAN, Abel dear!" Abel found that the scarecrow figure was the limit of his artist powers, and thenceforward it was Jan who "made pitchers."

He drew from dawn to dusk upon the little slate which he wore tied by a bit of string to the belt of his pinafore.

He drew his foster-mother, and Abel, and the kitten, and the clock, and the flower-pots in the window, and the windmill itself, and every thing he saw or imagined. And he drew till his slate was full on both sides, and then in very primitive fashion he spat and rubbed it all out and began again. And whenever Jan's face was washed, the two faces of his slate were washed too; and with this companion he was perfectly happy and constantly employed.

Now it was Abel who gave the subjects for the pictures, and Jan who made them, and it was good Abel also who washed the slate, and rubbed the well-worn stumps of pencil to new points upon the round-house floor.

They often went together to a mound at some little distance, where, seated side by side, they "made a mill" upon the slate, Jan drawing, and Abel dictating the details to be recorded.

"Put in the window, Jan," he would say; "and another, and another, and another, and another. Now put the sails. Now put the stage. Now put daddy by the door."

On one point Jan was obstinate. He steadily refused to "make Gearge" upon his slate in any capacity whatever.

Perhaps it was in this habit of constantly gazing at all things about him, in order to commit them to his slate, which gave a strange, dreamy expression to Jan's dark eyes. Perhaps it was sky-gazing, or the windmiller's trick of watching the clouds, or perhaps it was something else, from which Jan derived an erectness of carriage not common among the children about him, and a quaint way of carrying his little chin in the air as if he were listening to voices from a higher level than that of the round-house floor.

If he had lived farther north, he could hardly have escaped the suspicion of uncanniness. He was strangely like a changeling among the miller's children.

To gratify that old whim of his about the red shawl, his doting foster-mother made him little crimson frocks; and as he wandered over the downs in his red dress and a white pinafore, his yellow hair flying in the breeze, his chin up, his black eyes wide open, with slate in one hand, his pencil in the other, and the sandy kitten clinging to his shoulder (for Jan never lowered his chin to help her to balance herself), he looked more like some elf than a child of man.

He had queer, independent ways of his own, too; freaks, — not naughty enough for severe punishment, but sufficiently out of the routine and unexpected to cause Mrs. Lake some trouble.

He was no sooner firmly established on his own legs, with the power of walking, or rather toddling, independent of help, than he took to making expeditions on the downs by himself. He would watch his opportunity, and when his foster-mother's back was turned, and the door of the round-house opened by some grist-bringer, he would slip out and toddle off with a swiftness decidedly dangerous to a balance so lately acquired.

Sometimes Mrs. Lake would catch sight of him, and if

her hands were in the wash-tub, or otherwise engaged, she would cry to the nurse-boy, "Abel, he be off! Jan's off." A comic result of which was that Jan generally announced his own departure in the same words, though not always loud enough to bring detection upon himself.

When his chance came and the door was open, he would pause for half a moment on the threshold to say, in a tone of intense self-satisfaction, " He be off. Abel! Janny's off!" and forthwith toddle out as hard as he could go. As he grew older, he dropped this form; but the elfish habit of appearing and disappearing at his own whim was not cured.

It was a puzzle as well as a care to Mrs. Lake. All her own children had given trouble in their own way,— a way much the same with all of them. They squalled for what they wanted, and, like other mothers of her class, she served them whilst her patience lasted, and slapped them when it came to an end. They clung about her when she was cooking, in company with the cats, and she put tit-bits into their dirty paws, and threw scraps to the clean paws of the cats, till the nuisance became overwhelming, and she kicked the cats and slapped the children, who squalled for both. They dirted their clothes, they squabbled, they tore the gathers out of her dresses, and wailed and wept, and were beaten with a hazel-stick by their father, and pacified with treacle-stick by the mother; and so tumbled up, one after the other, through childish customs and misdemeanors, almost as uniform as the steps of the mill-ladders.

But the customs and misdemeanors of the foster-child were very different.

His appetite to be constantly eating, drinking, or sucking — if it were but a bennet or grass-stalk — was less voracious than that of the other children. Mrs. Lake gave him Benjamin's share of treacle-stick, but he has been known to give some of it away, and to exchange peppermint-drops for a slate-pencil rather softer than his own. He would have had Benjamin's share of "bits" from the cupboard, but that the other children begged so much oftener, and Mrs. Lake was not capable of refusing any thing to a steady tease. He could walk the whole length of a turnip-field without taking a munch, unless he were hungry, though even dear old Abel invariably exercised his jaws upon a "turmut." And he made himself ill with hedge-fruits and ground-roots seldomer than any other member of the family.

So far, Jan gave less trouble than the rest. But then he had a spirit of enterprise which never misled them. From the effects of this, Abel saved his life more than once. On one occasion he pulled him out of the wash-tub, into which he had plunged head-foremost, in a futile endeavor to blow soap-bubbles through a fragment of clay-pipe, which he had picked up on the road, and which made his lips sore for a week, besides nearly causing his death by drowning.

From diving into the deepest recesses of the windmill it became hopeless to try to hinder him, and when Abel was fairly taken into the business Mrs. Lake relied upon his care for his foster-brother. And Jan was wary and nimble, for his own part, and gave little trouble. His great delight was to gaze first out of one window, and then out of the opposite one; either blinking as the great sails drove by, as if they would strike him in the face, or watching the shadows of them invisible, as they passed like noon-day ghosts over the grass.

His habit of taking himself off on solitary expeditions neither the miller's hazel-stick nor Mrs. Lake's treacle-stick could cure by force or favor.

One November evening, just after tea, Jan disappeared, and the yellow kitten also. When his bed-time came, Mrs. Lake sought him high and low, and Abel went carefully, mill-candlestick in hand, through every floor, from the millstones to the machinery, but in vain. Neither he nor the kitten was to be found.

It was when the kitten, in chase of her own tail, tumbled in sideways through the round-house door, that Mrs. Lake remembered that Jan might possibly have gone out, and she ran out after him.

The air was chill and fresh, but not bitterly cold. The moon rode high in the dark heavens, and a flock of small white clouds passed slowly before its face and spread over the sky. The shadows of the driving sails fell clearly in the moonlight, and flitted over the grass more quickly than the clouds went by the moon.

Mrs. Lake was not susceptible to effects of scenery, and she was thinking of Jan. As she ran round the windmill, she struck her foot against what proved to be his body, and, stooping, saw that he was lying on his face. But when she snatched him up with a cry of terror, she found that he was not dead, nor even hurt, but only weeping pettishly.

In the first revulsion of feeling from her fright, she was rather disposed to shake her recovered treasure, as a relief to her own excitement. But Abel, whose first sight of Jan was as the light of the mill-candle fell on his tear-stained face, said tenderly, "What be amiss, Janny?"

"Jan can't make un," sobbed his foster-brother.

"What can't Janny make? Tell Abel, then," said the nurse-boy.

Jan stuck his fists into his eyes, which were drying fast, and replied, " Jan can't make the moon and the clouds, Abel dear!"

And Abel's candle being at that moment blown out by a gust of wind, he could see Jan's slate and pencil lying at some distance apart upon the short grass.

On the dark ground of the slate he had made a round, white, full moon with his soft slate-pencil, and had tried hard to draw each cloud as it passed. But the rapid changes had baffled him, and the pencil-marks were gray compared with the whiteness of the clouds and the brightness of the moon, and the slate, though dark, was a mockery of the deep, deep depths of the night-sky.

And in his despair he had flung the slate one way and the pencil another, and there they lay under the moonlight; and the sandy kitten, who could see more clearly on this occasion than any one else, was dancing a fandango upon poor Jan's unfinished sketch.

CHAPTER XII.

THE WHITE HORSE. — COMROGUES. — MOERDYK. — GEORGE CONFIDES IN THE CHEAP JACK — WITH RESERVATION.

WHEN the Cheap Jack's horse came to the brow of the hill, it stopped, and with drooping neck stood still as before. The Cheap Jack was busy with George, and it was at no word from him that the poor beast paused. It knew at what point to wait, and it waited. There was little temptation to go on. The road down the hill had just been mended with flints; some of these were the size of an average turnip, and the hill was steep. So the old horse poked out his nose, and stood almost dozing, till the sound of the Cheap Jack's shuffling footsteps caused him to prick his ears, and brace his muscles for a fresh start.

The miller's man came also, who was sulky, whilst the Cheap Jack was civil. He gave his horse a cut across the knees, to remind him to plant his feet carefully among the sharp boulders; and then, choosing a smooth bit by the side of the road, he and George went forward together.

"You've took to picters, I see," said George, nodding towards the cart.

"So I have, my dear," said the Cheap Jack; "anything for a livelihood; an *honest* livelihood, you know, George." And he winked at the miller's man, who relaxed his sulkiness for a guffaw.

"*You've* had so little in my way lately, George," the hunchback continued, looking sharply sideways up at his companion. "Sly business has been slack, my dear, eh?"

But George made no answer, and the Cheap Jack, after relieving his feelings by another cut at the horse, changed the subject.

"That's a sharp little brat of the miller's," said he, alluding to Jan. "And he ain't much like the others. Old-fashioned, too. Children mostly likes the gay picters, and worrits their mothers for 'em, bless 'em! But he picked out an ancient-looking thing, — came from a bankrupt pawn-shop, my dear, in a lot. I almost think I let it go too cheap; but that's my failing. And a beggarly place like this ain't like London. In London there's a place for every thing, my dear, and shops for old goods as well as new, and customers too; and the older and dirtier some things is, the more they fetches."

There was a pause, for George did not speak; and the Cheap Jack, bent upon amiability, repeated his remark, — "A sharp little brat, too!"

"What be 'ee harping on about him for?" asked George, suspiciously. "I knows what I knows about un, but that's no business of yours."

"You know about most things, my dear," said the Cheap Jack, flatteringly. "They'll have to get up very early that catch you napping. But what about the child, George?"

"Never you mind," said George. "But he ain't none of the miller's, I'll tell 'ee that; and he ain't the missus's neither."

"What is he to *you*, my dear?" asked the dwarf, curiously, and, getting no answer, he went on: "He'd be useful in a good many lines. He'd not do bad in a circus, but he'd draw prime as a young prodigy."

George looked round, "You be thinking of stealing *he* then, as well as " —

"Hush, my dear," said the dwarf. "No, no, I don't want him. But there was a good deal of snatching young kids done in my young days; for sweeps, destitute orphans, juvenile performers, and so on."

"*He* wouldn't suit you," grinned George. "A comes of genteel folk, and a's not hard enough for how you'd treat un."

"You're out there, George," said the dwarf. "Human beings is like 'osses; it's the genteelest as stands the most. 'Specially if they've been well fed when they was babies."

At this point the Cheap Jack was interrupted by his horse stumbling over a huge, jagged lump of flint, that, with the rest of the road-mending, was a disgrace to a highway of a civilized country. A rate-payer or a horse-keeper might have been excused for losing his temper with the authorities of the road-mending department; but the Cheap Jack's wrath fell upon his horse. He beat him over the knees for stumbling, and across the hind legs for slipping, and over his face for wincing, and accompanied his blows with a torrent of abuse.

What a moment that must have been for Balaam's ass, in which she found voice to remonstrate against the unjust blows, which have, nevertheless, fallen pretty thickly ever since upon her descendants and their fellow-servants of ungrateful man! From how many patient eyes that old reproach, of long service ill-requited, yet speaks almost as plainly as the voice that "rebuked the madness of the prophet!"

The Cheap Jack's white horse had a point of resemblance to the "genteel human beings" of whom he had been speaking. It had "come of a good stock," and had seen better and kinder days; and to it, also, in its misfortunes, there remained that nobility of spirit which rises in proportion to the ills it meets with. The poor old thing was miserably weak, and sore and jaded, and the flints were torture. But it rallied its forces, gave a desperate struggle, and got the cart safely to the bottom of the hill. Here the road turned sharply, and the horse went on. But after a few paces it stopped as before; this time in front of a small public-house, where trembling, and bathed in perspiration, it waited for its master.

The public-house was a small dark, dingy-looking hovel, with a reputation fitted to its appearance.

A dirty, grim-looking man nodded to the Cheap Jack and George as they entered, and a girl equally dirty, but much handsomer, brought glasses of spirits, to which the friends applied themselves, at the Cheap Jack's expense. George grew more sociable, and the Cheap Jack reproached him with want of confidence in his friends.

"You're so precious sharp, my dear," said the hunchback, who knew well on what point George liked to be flattered, "that you overreaches yourself. I don't complain—after all the business we've done together—that it's turned slack all of a sudden. You says they're down on you, and that's enough for me. I don't complain that you've got your own plans and keeps 'em as secret as the grave, but I says you'll regret it. If you was a good scholar, George, you could do without friends, you're so precious sharp. But you're no scholar, my dear, and you'll be let in yet, by a worse friend than Cheap John."

George so bitterly regretted his want of common learning, and the stupidity which made him still slow to decipher print, and utterly puzzled by writing, that the Cheap Jack's remarks told strongly. These, and the conversation they had had on the hill, recalled to his mind a matter which was still a mystery to the miller's man.

"Look here, Jack," said he, leaning across the dirty little table; "if you be such a good scholar, what do M O E R D Y K spell?"

"Say it again, George," said the dwarf. But when, after that, he still looked puzzled, George laughed long and loudly.

"You be a good scholar!" he cried. "You be a fine friend, too, for a iggerant man. If a can't tell the first word of a letter, 'tis likely 'ee could read the whole, too!"

"The first word of a *letter*, eh?" said the dwarf.

"The very first," said George. "'Tis a long way you 'd get in it, and stuck at the start!"

"Up in the corner, at the top, eh?" said the dwarf.

"So it be," said George, and he laughed no longer.

"It's the name of a place, then," said the Cheap Jack; "and it ain't to be expected I should know the names of all the places in the world, George, my dear."

It was a great triumph for the Cheap Jack, as George's face betrayed. If George had trusted him a little more, he might have known the meaning of the mysterious word years ago. The name of a place! The place from which the letter was written. The place where something might be learned about the writer of the letter, and of the gentleman to whom it was written. For George knew so much. It was written to a gentleman, and to a gentleman who had money, and who had secrets; and, therefore, a gentleman from whom money might be got, by interfering in his secrets.

The miller's man was very ignorant and very stupid, in spite of a certain low cunning not at all incompatible with gross ignorance. He had no knowledge of the world. His very knowledge of malpractices and mischief was confined to the evil doings of one or two other ill-conditioned country lads like himself, who robbed their neighbors on dark nights, and disposed of the spoil by the help of such men as the Cheap Jack and the landlord of the public-house at the bottom of the hill.

But by loitering about on that stormy night years ago, when he should have been attending to the mill, he had picked up enough to show him that the strange gentleman had no mind to have his proceedings as to the little Jan generally known. This and some sort of traditional idea that "sharp," though penniless men had at times wrung a great deal of money from rich people, by threatening to betray their secrets, was the sole foundation of George's hopes in connection with the letter. It was his very ignorance which hindered him from seeing the innumerable chances against his getting to know any thing important enough, even if he could use his information, to procure a bribe.

He had long given up the idea as hopeless, though he had kept the letter, but it revived when the Cheap Jack solved the puzzle which Abel could not explain, and George finally promised to let his friend read the whole letter for him. He also allowed that it concerned Jan, or that he supposed it to do so. He related Jan's history, and confessed that he had picked up the letter, which was being blown about near the mill, on the night of Jan's arrival.

In this statement there was some truth, and some falsehood; for in the opinion of the miller's man, if your own interest obliged you to confide in a friend, it was at least wise to hedge the confidence by not telling all the truth, or by qualifying it with lies.

This mental process was, however, at least equally familiar to the Cheap Jack, and he did not hesitate, in his own mind, to feel sure that the letter had not been found, but stolen. In which he was farther from the truth than if he had simply believed George.

But then he was not in the neighborhood five years back, and, as it happened, he had never heard of the lost pocket-book.

CHAPTER XIII.

GEORGE AS A MONEYED MAN. — SAL.— THE "WHITE HORSE."— THE WEDDING. — THE WINDMILLER'S WIFE FORGETS, AND REMEMBERS TOO LATE.

EXCITEMENT, the stifling atmosphere of the public-house, and the spirits he had drunk at his friend's expense, had somewhat confused the brains of the miller's man by the time that the Cheap Jack rose to go. George was, as a rule, sober beyond the wont of the rustics of the district, chiefly from parsimony. When he could drink at another man's expense, he was not always prudent.

"So you've settled to go, my dear?" said the dwarf, as they stood together by the cart. "Business being slack, and parties unpleasantly suspicious, eh?"

"Never you mind," said George, who felt very foolish, and hoped himself successful in looking very wise; "I be going to set up for myself; I'm tired of slaving for another man."

"Quite right, too," said the dwarf; "but all businesses takes money, of which, my dear, I doesn't doubt you've plenty. You always took care of Number One, when you did business with Cheap John."

At that moment, George felt himself a sort of embodiment of shrewd wisdom; he had taken another sip from the glass, which was still in his hand, and the only drawback to the sense of magnified cunning by which his ideas seemed to be illumined was a less pleasant feeling that they were perpetually slipping from his grasp. To the familiar idea of outwitting the Cheap Jack he held fast, however.

"It be nothin' to thee what a have," he said slowly; "but a don't mind 'ee knowin' so much, Jack, because 'ee can't get at un; haw, haw! Not unless 'ee robs the savings-bank."

The dwarf's eyes twinkled, and he affected to secure some pictures that hung low, as he said carelessly,—

"Savings-banks be good places for a poor man to lay by in. They takes small sums, and a few shillings comes in useful to a honest man, George, my dear, if they doesn't go far in business."

"Shillings!" cried George, indignantly; "pounds!" And then, doubtful if he had not said too much, he added, "A don't so much mind 'ee knowing, Jack, because 'ee can't get at 'em!"

"It's a pity you're such a poor scholar, George," said the Cheap Jack, turning round, and looking full at his friend; "you're so sharp, but for that, my dear. You don't think you counts the money over in your head till you makes it out more than it is, now, eh?"

"A can keep things in my yead," said George, "better than most folks can keep a book; I knows what I has, and what other folks can't get at. I knows how I put un in. First, the five-pound bill"—

"They must have stared to see you bring five pound in a lump, George, my dear!" said the hunchback. "Was it wise, do you think?"

"Gearge bean't such a vool as a looks," replied the miller's man. "A took good care to change it first, Cheap John, and a put it in by bits."

"You're a clever customer, George," said his friend. "Well, my dear? First, the five-pound bill, and then?"

George looked puzzled, and then, suddenly, angry. "What be that to you?" he asked, and forthwith relapsed into a sulky fit, from which the Cheap Jack found it impossible to rouse him. All attempts to renew the subject, or to induce the miller's man to talk at all, proved fruitless. The Cheap Jack insisted, however, on taking a friendly leave.

"Good-by, my dear," said he, "till the mop. You knows my place in the town, and I shall expect you."

The miller's man only replied by a defiant nod, which possibly meant that he would come, but had some appearance of expressing only a sarcastic wish that the Cheap Jack might see him on the occasion alluded to.

In obedience to a yell from its master, the white horse now started forward, and it is not too much to say that the journey to town was not made more pleasant for the poor beast by the fact that the Cheap Jack had a good deal of long-suppressed fury to vent upon somebody.

It was perhaps well for the bones of the white horse that, just as they entered the town, the Cheap Jack brushed against a woman on the narrow foot-path, who having turned to remonstrate in no very civil terms, suddenly checked herself, and said in a low voice, "Juggling Jack!"

The dwarf started, and looked at the woman with a puzzled air.

She was a middle-aged woman, in the earlier half of middle age; she was shabbily dressed, and had a face that would not have been ill-looking, but that the upper lip was long and cleft, and the lower one unusually large. As the Cheap Jack still stared in silence, she burst into a noisy laugh, saying, "More know Jack the Fool than Jack the Foo'. knows." But, even as she spoke, a gleam of recognition suddenly spread over the hunchback's face, and, putting out his hand, he said, "Sal! *you here*, my dear?"

"The air of London don't agree with me just now," was the reply; "and how are you, Jack?"

"The country air's just beginning to disagree with me, my dear," said the hunchback; "but I'm glad to see you, Sal. Come in here, my dear, and let's have a talk, and a little refreshment."

The place of refreshment to which the dwarf alluded was another public-house, the White Horse by name. There was no need to bid the Cheap Jack's white horse to pause here; he stopped of himself at every public-house; nineteen times out of twenty to the great convenience of his master, for which he got no thanks; the twentieth time the hunchback did not want to stop, and he was lavish of abuse of the beast's stupidity in coming to a standstill.

The white horse drooped his soft white nose and weary neck for a long, long time under the effigy of his namesake swinging overhead, and when the Cheap Jack did come out, he seemed so preoccupied that the tired beast got home with fewer blows than usual.

He unloaded his cart mechanically, as if in a dream; but when he touched the pictures, they seemed to awaken a fresh train of thought. He stamped one of his little feet spitefully on the ground, and, with a pretty close imitation of George's dialect, said bitterly, "Gearge bean't such a vool as a looks!" adding, after a pause, "I'd do a deal to pay *him* off!"

As he turned into the house, he said thoughtfully, " Sal's precious sharp; she allus was. And a fine woman, too, is Sal!"

Not long after the incidents just related, it happened that business called Mrs. Lake to the neighboring town. She seldom went out, but a well-to-do aunt was sick, and wished to see her; and the miller gave his consent to her going.

She met the milk-cart at the corner of the road, and so was driven to the town, and she took Jan with her.

He had begged hard to go, and was intensely amused by all he saw. The young Lakes were so thoroughly in the habit of taking every thing, whether commonplace or curious, in the same phlegmatic fashion, that Jan's pleasure was a new pleasure to his foster-mother, and they enjoyed themselves greatly.

As they were making their way towards the inn where they were to pick up a neighbor, in whose cart they were to be driven home, their progress was hindered by a crowd, which had collected near one of the churches.

Mrs. Lake was one of those people who lead colorless lives, and are without mental resources, to whom a calamity is almost delightful, from the stimulus it gives to the imagination, and the relief it affords to the monotony of existence.

"Oh, dear! oh, dear!" she cried, peering through the crowd: "I wonder what it is. 'Tis likely 'tis a man in a fit now, I shouldn't wonder, or a cart upset, and every soul killed, as it might be ourselves going home this very evening. Dear, dear! 'tis a venturesome thing to leave home, too!"

"'Ere they be! 'ere they be!" roared a wave of the crowd, composed of boys, breaking on Mrs. Lake and Jan at this point.

"'Tis the body, sure as death!" murmured the windmiller's wife; but, as she spoke, the street boys set up a lusty cheer, and Jan, who had escaped to explore on his own account, came running back, crying, —

"'Tis the Cheap Jack, mammy! and he's been getting married."

If any thing could have rivalled the interest of a sudden death for Mrs. Lake, it must have been such a wedding as this. She hurried to the front, and was just in time to catch sight of the happy couple as they passed down the street, escorted by a crowd of congratulating boys.

"Well done, Cheap John!" roared one. "You've chose a beauty, you have," cried another. "She's 'arf a 'ead taller, anyway," added a third. "Many happy returns of the day, Jack!" yelled a fourth.

Jan was charmed, and again and again he drew Mrs. Lake's attention to the fact that it really *was* the Cheap Jack.

But the windmiller's wife was staring at the bride. Not merely because the bride is commonly considered the central figure of a wedding-party, but because her face seemed familiar to Mrs. Lake, and she could not remember where she had seen her. Though she could remember nothing, the association seemed to be one of pain. In vain she beat her brains. Memory was an almost uncultivated quality with her, and, like the rest of her intellectual powers, had a nervous, skittish way of deserting her in need, as if from timidity.

Mrs. Lake could sometimes remember things when she got into bed, but on this occasion her pillow did not assist her; and the windmiller snubbed her for making "such a caddle" about a woman's face she might have seen anywhere or nowhere, for that matter; so she got no help from him.

And it was not till after the Cheap Jack and his wife had left the neighborhood, that one night (she was in bed) it suddenly "came to her," as she said, that the dwarf's bride was the woman who had brought Jan to the mill, on the night of the great storm.

CHAPTER XIV.

SUBLUNARY ART. — JAN GOES TO SCHOOL. — DAME DATCHETT AT HOME. — JAN'S FIRST SCHOOL SCRAPE. JAN DEFENDS HIMSELF.

EVEN the hero of a tale cannot always be heroic, nor of romantic or poetic tastes.

The wonderful beauty of the night sky and the moon had been fully felt by the artist-nature of the child Jan; but about this time he took to the study of a totally different subject, — pigs.

It was the force of circumstances which led Jan to "make pigs" on his slate so constantly, instead of nobler subjects; and it dated from the time when his foster-mother began to send him with the other children to school at Dame Datchett's.

Dame Datchett's cottage was the last house on one side of the village main street. It was low, thatched, creeper-covered, and had only one floor, and two rooms, — the outer room where the Dame kept her school, and the inner one where she slept. Dame Datchett's scholars were very young, and it is to be hoped that the chief objects of their parents in paying for their schooling were to insure their being kept safely out of the way for a certain portion of each day, and the saving of wear and tear to clothes and shoes. It is to be hoped so, because this much of discipline

"'Tis a Q, not a F," he said boldly and aloud. — PAGE 99.

was to some extent accomplished. As to learning, Dame Datchett had little enough herself, and was quite unable to impart even that, except to a very industrious and intelligent pupil.

Her school appurtenances were few and simple. From one of them arose Jan's first scrape at school. It was a long, narrow blackboard, on which the alphabet had once been painted white, though the letters were now so faded that the Dame could no longer distinguish them, even in spectacles.

The scrape came about thus.

As he stood at the bottom of the little class which gathered in a semicircle around the Dame's chair, his young eyes could see the faded letters quite clearly, though the Dame's could not.

"Say th' alphabet, childern!" cried Dame Datchett; and as the class shouted the names of the letters after her, she made a show of pointing to each with a long "sallywithy" wand cut from one of the willows in the water-meadows below. She ran the sallywithy along the board at what she esteemed a judicious rate, to keep pace with the shouted alphabet, but, as she could not see the letters, her tongue and her wand were not in accord. Little did the wide-mouthed, white-headed youngsters of the village heed this, but it troubled Jan's eyes; and when — in consequence of her rubbing her nose with her disengaged hand — the sallywithy slipped to Q as the Dame cried F, Jan brought the lore he had gained from Abel to bear upon her inaccuracy.

" 'Tis a Q, not a F," he said, boldly and aloud.

A titter ran through the class, and the biggest and stupidest boy found the joke so overwhelming that he stretched his mouth from ear to ear, and doubled himself up with laughter, till it looked as if his corduroy-breeched knee were a turnip, and he about to munch it.

The Dame dropped her sallywithy and began to feel under her chair.

"Which be the young varment as said a F was a Q?" she rather unfairly inquired.

"A didn't say a F was a Q"— began Jan; but a chorus of cowardly little voices drowned him, and curried favor with the Dame by crying, "'Tis Jan Lake, the miller's son, missus."

And the big boy, conscious of his own breach of good manners, atoned for it by officiously dragging Jan to Dame Datchett's elbow.

"Hold un vor me," said the Dame, settling her spectacles firmly on her nose.

And with infinite delight the great booby held Jan to receive his thwacks from the strap which the Dame had of late years substituted for the birch rod. And as Jan writhed, he chuckled as heartily as before, it being an amiable feature in the character of such clowns that, so long as they can enjoy a guffaw at somebody's expense, the subject of their ridicule is not a matter of much choice or discrimination.

After the first angry sob, Jan set his teeth and bore his punishment in a proud silence, quite incomprehensible by the small rustics about him, who, like the pigs of the district, were in the habit of crying out in good time before they were hurt as a preventive measure.

Strangely enough, it gave the biggest boy the impression that Jan was "poor-spirited," and unable to take his own part,— a temptation to bully him too strong to be resisted

So when the school broke up, and the children were scattering over the road and water-meads, the wide-mouthed boy came up to Jan and snatched his slate from him.

"Give Jan his slate!" cried Jan, indignantly.

He was five years old, but the other was seven, and he held the slate above his head.

"And who be *Jan*, then, thee little gallus-bird?" said he, tauntingly.

"I be Jan!" answered the little fellow, defiantly. "Jan Lake, the miller's son. Give I his slate!"

"Thee's not a miller's son," said the other; and the rest of the children began to gather round.

"I be a miller's son," reiterated Jan. "And I've got a miller's thumb, too;" and he turned up his little thumb for confirmation of the fact.

"Thee's not a miller's son," repeated the other, with a grin. "Thee's nobody's child, thee is. Master Lake's not thy vather, nor Mrs. Lake bean't thy mother. Thee was brought to the mill in a sack of grist, thee was."

In saying which, the boy repeated a popular version of Jan's history.

If any one had been present outside Dame Datchett's cottage at that moment who had been in the windmill when Jan first came to it, he would have seen a likeness so vivid between the face of the child and the face of the man who brought him to the mill as would have seemed to clear up at least one point of the mystery of his parentage.

Pride and wrath convulsed every line of the square, quaint face, and seemed to narrow it to the likeness of the man's, as, with his black eyes blazing with passion, Jan flew at his enemy.

The boy still held Jan's slate on high, and with a derisive "haw! haw!" he brought it down heavily above Jan's head. But Jan's eye was quick, and very true. He dodged the blow, which fell on the boy's own knees, and then flew at him like a kitten in a tiger fury.

They were both small and easily knocked over, and in an instant they were sprawling on the road, and cuffing, and pulling, and kicking, and punching with about equal success, except that the bigger boy prudently roared and howled all the time, in the hope of securing some assistance in his favor.

"Dame Datchett! Missus! Murder! Yah! Boohoo! The little varment be a throttling I."

But Mrs. Datchett was deaf. Also, she not unnaturally considered that, in looking after "the young varments" in school-hours, she fully earned their weekly pence, and was by no means bound to disturb herself because they squabbled in the street.

Meanwhile Jan gradually got the upper hand of his lubberly and far from courageous opponent, whose smock he had nearly torn off his back. He had not spent any of his breath in calling for aid, but now, in reply to the boy's cries for mercy and release, he shouted, "What be my name, now, thee big gawney? Speak, or I'll drottle 'ee."

"Jan Lake," said his vanquished foe. "Let me go! Yah! yah!"

"Whose son be I?" asked the remorseless Jan.

"Abel Lake's, the miller! Boohoo, boohoo!" sobbed the boy.

"And what be this, then, Willum Smith?" was Jan's final question, as he brought his thumb close to his enemy's eye.

"It be the miller's thumb thee's got, Jan Lake," was the satisfactory answer.

CHAPTER XV.

WILLUM GIVES JAN SOME ADVICE. — THE CLOCK FACE. — THE HORNET AND THE DAME. — JAN DRAWS PIGS. — JAN AND HIS PATRONS. — KITTY CHUTER. — THE FIGHT. — MASTER CHUTER'S PREDICTION.

JAN went back to school. Though his foster-mother was indignant, and ready to do battle both with Dame Datchett and with William Smith's aunt (with whom, in lieu of parents, the boy lived), and though Abel expressed his anxiety to go down and "teach Willum to vight one of his own zize," Jan steadily rejected their help, and said manfully, "Jan bean't feared of un. I whopped un, I did."

So Mrs. Lake doctored his bruises, and sent him off to school again. She yielded the more readily that she felt certain that the windmiller would not take the child's part against the Dame.

No further misfortune befell him. William, if loutish and a bit of a bully on occasion, was not an ill-natured child; and, having a turn for humor of a broad, unintellectual sort, he and Jan became rather friendly on the common, but reprehensible ground of playing pranks, which kept the school in a titter and the Dame in doubt. And, if detected, they did not think a dose of the strap by any means too high a price to pay for their fun.

For William's sufferings under that instrument of discipline were not to be measured by his doleful howlings and roarings, nor even by his ready tears.

"What be 'ee so voolish for as to say nothin' when her wollops 'ee?" he asked of Jan, in a very friendly spirit, one day. "Thee should holler as loud as 'ee can. Them that hollers and cries murder she soon stops for, does Dame Datchett. She be feared of their mothers hearing 'em, and comin' after 'em."

Jan could not lower himself to accept such base advice; but his superior adroitness did much to balance the advantage William had over him, in a less scrupulous pride.

As to learning, I fear that, after the untoward consequences of his zeal for the alphabet, Jan made no effort to learn any thing but cat's-cradle from his neighbors.

On one other occasion, indeed, he was somewhat over-zealous, and only escaped the strap for his reward by a friendly diversion on the part of his friend. The Dame had a Dutch clock in the corner of her kitchen, the figures on the face of which were the common Arabic ones, and not Roman. And as one of the few things the Dame professed was to "teach the clock," she would, when the figures had been recited after the fashion in which her scholars shouted over the alphabet, set those who had advanced to the use of slates to copy the figures from the clock-face.

Slowly and sorrowfully did William toil over this lesson. Again and again did he rub out his ill-proportioned fives, with so greasy a finger and such a superabundance of moisture as to make a sort of puddle, into which he dug heavily, and broke two pencils.

"A vive be such an akkerd vigger," he muttered, in reply to Jan, who had looked up inquiringly as the second pencil snapped. "'Twill come aal right, though, when a dries."

It did dry, but any thing but right. Jan rubbed out the mass of thick and blotted strokes, and when the Dame was not looking, he made William's figures for him. Jan was behindhand in spelling, but to copy figures was no difficulty to him.

Having helped his friend thus, he pulled his smock, to draw attention to his own slate. The other children wrote so slowly that time had hung heavy on his hands; and, instead of copying the figures in a row, he had made a drawing of the clock-face, with the figures on it; but instead of the hands, he had put eyes, nose, and mouth, and below the mouth a round gray blot, which William instantly recognized for a portrait of the mole on Dame Datchett's chin. This brilliant caricature so tickled him, that he had a fit of choking from suppressed laughter; and he and Jan, being detected "in mischief," were summoned with their slates to the Dame's chair.

William came off triumphant; but when the Dame caught sight of Jan's slate, without minutely examining his work, she said, "Zo thee's been scraaling on thee slate, instead of writing thee figures," and at once began to fumble beneath her chair.

But William had slightly moved the strap with his foot, as he stood with a perfectly unmoved and vacant countenance beside the Dame, which made some delay; and as Mrs. Datchett bent lower on the right side of her chair, William began upon the left a "hum," which, with a close imitation of the crowing of a cock, the grunting of a pig, and the braying of a donkey, formed his chief stock of accomplishments.

"Drat the thing! Where be un?" said the Dame, endangering her balance in the search.

"B-z-z-z-z!" went William behind the chair; and he added, *sotto voce*, to Jan, "She be as dunch as a bittle."

At last the Dame heard, and looked round. "Be that a harnet, missus, do 'ee think?" said William, with a face as guileless as a babe's.

Dame Datchett rose in terror. William bent to look beneath her chair for the hornet, and of course repeated his hum. As the hornet could neither be found nor got rid of, the alarmed old lady broke up the school, and went to lay a trap of brown sugar outside the window for her enemy. And so Jan escaped a beating.

But this and the story of his first fight are digressions. It yet remains to be told how he took to drawing pigs.

Dame Datchett's cottage was the last on one side of the street; but it did not face the street, but looked over the water-meadows, and the little river, and the bridge.

As Jan sat on the end of the form, he could look through the Dame's open door, the chief view from which was of a place close by the bridge, and on the river's bank, where the pig-minders of the village brought their pigs to water. Day after day, when the tedium of doing nothing under Dame Datchett's superintendence was insufficiently relieved to Jan's active mind by pinching "Willum" till he giggled, or playing cat's-cradle with one of his foster-brothers, did he welcome the sight of a flock of pigs with their keeper, scuttling past the Dame's door, and rushing snorting to the stream.

Much he envied the freedom of the happy pig-minder, whilst the vagaries of the pigs were an unfailing source of amusement.

The degree and variety of expression in a pig's eye can only be appreciated by those who have studied pigs as Morland must have studied them. The pertness, the liveliness, the humor, the love of mischief, the fiendish ingenuity and perversity of which pigs are capable, can be fully known to the careworn pig-minder alone. When they are running away, — and when are they not running away? — they have an action with the hind legs very like a donkey in a state of revolt. But they have none of the donkey's too numerous grievances. And if donkeys squealed at every switch, as pigs do, their undeserved sufferings would have cried loud enough for vengeance before this.

Jan's opportunities for studying pigs were good. As the smallest and swiftest of the flock, his tail tightly curled, and indescribable jauntiness in his whole demeanor, came bounding to the river's brink, followed by his fellows, driving, pushing, snufling, winking, and gobbling, and lastly by a small boy in a large coat, with a long switch, Jan was witness of the whole scene from Dame Datchett's door. And, as he sat with his slate and pencil before him, he naturally took to drawing the quaint comic faces and expressive eyes of the herd, and their hardly less expressive backs and tails; and to depicting the scenes which took place when the pigs had enjoyed their refreshment, and with renewed vigor led their keeper in twenty different directions, instead of going home. Back, up the road, where he could hardly drive them at the point of the switch a few hours before; by sharp turns into Squire Ammaby's grounds, or the churchyard; and helter-skelter through the water-meadows.

The fame of Jan's "pitcher-making" had gone before him to Dame Datchett's school by the mouths of his foster-

-brothers and sisters, and he found a dozen little voices ready to dictate subjects for his pencil.

"Make a 'ouse, Janny Lake." "Make thee vather's mill, Janny Lake.' " Make a man. Make Dame Datchett. Make the parson. Make the Cheap Jack. Make Daddy Angel. Make Master Chuter. Make a oss — cow — ship — pig!"

But the popularity obtained by Jan's pigs soon surpassed that of all his other performances.

"Make pigs for I, Janny Lake!" and "Make pigs for I, too!" was a sort of whispering chorus that went on perpetually under the Dame's nose. But when she found that it led to no disturbance, that the children only huddled round the child Jan and his slate like eager scholars round a teacher, Dame Datchett was wise enough to be thankful that Jan possessed a power she had never been able to acquire, — that he could "keep the young varments quiet."

"He be most 's good 's a monitor," thought the Dame; and she took a nap, and Jan's genius held the school together.

The children tried other influences besides persuasion.

"Jan Lake, I've brought thee an apple. Draa out a pig for I on a's slate."

Jan had a spirit of the most upright and honorable kind. He never took an unfair advantage, and to the petty cunning which was "Willum's" only idea of wisdom he seemed by nature incapable of stooping. But in addition to, and alongside of, his artistic temperament, there appeared to be in him no small share of the spirit of a trader. The capricious, artistic spirit made him fitful in his use even of the beloved slate; but, when he was least inclined to draw, the offer of something he very much wanted would spur him to work; and in the spirit of a true trader, he worked well.

He would himself have made a charming study for a painter, as he sat surrounded by his patrons, who watched him with gaping mouths of wonderment, as his black eyes moved rapidly to and fro between the river's brink and his slate, and his tiny fingers steered the pencil into cunning lines which " made pigs." " The very moral!" as William declared, smacking his corduroy breeches with delight.

Sometimes Jan hardly knew that they were there, he was so absorbed in his work. His eyes glowed with that strong pleasure which comes in the very learning of any art, perhaps of any craft. Now and then, indeed, his face would cloud with a different expression, and in fits of annoyance, like that in which his foster-mother found him outside the windmill, he would break his pencils, and ruthlessly destroy sketches with which his patrons would have been quite satisfied. But at other moments his face would twinkle with a very sunshine of smiles, as he was conscious of having caught exactly the curve which expressed obstinacy in this pig's back, or the air of reckless defiance in that other's tail.

And so he learned little or nothing, and improved in his drawing, and kept the school quiet, and had always a pocket well filled with sweet things, nails, string, tops, balls, and such treasures, earned by his art.

One day as he sat " making pigs " for one after another of the group of children round him, a pig of especial humor having drawn a murmur of delight from the circle, this murmur was dismally echoed by a sob from a little maid on the outside of the group. It was Master Chuter's little daughter, a pretty child, with an oval, dainty featured face, and a prim gentleness about her, like a good little girl in a good little story. The intervening young rustics began to nudge each other and look back at her.

"Kitty Chuter be crying!" they whispered.

"What be amiss with 'ee, then, Kitty Chuter?" said Jan, looking up from his work; and the question was passed on with some impatience, as her tears prevented her reply. "What be amiss with 'ee?"

"Janny Lake have never made a pig for I," sobbed the little maid, with her head dolefully inclined to her left shoulder, and her oval face pulled to a doubly pensive length. "I axed my vather to let me get him a posy, and a said I might. And I got un some vine Bloody Warriors, and a heap of Boy's Love off our big bush, that smelled beautiful. And vather says a can have some water-blobs off our pond when they blows. But Tommy Green met I as a was coming down to school, and a snatched my vlowers from me, and I begged un to let me keep some of un, and a only laughed at me. And I daren't go back, for I was late; and now I've nothin' to give Janny Lake to make a draft of a pig for I." And, having held up for the telling of her tale, the little maid broke down in fresh tears.

Jan finished off the tail of the pig he was drawing with a squeak of the pencil that might have come from the pig itself, and, stuffing the slate into its owner's hands, he ran up to Kitty Chuter and kissed her wet cheeks, saying, "Give I thee slate, Kitty Chuter, and I'll make thee the best pig of all. I don't want nothing from thee for 't. And when school's done, I'll whop Tommy Green, if I sees him."

And forthwith, without looking from the door for studies, Jan drew a fat sow with her little ones about her; the other children clustering round to peep, and crying, " He 've made Kitty Chuter one, two, three, vour, *vive* pigs!"

"Ah, and there be two more you can't see, because the old un be lying on 'em," said Jan.

"Six, seven!" William counted; and he assisted the calculation by sticking up first a thumb and then a forefinger as he spoke.

Some who had not thought half a ball of string, or a dozen nails as good as new, too much to pay for a single pig drawn on one side of their slates, and only lasting as long as they could contrive to keep the other side in use without quite smudging that one, were now disposed to be dissatisfied with their bargains. But as the school broke up, and Tom Green was seen loitering on the other side of the road, every thing was forgotten in the general desire to see Jan carry out his threat, and " whop " a boy bigger than himself for bullying a little girl.

Jan showed no disposition to shirk, and William acted as his friend, and held his slate and book.

Success is not always to the just, however; and poor Jan was terribly beaten by his big opponent, though not without giving him some marks of the combat to carry away.

Kitty Chuter wept bitterly for Jan's bloody nose; but he comforted her, saying, " Never mind, Kitty; if he plagues thee again, 'll fight un again and again, till I whops he."

But his valor was not put to the proof, for Tommy Green molested her no more.

Jan washed his face in the water-meadows, and went stout-heartedly home, where Master Lake beat him afresh, as he ironically said, " to teach him to vight young varments like himself instead of minding his book."

But upon Master Chuter, of the Heart of Oak, the incident made quite a different impression. He was naturally pleased by Jan's championship of his child, and, added to this, he was much impressed by the sketch on the slate. It was, he said, the "living likeness" of his own sow; and, as she had seven young pigs, the portrait was exact, allowing for the two which Jan had said were out of sight.

He gave Kitty a new slate, and kept the sketch, which he showed to all in-comers. He displayed it one evening to the company assembled round the hearth of the little inn, and took occasion to propound his views on the subject of Jan's future life.

(Master Chuter was fond of propounding his views,— a taste which was developed by always being sure of an audience.)

"It's nothing to me," said Master Chuter, speaking of Jan, "who the boy be. It be no fault of his'n if he's a fondling. And one thing's sure enough. Them that left him with Master Lake left something besides him. There was that advertisement,— you remember that about the five-pound bill in the paper, Daddy Angel?"

"Ay, ay, Master Chuter," said Daddy Angel; "after the big storm, five year ago. Sartinly, Master Chuter."

"Was it ever found, do ye think?" said Master Linseed, the painter and decorator.

"It must have been found," said the landlord; "but I bean't so sure about it's having been given up, the notice was in so long. And whoever did find un must have found un at once. But what 1 says is, five-pound notes lost as easy as that comes from where there's more of the same sort. And, if Master Lake be paid for the boy, he can 'fford to 'prentice him when his time comes. He 've boys enough of his own to take to the mill, and Jan do seem to have such an uncommon turn for drawing things out, I'd try him with painting and varnishing, if he was mine. And I believe he'd come to signs, too! Look at that, now! It be small, and the boy 've had no paint to lay on, but there's the sign of the Jolly Sow for you, as natteral as life. You know about signs, Master Linseed," continued the landlord. For there was a tradition that the painter could "do picture-signs," though he had only been known to renew lettered ones since he came to the neighborhood. "Master Lake should 'prentice him with you when he's older," Master Chuter said in conclusion.

But Master Linseed did not respond warmly. He felt it a little beneath his dignity as a sign-painter to jump at the idea, though the rest of the company assented in a general murmur.

"Scrawling on a slate," the painter and decorator began — and at this point he paused, after the leisurely customs of the district, to light his pipe at the leaden-weighted candlestick which stood near; and then, as his hearers sat expectant, but not impatient, proceeded: "Scrawling on a slate is one thing, Master Chuter: painting and decorating's another. Painting's a trade; and not rightly to be understood by them that's not larned it, nor to be picked up by all as can scrawl a line here and a line there, as the whim takes 'em. Take oak-graining," — and here Master Linseed paused again, with a fine sense of effect, — "who'd ever think of taking a comb to it as didn't know? And for the knots, I've worked 'em — now with a finger and now a thumb — over a shutter-front till it looked that beautiful the man it was done for telled me himself,—'I 'd rather,' says he, ' have 'em as you 've done 'em than the real thing.' But young hands is nowhere with the knots. They puts 'em in too thick."

The company said, "Ay, ay!" in a tone of unbroken assent, for Master Linseed was understood to have "come from a distance," and to "know a good deal." But an innkeeper stands above a painter and decorator anywhere, and especially on his own hearth, and Master Chuter did not mean to be put down.

"I suppose old hands were young uns once, Master Linseed," said he; "and if the boy were never much at oak-graining, I 'd back him for sign-painting, if he were taught. Why, the pigs he draas out, look you. I could cut 'em up, and not a piece missing; not a joint, nor as much as would make a pound of sausages. And if a draas pigs, why not osses, why not any other kind?"

"Ay, ay!" said the company.

"I be thinking," continued Master Chuter, "of a gentlemen as draad out that mare of my father's that ran in the mail. You remember the coaches, Daddy Angel?"

" Ay, ay, Master Chuter. Between Lonnon and Exeter a ran. Fine days at the Heart of Oak, then, Master Chuter."

" He weren't a sign-painter, that I knows on. A were somethin' more in the gentry way," said Master Chuter, not, perhaps, quite without malice in the distinction. "He were what they calls in genteel talk a"—

"Artis'," said Master Linseed, removing his pipe, to supply the missing word with a sense of superiority.

"No, not a artis'," said Master Chuter, " though it do begin with a A, too. 'Twasn't a artis' he was, 'twas a"—

" Ammytoor," said the travelled sign-painter.

"That be it," said the innkeeper. "A ammytoor. And he was short of money, I fancy, and so 'twas settled a should paint this mare of my father's to set against the bill. And a draad and a squinted at un, and a squinted at un and a draad, and laid the paint on till the pictur' looked all in a mess, and then he took un away to vinish. But when a sent it home, I thought my vather would have had the law of un. I'm blessed if a hadn't given the mare four white feet, and shoulders that wouldn't have pulled a vegetable cart; and she near-wheeler of the mail! I'd lay a pound bill Jan Lake would a done her ever so much better, for as young a hand as a is, if a'd squinted at her as long."

"Well, well, Master Chuter," said the painter and decorator, rising to go, "let the boy draw pigs and osses for his living. And I wish he may find paint as easy as slate pencil."

Master Linseed's parting words produced upon the company that somewhat unreasonable depression which such ironical good wishes are apt to cause; but they only roused the spirit of contradiction in Master Chuter, and heightened his belief in Jan's talents more than any praise from the painter could have done.

"Here's a pretty caddle about giving a boy's due!" said the innkeeper. "But I knows the points of a oss, and the makings of a pig, if I bean't a sign-painter. And, mark my words, the boy Jan 'ull out-paint Master Linseed yet."

Master Chuter spoke with triumph in his tone, but it was the triumph of delivering his sentiments to unopposing hearers.

There were moments of greater triumph to come, of which he yet wotted not, when the sevenfold fulfilment of his prediction should be past dispute, and attested from his own walls by more lasting monuments of Jan's skill than the too perishable sketch which now stood like a text for the innkeeper on the mantelpiece of the Heart of Oak.

CHAPTER XVI.

THE MOP. — THE SHOP. — WHAT THE CHEAP JACK'S WIFE HAD TO TELL. — WHAT GEORGE WITHHELD.

A MOP is a local name for a hiring-fair, at which young men and women present themselves to be hired as domestic servants or farm laborers for a year. It was at a mop that the windmiller had hired George, and it was at that annual festival that his long service came to an end. He betook himself to the town, where the fair was going on, not with any definite intention of seeking another master, but from a variety of reasons: partly for a holiday, and to "see the fun;" partly to visit the Cheap Jack, and hear what advice he had to give, and to learn what was in the letter; partly with the idea that something might suggest itself in the busy town as a suitable investment for his savings and his talents. At the worst, he could but take another place.

The sun shone brightly on the market-place as George passed through it. The scene was quaint and picturesque. Booths, travelling shows, penny theatres, quack doctors, tumblers, profile cutters, exhibitors and salesmen of all sorts, thronged the square, and overflowed into a space behind, where some houses had been burnt down and never rebuilt; whilst round the remains of the market cross in the centre were grouped the lads and lasses "on nire." The girls were smartly dressed, and the young men in snowy smocks, above which peeped waistcoats of gay colors, looked in the earlier part of the day so spruce, that it was as lamentable to see them after the hours of beer-drinking and shag tobacco-smoking which followed, as it was to see what might have been a neighborly and cheerful festival finally swamped in drunkenness and debauchery.

George's smock was white, and George's waistcoat was red, and he had made himself smart enough, but he did not linger amongst his fellow-servants at the Cross. He hurried through the crowd, nodding sheepishly in answer to a shower of chaff and greetings, and made his way to the by-street where the Cheap Jack had a small dingy shop for the sale of coarse pottery. Some people were spiteful enough to hint that the shop-trade was of much less value to him than the store-room attached, where the goods were believed to be not all of one kind.

The red bread-pans, pipkins, flower-pots, and so forth, were grouped about the door with some attempt at effective display, and with cheap prices marked in chalk upon their sides. The window was clean, and in it many knickknacks of other kinds were mixed with the smaller china ware. And, when George entered the shop, the hunchback's wife was behind the counter. Like Mrs. Lake, he paused to think where he could have seen her before; the not uncomely face marred by an ugly mouth, in which the upper lip was long and cleft, and the lower lip large and heavy, seemed familiar to him. He was still beating his brains when the Cheap Jack came in.

George had been puzzled that the woman's countenance did not seem new to him, and he was puzzled and disturbed also that the expression on the face of the Cheap Jack was quite new. Whatever the hunchback had in his head, however, he was not unfriendly in his manner.

"Good morning, George, my dear!" he cried, cheerfully; "you've seen my missus before, eh, George?"

George was just about to say no, when he remembered that he had seen the woman, and when and where.

"Dreadful night that was, Mr. Sannel!" said the Cheap Jack's wife, with a smile on her large mouth. George assented, and by the hospitable invitation of the newly married couple he followed them into the dwelling part of the house, trying as he did so to decide upon a plan for his future conduct.

Here at last was a woman who could probably tell all that he wanted to know about the mystery on which he had hoped to trade, and — the Cheap Jack had married her. If any thing could be got out of the knowledge of Jan's history, the Cheap Jack, and not George, would get it now. The hasty resolution to which George came was to try to share what he could not keep entirely to himself. He flattered himself he could be very civil, and — he had got the letter.

It proved useful. George was resolved not to show it until he had got at something of what the large-mouthed woman had to tell; and, as she wanted to see the letter, she made a virtue of necessity, and seemed anxious to help the miller's man to the utmost of her power.

The history of her connection with Jan's babyhood was soon told, and she told it truthfully.

Five years before her marriage to the Cheap Jack, she was a chambermaid in a small hotel in London, and " under notice to leave." Why — she did not deem it necessary to tell George. In this hotel Jan was born, and Jan's mother died. She was a foreigner, it was supposed, and her husband also, for they talked a foreign language to each other. He was not with her when she first came, but he joined her afterwards, and was with her at her death. So far the Cheap Jack's wife spoke upon hearsay. Though employed at the hotel, which was very full, she was not sleeping in the house; she was not on good terms with the landlady, nor even with the other servants, and her first real connection with the matter was when the gentleman, overhearing some "words" between her and the landlady at the bar, abruptly asked her if she were in want of employment. He employed her, — to take the child to the very town where she was now living as the Cheap Jack's wife. He did not come with her, as he had to attend his wife's funeral. It was understood at the hotel that he was going to take the body abroad for interment. So the porter had said. The person to whom she was directed to bring the child was a respectable old woman, living in the outskirts of the town, whose business was sick-nursing. She seemed, however, to be comfortably off, and had not been out for some time. She had been nurse to the gentleman in his childhood, so she once told the Cheap Jack's wife with tears. But she was always shedding tears, either over the baby, or as she sat over her big Bible, "for ever having to wipe her spectacles, and tears running over her nose ridic' lus to behold." She was pious, and read the Bible aloud in the evening. Then she had fainting fits; she could not go uphill or upstairs without great difficulty, and she had one of her fits when she first saw the child. If with these infirmities of body and mind the ex-nurse had been easily managed, the Cheap Jack's wife professed that she could have borne it with patience. But the old woman was painfully shrewd, and there was no hoodwinking her. She never allowed the Cheap Jack's wife to go out without her, and contrived, in spite of a hundred plans and excuses, to prevent her from speaking to any of the townspeople alone. Never, said Sal, never could she have put up with it, even for the short time before the gentleman came down to them, but for knowing it would be a paying job. But his arrival was the signal for another catastrophe, which ended in Jan's becoming a child of the mill.

If the sight of the baby had nearly overpowered the old nurse, the sight of the dark-eyed gentleman overwhelmed her yet more. Then they were closeted together for a long time, and the old woman's tongue hardly ever stopped. Sal explained that she would not have been such a fool as to let this conversation escape her, if she could have helped it. She took her place at the keyhole, and had an excuse ready for the old woman, if she should come out suddenly. The old woman came out suddenly, but she did not wait for the excuse. She sent the Cheap Jack's wife civilly on an errand into the kitchen, and then followed her, and shut the door and turned the key upon her without hesitation, leaving her unable to hear any thing but the tones of the conversation through the parlor-wall. She never opened the door again. As far as the Cheap Jack's wife could tell, the old woman seemed to be remonstrating and pleading; the gentleman spoke now and then. Then there was a lull, then a thud, then a short pause, and then the parlor-door was burst open, and the gentleman came flying towards the kitchen, and calling for the Cheap Jack's wife. The fact that the door was locked caused some delay, and delay was not desirable The old nurse had had "a fit." When the doctor came, he gave no hope of her life. She had had heart disease for many years, he said. In the midst of this confusion, a letter came for the gentleman, which seemed absolutely to distract him. He bade Sal get the little Jan ready, and put his clothes together, and they started that evening for the mill. Sal believed it was the doctor who recommended Mrs. Lake as a foster-mother for the baby, having attended her child. The storm came on after they started. The child had been very sickly ever since they left London. The gentleman took the Cheap Jack's wife straight back to the station, paid her handsomely, and sent her up to town again. She had never seen him since. As to his name, it so happened she had never heard it at the hotel; but when he was setting her off to the country with the child, she asked it, and he told her that it was Ford. The old nurse also spoke of him as Mr. Ford, but — so Sal fancied — with a sort of effort, which made her suspect that it was not his real name.

"Yes, it be!" said George, who had followed the narrative with open-mouthed interest. "It be aal right. I knows. 'Twas a gentleman by the name of Ford as cried his pocket-book, and the vive-pound bill in the papers. 'Tis aal right. Ford — Jan Ford be the little varment's name then, and he be gentry-born, too! Missus Lake she allus said so, she did, sartinly."

George was so absorbed by the flood of information which had burst upon him all at once, and by adjusting his clumsy thoughts to the new view of Jan, that he did not stop to think whether the Cheap Jack and his wife had known of the lost pocket-book and the reward. They had not. The dark gentleman had no wish to reopen communication with the woman he had employed. He thought (and rightly) that the book had fallen when he stumbled over his cloak in getting into the carriage, and he had refused to advertise it except in the local papers. And at that time the Cheap Jack and Sal were both in London.

But George's incautious speech recalled one or two facts to them, and whilst George sat slowly endeavoring to realize that new idea, "Master Jan Ford, full young gentleman, and at least half Frenchman" (for of any other foreigners George knew nothing), the Cheap Jack was pondering the words "five-pound bill," and connecting them with George's account of his savings when they last met; and his quicker spouse was also putting two and two together, but with a larger sum. At the same instant the Cheap Jack inquired after George's money, and his wife asked about the letter. But George had hastily come to a decision. If the tale told by the woman were true, he had got a great deal of information for nothing, and he saw no reason for sharing whatever the letter might contain with those most likely to profit by it. As to letting the Cheap Jack have any thing whatever to do with the disposal of his savings, nothing could be further from his intentions.

"Gearge bean't such a vool as a looks," thought that worthy, and aloud he vowed, with unnecessary oaths, that the money was still in the bank, and that he had forgotten to bring the letter, which was in a bundle that he had left at the mill.

This disappointment did not, however, diminish the civility of the Cheap Jack's wife. She was very hospitable, and even pressed George to spend the night at their house, which he declined. He had a dread of the Cheap Jack, which was almost superstitious.

For her civility, indeed, the Cheap Jack's wife was taken to task by her husband in a few moments when they were alone together.

"I thought you was sharper than to be took in by him!" said the hunchback, indignantly. "Do you believe all that gag about the bank and the bundle? and you, as soft to him, telling him every blessed thing, and he stowed the cash and the letter somewheres where we shall never catch a sight of 'em, and got every thing out of you as easy as shelling a pod of peas." And in language as strong as that of the miller's man the Cheap Jack swore he could have done better himself a hundred times over.

"Could you?" said the large-mouthed woman, contemptuously. "I wouldn't live long in the country, I wouldn't, if it was to make me such a owl as you 've turned into. It ain't much farther than your nose *you* sees!"

"Never mind me, Sal, my dear," said the hunchback, anxiously. "I trusts you, my dear. And it seems to me as if you thought he 'd got 'em about him. Do you, my dear, and why? And why did you tell him the truth, straight on end, when a made-up tale would have done as well, and kept him in the dark?"

"Why did I tell him the truth?" repeated the woman. "'Cos I ain't such a countrified fool as to think lies is allus the cleverest tip, 'cos the truth went farthest this time. Why do I think he 's got 'em about him? First, 'cos he swore so steady he hadn't. For a ready lie, and for acting a lie, and over-acting it at times, give me townspeople; but for a thundering big un, against all reason, and for sticking to it stupid when they 're downright convicted, and with a face as innercent as a baby's, give me a country lump! And next, because I can tell with folks a deal sharper than him, even to which side of 'em the pocket is they've got what they wants to hide in, by the way they moves their head and their hands."

"Which side is it of him, Sal?" said the hunchback, with ugly eagerness.

"The left," said Sal; "but it won't be there long."

CHAPTER XVII.

THE MILLER'S MAN AT THE MOP. — A LIVELY COMPANION. — SAL LOSES HER PURSE. — THE RECRUITING SERGEANT. — THE POCKET-BOOK TWICE STOLEN. — GEORGE IN THE KING'S ARMS. — GEORGE IN THE KING'S SERVICE. — THE LETTER CHANGES HANDS, BUT KEEPS ITS SECRET.

FOR some years the ex-servant of the windmill had been rather favored by fortune than otherwise. He found the pocket-book, and, though he could not read the letter, he got the five-pound note. Since then, his gains, honest and dishonest, had been much beyond his needs, and his savings were not small. Suspicion was just beginning to connect his name and that of the Cheap Jack with certain thefts committed in the neighborhood, when he made up his mind to go.

His wealth was not generally known. Many a time had he been tempted to buy pigs (a common speculation in the district, and the first stone of more than one rustic fortune), but the dread of exciting suspicion balanced the almost certain profit, and he could never make up his mind. For Master Lake paid only five pounds a yeaı for his man's valuable services, which, even in a district where at that time habits were simple, and boots not made of brown paper, did not leave much margin for the purchase of pigs. The pig speculation, though profitable, was not safe. George had made money, however, and he had escaped detection. On the whole, he had been fortunate. But that mop saw a turn in the tide of his affairs, and ended strangely with him.

It began otherwise. George had never felt more convinced of his power to help himself at the expense of his neighbors than he did after getting Sal's information, and keeping back his own, before they started to join in the amusements of the fair. He was on good terms with himself; none the less so that he had not failed to see the Cheap Jack's chagrin, as the woman poured forth all she knew for George's benefit, and got nothing in return.

The vanity of the ignorant knows no check except from without; under flattery, it is boundless, and the Cheap Jack's wife found no difficulty in fooling George to the top of his bent.

George was rather proud, too, of his companion. She was not, as has been said, ill-looking but for her mouth, and beauty was not abundant enough in the neighborhood to place her at much disadvantage. Fashionable finery was even less common, and the Cheap Jack's wife was showily dressed. And George found her a very pleasant companion; much livelier than the slow-witted damsels of the country-side. For him she had nothing but flattery; but her smart speeches at the expense of other people in the crowd caused the miller's man to double up his long back with laughter.

A large proportion of the country wives and sweethearts tramped up and down the fair at the heels of their husbands and swains, like squaws after their Indian spouses. But the Cheap Jack's wife asked George for his arm,—the left one,—and she clung to it all the day. "Quite the lady in her manners she be," thought George. She called him "Mr. Sannel," too. George felt that she admired him. For a moment his satisfaction was checked, when she called his attention to the good looks of a handsome recruiting sergeant, who was strutting about the mop with an air expressing not so much that it all belonged to him as that he didn't at all belong to it.

"But there, he ain't to hold a candle to you, Mr. Sannel, though his coat do sit well upon him," said the Cheap Jack's wife.

It gratified George's standing ill-will to the Cheap Jack to have "cut him out" with this showy lady, and to laugh loudly with her upon his arm, whilst the hunchback followed, like a discontented cur, at their heels. If there was a drawback to the merits of his lively companion, it was her power of charming the money out of George's pocket.

The money that he disbursed came from the right-hand pocket of his red waistcoat. In the left-hand pocket (and the pockets, like the pattern of the waistcoat, were large) was the lost pocket-book. It was a small one, and just fitted in nicely. In the pocket-book were George's savings, chiefly in paper. Notes were more portable than coin, and, as George meant to invest them somewhere where he was not known, no suspicions need be raised by their value. The letter was there also.

There were plenty of shows at the mop, and the Cheap Jack's wife saw them all. The travelling wax-works; the menagerie with a very mangy lion in an appallingly rickety cage; the fat Scotchman, a monster made more horrible to view by a dress of royal Stuart tartan; the penny theatre, and a mermaid in a pickling-tub.

One treat only she declined. The miller's man would have paid for a shilling portrait of her, but she refused to be taken.

The afternoon was wearing away, when Sal caught sight of some country bumpkins upon a stage, who were preparing to grin through horse-collars against each other for the prize of a hat. As she had never seen or heard of the entertainment, George explained it to her.

It was a contest in which the ugliest won the prize. Only the widest-mouthed, most grotesque-looking clowns of the place attempted to compete; and he won who, besides being the ugliest by nature, could " grin " and contort his features in the mode which most tickled the fancy of the beholders. George had once competed himself, and had only failed to secure the hat because his nearest rival could squint as well as grin; and he was on the point of boasting of this, but on second thoughts he kept the fact to himself.

Very willing indeed he was to escort his companion to a show in the open air for which nothing was charged, and they plunged valiantly into the crowd. The crowd was huge, but George's height and strength stood him in good stead, and he pushed on, and dragged Sal with him. There was some confusion on the stage. A nigger, with a countenance which of itself moved the populace to roars of laughter, had applied to be allowed to compete. Opinions were divided as to whether it would be fair to native talent, whilst there was a strong desire to see a face that in its natural condition was "as good as a play," with the additional attractions of a horse-collar and a grin.

The country clowns on the stage fumed, and the nigger grinned and bowed, and the crowd yelled, and surged, and swayed, and weak people got trampled, and everybody was tightly squeezed, and the Cheap Jack's wife was alarmed, and withdrew her hand from George's arm, and begged him to hold her up, which he gallantly did, she meanwhile clinging with both hands to his smock.

As to the hunchback, it is hardly necessary to say that he did not get very far into the crowd, and when his wife and George returned, laughing gayly, they found him standing outside, with a sulky face. "Look here, missus," said he; "you're a enjoying of yourself, but I'm not. You've got the blunt, so just hand over a few coppers, and I'll get a pint at the King's Arms."

Sal began fumbling to find her pocket, but when she found it, she gave a shriek, and turned it inside out. It was empty!

If the miller's man had enjoyed himself before, he was not to be envied now. The Cheap Jack's wife poured forth her woes in a continuous stream of complaint. She minutely described the purse which she had lost, the age and quality of her dress, and the impossibility of there being a hole in her pocket. She took George's arm once more, and insisted upon revisiting every stall and show where they had been, to see if her purse had been found. Up and down George toiled with her, wiping his face and feeling that he looked like a fool, as at each place in turn they were told that they might as well "look for a needle in a bottle of hay," and that pickpockets were as plenty at a mop as blackberries in September.

He was tired of the woman now she was troublesome, and fidgetingly persevering, as women are apt to be, and he was vexed to feel how little money was left in his right-hand pocket. He did not think of feeling in the left one.

not merely because the Cheap Jack was standing in front of him, but because no fear for the safety of its contents had dawned upon him. It was easy for a woman to lose her purse out of a pocket flapping loosely in the drapery of her skirts, but that any thing stowed tightly away in a man's waistcoat under his smock could be stolen in broad daylight without his knowledge did not occur to him. As little did he guess that of all the pickpockets who were supposed to drive a brisk trade at the fair, the quickest, the cleverest, the most practised professional was the Cheap Jack's wife.

She had feigned to see "something" on the ground near an oyster stall, which she said "might be" her purse. As indeed it might as well as any thing else, seeing that the said purse had no existence.

As she left them, George turned to the Cheap Jack.

"Look 'ee here, Jack," said he; "take thee missus whoam. She do seem to be so put about, 'tis no manner of use her stopping in the mop. And I be off for a pint of something to wash my throat out. I be mortal dry with running up and down after she. Women does make such a caddle about things."

"You might stand a pint for an old friend, George, my dear," said the Cheap Jack, following him. But George hurried on, and shook his head. "No, no," said he; "tak' thee missus whoam, I tell 'ee. She've not seen much at your expense to day, if she have lost her pus."

With which the miller's man escaped into the King's Arms, and pushed his way to the farthest end of the room, where a large party of men were drinking and smoking.

At a table near him sat the recruiting sergeant whom

he had noticed before, and he now examined him more closely.

He was of a not uncommon type of non-commissioned officers in the English service. Not of a very intellectual — hardly perhaps of an interesting — kind of good looks, he was yet a strikingly handsome man. His features were good and clearly cut; his hair and moustache were dark, thick, short and glossy; his dark eyes were quick and bright; his figure was well-made, and better developed; his shapely hands were not only clean, they were fastidiously trimmed about the nails (a daintiness common below the rank of sergeant, especially among men acting as clerks); and if the stone in his signet ring was not a real onyx, it looked quite as well at a distance, and the absence of a crest was not conspicuous. He spoke with a very good imitation of the accent of the officers he had served with, and in his alertness, his well-trained movements, his upright carriage, and his personal cleanliness, he came so near to looking like a gentleman that he escaped it only by a certain swagger, which proved an ill-chosen substitute for well-bred ease.

To George's eyes this was not visible as a fault. The sergeant was as much "the swell" as George could imagine any man to be.

George Sannel could never remember with distinctness the ensuing events of that afternoon. Dim memories remained with him of the sergeant meeting his long stare with some civilities, to which he was conscious of having replied less suitably than he might have wished. At one period, certainly, bets were made upon the height of himself and the handsome soldier, respectively, and he was sure that they were put back to back, and that he proved the taller man; and that it was somehow impressed upon him that he did not look so, because the other carried himself so much better. It was also impressed upon him, somehow, that if he would consent to be well-dressed, well-fed, and well-lodged, at the expense of the country, his own appearance would quickly rival that of the sergeant, and that the reigning Sovereign would gladly pay, as well as keep and clothe, such an ornamental bulwark of the state. At some other period the sergeant had undoubtedly told him to "give it a name," and the name he gave it was sixpenny ale, which he drank at the sergeant's expense, and which was followed by shandy-gaff, on the same footing.

At what time and for what reason George put his hand into his left-hand waistcoat pocket he never could remember. But when he did so, and found it empty, the cry he raised had such a ring of anguish as might have awakened pity for him, even where his ill deeds were fully known.

The position was perplexing, if he had had a sober head to consider it with. That pickpockets abounded had been well impressed upon his slow intellect, and that there was no means of tracing property so lost, in the crowd and confusion of the mop. True, his property was worth "crying," worth offering a reward for. But the pocketbook was not his, and the letter was not addressed to him; and it was doubtful if he even dare run the risk of claiming them.

His first despair was succeeded by a sort of drunken fury, in which he accused the men sitting with him of robbing him, and then swore it was the Cheap Jack, and so raved till the landlord of the King's Arms expelled him as "drunk and disorderly," and most of the company refused to believe that he had had any such sum of money to lose.

Exactly how or where, after this, the sergeant found him, George could not remember, but his general impression of the sergeant's kindness was strong. He could recall that he pumped upon his head in the yard of the King's Arms, to sober him, by George's own request; and that it did somewhat clear his brain, his remembrance of seeing the sergeant wipe his fingers on a cambric handkerchief seems to prove. They then paced up and down together arm in arm, if not as accurately in step as might have been agreeable to the soldier. George remembered hearing of prize money, to which his own loss was a bagatelle, and gathering on the whole that the army, as a profession, opened a sort of boundless career of opportunities to a man of his peculiar talents and appearance. There was something infectious, too, in the gay easy style in which the soldier seemed to treat fortune, good or ill; and the miller's man was stimulated at last to vow that he was not such a fool as he looked, and would "never say die." To the best of his belief, the sergeant replied in terms which showed that, had he been "in cash," George's loss would have been made good by him, out of pure generosity, and on the spot.

As it was, he pressed upon his acceptance the sum of one shilling, which the miller's man pocketed with tears.

What recruit can afterwards remember which argument of the skilful sergeant did most to melt his discretion into valor?

The sun had not dried the dew from the wolds, and the sails of the windmill hung idle in the morning air, when George Sannel made his first march to the drums and fifes with ribbons flying from his hat, a recruit of the 206th (Royal Wiltshire) Regiment of Foot.

As the Cheap Jack and his wife hastened home from the mop, Sal had some difficulty in restraining her husband's impatience to examine the pocket-book as they walked along.

Prudence prevailed, however, and it was not opened till they were at home and alone.

In notes and money, George's savings amounted to more than thirteen pounds.

"Pretty well, my dear," said the Cheap Jack, grinning hideously. "And now for the letter. Read it aloud, Sal, my dear; you're a better scholar than me."

Sal opened the thin, well-worn sheet, and read the word "Moerdyk," but then she paused. And, like Abel, she paused so long that the hunchback pressed impatiently to look over her shoulder.

But the letter was written in a foreign language, and the Cheap Jack and his wife were no wiser for it than the miller's man.

CHAPTER XVIII.

MIDSUMMER HOLIDAYS. — CHILD FANCIES. — JAN AND THE PIG-MINDER. — MASTER SALTER AT HOME. — JAN HIRES HIMSELF OUT.

MIDSUMMER came, and the Dame's school broke up for the holidays. Jan had longed for them intensely. Not that he was oppressed by the labors of learning, but that he wanted to be out of doors. Many a little one was equally eager for the freedom of the fields, but the common child-love for hedges and ditches, and flower-picking, and the like, was intensified in Jan by a deeper pleasure which country scenes awoke from the artist nature within him. That it is no empty sentimentality to speak of an artist nature in a child, let the child-memories of all artists bear witness! That they inspired the poet Wordsworth with one of his best poems, and that they have dyed the canvas of most landscape painters with the indestructible local coloring of the scenes of each man's childhood, will hardly be denied.

That this is against the wishes and the theories of many excellent people has nothing to do with its truth. If all children were the bluff, hearty, charmingly naughty, enviably happy, utterly simple and unsentimental beings that some of us wish, and so assert them to be, it might be better for them, or it might not — who can say? That the healthy, careless, rough and ready type is the one to encourage, many will agree, who cannot agree that it is universal, or even much the most common. It is probably from an imperfect remembrance of their nursery lives that some people believe that the griefs of one's childhood are light, its joys uncomplicated, and its tastes simple. A clearer recollection of the favorite poetry and the most cherished day-dreams of very early years would probably convince them that the strongest taste for tragedy comes before one's teens, and inclines to the melodramatic; that sentimentality (of some kind) is grateful to the verge of mawkishness; and that simple tastes are rather a result of culture and experience than natural gifts of infancy.

But in this rummaging up of the crude tastes, the hot little opinions, the romance, the countless visions, the many affectations of nursery days, there will be recalled also a very real love of nature; varying, of course, in its intensity from a mere love of fresh air and free romping, and a destructive taste for nosegays, to a living romance about the daily walks of the imaginative child, — a world apart, peopled with invisible company, such as fairies, and those fancy friends which some children devise for themselves, or with the beasts and flowers, to which love has given a personality.

To the romance child-fancy weaves for itself about the meadows where the milkmaids stand thick and pale, and those green courts where lords and ladies live, Jan added that world of pleasure open to those gifted with a keen sense of form and color. Strange gleams under a stormy sky, sunshine on some kingfisher's plumage rising from the river, and all the ever-changing beauties about him, stirred his heart with emotions that he could not have defined.

There was much to see even from Dame Datchett's open

door, but there was more to be imagined. Jan's envy of the pig-minder had reached a great height when the last school-day came.

He wanted to be free by the time that the pig-herd brought his pigs to water, and his wishes were fulfilled. The Dame's flock and the flock of the swineherd burst at one and the same moment into the water-meadows, and Jan was soon in conversation with the latter.

"Thee likes pig-minding, I reckon?" said Jan, stripping the leaves from a sallywithy wand, which he had picked to imitate that of the swineherd.

"Do I?" said the large-coated urchin, wiping his face with the big sleeve of his blue coat. "That's aal thee knows about un. I be going to leave to-morrow, I be. And if so be Master Salter's got another bwoy, or if so be he's not, I dunno, it ain't nothin' to I."

Jan learned that he had eighteen pence a week for driving the pigs to a wood at some little distance, where they fed on acorns, beech-mast, &c.; for giving them water, keeping them together, and bringing them home at teatime. He allowed that he could drive them as slowly as he pleased, and that they kept pretty well together in the wood; but that, as a whole, the perversity of pigs was such that— "Well, wait till ee tries it theeself, Jan Lake, that's aal."

Jan had resolved to do so. He did not return with his foster-brothers to the mill. He slipped off on one of his solitary expeditions, and made his way to the farm-house of Master Salter.

Master Salter and his wife sat at tea in the kitchen. In the cheerful clatter of cups, they had failed to hear Jan's knock; but the sunshine streaming through the open doorway being broken by some small body, the farmer's wife looked hastily up, thinking that the new-born calf had got loose, and was on the threshold.

But it was Jan. The outer curls of his hair gleamed in the sunlight like an aureole about his face. He had doffed his hat, out of civility, and he held it in one hand, whilst with the other he fingered the slate that hung at his waist.

"Massey upon us!" said the farmer, looking up at the same instant. "And who be thee?"

"Jan Lake, the miller's son, maester."

"Come in, come in!" cried Master Salter, hospitably. "So Master Lake have sent thee with a message, eh?"

"My father didn't send me," said Jan, gravely. "I come myself. Do 'ee want a pig-minder, Master Salter?"

"Ay, I wants a pig-minder. But I reckon thee father can't spare Abel for that now. A wish he could. Abel was careful with the pigs, he was, and a sprack boy, too."

"I'll be careful, main careful, Master Salter," said Jan, earnestly. "I likes pigs." But the farmer was pondering.

"Jan Lake — Jan," said he. "Be thee the boy as draad out the sow and her pigs for Master Chuter's little gel?" Jan nodded.

"Lor massey!" cried Master Salter. "I told 'ee, missus, about un. Look here, Jan Lake. If thee'll draa me out some pigs like them, I'll give 'ee sixpence and a new slate, and I'll try thee for a week, anyhow."

Jan drew the slate-pencil from his pocket without reply. Mrs. Salter, who had been watching him with motherly eyes, pushed a small stool towards him, and he began to draw a scene such as he had been studying daily for months past, — pigs at the water-side. He had made dozens of such sketches. But the delight of the farmer knew no bounds.

He slapped his knees, he laughed till the tears ran down his cheeks, and, as Jan put a very wicked eye into the face of the hindmost pig, he laughed merrily also. He was not insensible of his own talents, and the stimulus of the farmer's approbation gave vigor to his strokes.

"Here, missus," cried Master Salter; "get down our Etherd's new slate, and give it to un; I'll get another for he. And there's the sixpence, Jan; and if thee minds pigs as well as 'ee draas 'em, I don't care how long 'ee minds mine."

The object of his visit being now accomplished, Jan took up his hat to depart, but an important omission struck him, and he turned to say, "What 'll 'ee give me for minding your pigs, Master Salter?"

Master Salter was economical, and Jan was small, and anxious for the place.

"A shilling a week," said the farmer.

"And his tea?" the missus gently suggested.

"Well, I don't mind," said Master Salter. "A shilling a week and thee tea."

Jan paused. His predecessor had had eighteen pence for very imperfect services. Jan meant to be beyond reproach, and felt himself worth quite as much.

"I give the other boy one and sixpence," said the farmer, "but thee's very small."

"I'm sprack," said Jan, confidently. "And I be fond of pigs."

"Massey upon me," said Master Salter, laughing again. "'Tis a peart young toad, sartinly. A might be fifty year old, for the ways of un. Well, thee shall have a shilling and thee tea, or one and sixpence without, then." And seeing that Jan glanced involuntarily at the table, the farmer added, " Give un some now, missus. I'll lay a pound bill the child be hungry."

Jan was hungry. He had bartered the food from his "nunchin bag" at dinner-time for another child's new slate-pencil. The cakes were very good, too, and Mrs. Salter was liberal. He rose greatly in her esteem by saying grace before meat. He cooled his tea in his saucer too, and raised it to his lips with his little finger stuck stiffly out (a mark of gentility imparted by Mrs. Lake), and in all points conducted himself with the utmost propriety. "For what we have received the Lord be praised," was his form of giving thanks; to which Mrs. Salter added, "Amen," and "Bless his heart!" And Jan, picking up his hat, lifted his dark eyes candidly to the farmer's face, and said with much gravity and decision, —

"I'll take a shilling a week and me tea, Master Salter, if it be all the same to you. And thank you kindly, sir, and the missus likewise."

CHAPTER XIX.

THE BLUE COAT. — PIG-MINDING AND TREE-STUDYING.
—LEAF PAINTINGS. — A STRANGER. — MASTER SWIFT
IS DISAPPOINTED.

WHEN Jan returned to the windmill, and gravely announced that he had hired himself out as pig-minder to Master Salter, Mrs. Lake was, as she said, "put about." She considered pig-minding quite beneath the dignity of her darling, and brought forward every objection she could think of except the real one. But the windmiller had no romantic dreams on Jan's behalf, and he decided that "'twas better he should be arning a shillin' a week than gettin' into mischief at whoam." Jan's ambition, however, was not satisfied. He wanted a blue coat, such as is worn by the shepherd-boys on the plains. He did not mind how old it was, but it must be large; long in the skirt and sleeves. He had woven such a romance about Master Salter's swineherd and his life, as he watched him week after week from Dame Datchett's door with envious eyes, that even his coat, with the tails almost sweeping the ground, seemed to Jan to have a dignified air. And there really was something to be said in favor of sleeves so long that he could turn them back into a huge cuff in summer, and turn them down, Chinese fashion, over his hands in winter, to keep them warm.

Such a blue coat Abel had possessed, but it was not suitable for mill work, and Mrs. Lake was easily persuaded to give it to Jan. He refused to have it curtailed, or in any way adapted to his figure, and in it, with a switch of his own cutting, he presented himself at Master Salter's farm in good time the following morning.

It could not be said that Jan's predecessor had exaggerated the perversity of the pigs he drove. If the coat of his choice had a fault in Jan's estimation, it was that it helped to make him very hot as he ran hither and thither after his flock. But he had not studied pig-nature in vain. He had a good deal of sympathy with its vagaries, and he was quite able to outwit the pigs. Indeed, a curious attachment grew up between the little swineherd and his flock, some of whom would come at his call, when he rewarded their affection, as he had gained it, by scratching their backs with a rough stick.

But there were times when their playful and errant peculiarities were no small annoyance to him. Jan was growing fast both in mind and body. Phases of taste and occupation succeed each other very rapidly when one is young; and there are, perhaps, no more distinct phases, more sudden strides, than in the art of painting. With Jan the pig phase was going, and it was followed by landscape-sketching.

Jan was drawing his pigs one day in the little wood, when he fancied that the gnarled elbow of a branch near him had, in its outline, some likeness to a pig's face, and he began to sketch it on his slate. But in studying the tree the grotesque likeness was forgotten, and there burst upon his mind, as a revelation, the sense of that world of beauty which lies among stems and branches, twigs and leaves.

Painfully, but with happy pains, he traced the branch joint by joint, curve by curve, as it spread from the parent stem and tapered to its last delicate twigs. It was like following a river from its source to the sea. But to that sea of summer sky, in which the final ramifications of his branch were lost, Jan did not reach. He was abruptly stopped by the edge of his slate, which would hold no more.

To remedy this, when next he drew trees, he began the branches from the outer tips, and worked inwards to the stem. It was done for convenience, but to this habit he used afterwards to lay some of the merit of his admirable touch in tree-painting. And so "pig-making" became an amusement of the past, and the spell of the woods fell on Jan.

It was no very wonderful wood either, this one where he first herded pigs and studied trees. It was composed chiefly of oaks and beeches, none of them of very grand proportions. But it was little cut and little trodden. The bramble-bowers were unbroken, the leaf-mould was deep and rich, and a very tiny stream, which trickled out of sight, kept mosses ever green about its bed. The whole wood was fragrant with honeysuckle, which pushed its way everywhere, and gay with other wild flowers. But the trees were Jan's delight. He would lie on his back and gaze up into them with unwearying pleasure. He looked at his old etching with new interest, to see how the artist had done the branches of the willows by the water-mill. And then he would get Abel to put a very sharp point to his own slate-pencil, and would go back to the real oaks and beeches, which were so difficult and yet so fascinating to him.

He was very happy in the wood, with two drawbacks.

The pigs would stray when he became absorbed in his sketching, and the slate and slate-pencil, which did very well to draw pigs in outline, were miserable implements, when more than half the beauty of the subject to be represented was in its color. For the first evil there was no remedy but to give chase. Out of the second came an amusement in favor of which even the beloved slate hung idle.

In watching beautiful bits of coloring in the wood, contrasted greens of many hues, some jutting branch with yellowish foliage caught by the sun, and relieved by a distance of blue grays beyond, — colors and contrasts which only grew lovelier as the heavy green of midsummer was broken by the inroad of autumnal tints, — Jan noticed also that among the fallen leaves at his feet there were some of nearly every color in the foliage above. At first it was by a sort of idle trick that he matched one against the other, as a lady sorts silks for her embroidery; then he arranged bits of the leaves upon the outline on his slate, and then, the slate being too small, he amused himself by grouping the leaves upon the path in front of him into woodland scenes. The idea had been partly suggested to him by a bottle which stood on Mrs. Salter's mantelpiece, containing colored sands arranged into landscapes; a work of art sent by Mrs. Salter's sister from the Isle of Wight.

The slate would have been quite unused, but for the difficulties Jan got into with his outlines. At last he adopted the plan of making a sketch upon his slate, which he then laid beside him on the walk, and copied it in leaves. More perishable even than the pig-drawings, the evening breeze generally cast these paintings to the winds, but none the less was Jan happy with them, and sometimes in quiet weather, or a sheltered nook, they remained undisturbed for days.

Dame Datchett's school reopened, but Jan would not leave his pigs. He took the shilling faithfully home each week to his foster-mother. She found it very useful, and she had no very high ideas about education. She had some twinges of conscience in the matter, but she had no strength of purpose, and Jan went his own way.

The tints had grown very warm on trees and leaves, when Jan one day accomplished, with much labor, the best painting he had yet done. It was of a scene before his eyes. The trees were admirably grouped; he put little bits of twigs for the branches, which now showed more than hitherto, and he added a glimpse of the sky by neatly dovetailing the petals of some bluebells into a mosaic. He had turned back the long sleeves of his coat, and had with difficulty kept the tail of it from doing damage to his foreground, and had perseveringly kept the pigs at bay, when, as he returned with a last instalment of bluebells to finish his sky, he saw a man standing on the path, with his back to him, completely blotting out the view by his very broad body, and with one heel not half an inch from Jan's picture.

He was a coarsely built old man, dressed in threadbare black. The tones of his voice were broad, and quite unlike the local dialect. He was speaking as Jan came up, but to no companion that Jan could see, though his hand was outstretched in sympathy with his words. He was looking upwards, too, as Jan was wont to look himself, into that azure sky which he was trying to paint in bluebell flowers.

In truth, the stranger was spouting poetry, and poems and recitations were alike unknown to Jan; but something caught his fancy in what he heard, and the flowers dropped from his fingers as the broad but not ungraceful accents broke upon his ear: —

> "The clouds were pure and white as flocks new shorn,
> And fresh from the clear brook; sweetly they slept
> On the blue fields of heaven, and then there crept
> A little noiseless noise among the leaves,
> Born of the very sigh that silence heaves;
> For not the faintest motion could be seen
> Of all the shades that slanted o'er the green."

The old man paused for an instant, and, turning round, saw Jan, and put his heavy foot into the sky of Jan's picture. He drew it back at Jan's involuntary cry, and, after a long look at the quaint figure before him, said, "Are ye one of the fairies, little man?"

But Jan knew nothing of fairies. "I be Jan Lake, from the mill," said he.

"Are ye so? But that's not a miller's coat ye've on," said the old man, with a twinkle in his eye.

Jan looked seriously at it, and then explained. "I be Master Salter's pig-minder just now, but I've got a miller's thumb, I have."

"That's well, Master Pig-minder; and now would ye tell an old man what ye screamed out for. Did I scare ye?"

"Oh, no, sir," said Jan, civilly; and he added, "I liked that you were saying."

"Are ye a bit of a poet as well as a pig-minder, then?" and waving his hand with a theatrical gesture up the wood, the old man began to spout afresh: —

> "A filbert hedge with wild briar overtwined,
> And clumps of woodbine taking the soft wind
> Upon their summer thrones; there too should be
> The frequent chequer of a youngling tree,
> That with a score of light green brethren shoots
> From the quaint mossiness of aged roots:
> Round which is heard a spring-head of clear waters
> Babbling so wildly of its lovely daughters,
> The spreading bluebells; it may haply mourn
> That such fair clusters should be rudely torn
> From their fresh beds, and scattered thoughtlessly
> By infant hands, left on the path to die."

Between the strange dialect and the unfamiliar terseness of poetry, Jan did not follow this very clearly, but he caught the allusion to bluebells, and the old man brought his hand back to his side with a gesture so expressive towards the bluebell fragments at his feet, that it hardly needed the tone of reproach he gave to the last few words — "left on the path to die" — to make Jan hang his head.

"'Twas the only blue I could find," he said, looking ruefully at the fading flowers.

"And what for did ye want blue, then, my lad?"

"To make the sky with," said Jan.

"The powers of the air be good to us!" said the stranger, setting his broad hat back from his face, as if to obtain a clearer view of the little pig-minder. "Are ye a sky-maker as well as a swineherd? And while I'm catechising ye, may I ask for what do ye bring a slate out pig-minding and sky-making?"

"I draws out the trees on it first," said Jan, "and then I does them in leaves. If you'll come round," he added, shyly, "you'll see it. But don't tread on un, please, sir."

The old man fumbled in his pocket, from which he drew

a shagreen spectacle-case, as substantial looking as himself, and, planting the spectacles firmly on his heavy nose, he held out his hand to Jan.

"There," said he, "take me where ye will. To bonnie Elf-land, if that's your road, where withered leaves are gold."

Jan ran round willingly to take the hand of his new friend. He felt a strange attraction towards him. His speech was puzzling and had a tone of mockery, but his face was unmistakably kind.

"Now then, lad, which path do we go by?" said he.

"There's only one," said Jan, gazing up at the old man, as if by very staring with his black eyes he could come to understand him. But in an instant he was spouting again, holding Jan before him with one hand, whilst he used the other as a sort of *bâton* to his speech:—

> "And know'st thou not yon broad, broad road
> That lies across the lily levin?
> That is the path of sinfulness,
> Though some think it the way to heaven."

"Go on, please!" Jan cried, as the old man paused. His rugged speech seemed plainer in the lines it suited so well, and a touch of enthusiasm in his voice increased the charm.

> "And know'st thou not that narrow path
> So thick beset with thorns and briars?
> It is the path of righteousness,
> And after it but few aspires.

> "And know'st thou not the little path
> That winds about the ferny brae?
> That is the road to bonnie Elf-land,
> Where thou and I this night maun gae."

"Where is it?" said Jan, earnestly. "Is't a town?"

The old man laughed. "I'm thinking it would be well to let that path be, in your company. We'd hardly get out under a year and a day."

"I'd go — with you," said Jan, confidently. Many an expedition had he undertaken on his own responsibility, and why not this?

"First, show me what ye were going to show me," said the old man. "Where's this sky you've been manufacturing?"

"It's on the ground, sir."

"On the ground! And are ye for turning earth into heaven among your other trades?" What this might mean Jan knew not; but he led his friend round, and pointed out the features of his leaf-picture. He hoped for praise, but the old man was silent, — long silent, though he seemed to be looking at what Jan showed him. And when he did speak, his broken words were addressed to no one.

"Wonderful! wonderful! The poetry of 't. It's no child's play, this. It's genius. Ay! we mun see to it!" And then, with clasped hands, he cried, "Good Lord' Have I found him at last?"

"Have you lost something?" said Jan.

But the old man did not answer. He did not even speak of the leaf-picture, to Jan's chagrin. But, stroking the boy's shoulder almost tenderly, he asked, "Did ye ever go to school, laddie?"

Jan nodded. "At Dame Datchett's," said he.

"Ah! ye were sorry to leave school for pig-minding, weren't ye?"

Jan shook his head. "I likes pigs," said he. "I axed

Master Salter to let me mind his. I gets a shilling a week and me tea."

" But ye like school better? Ye love your books, don't ye?"

Jan shook his head again.

" I don't like school," said he, " I likes being in the wood."

The old man winced as if some one had struck him in the face, then he muttered, " The wood! Ay, to be sure! And such a school, too!"

Then he suddenly addressed Jan. " Do ye know me, my lad?"

" No, sir," said Jan.

" Swift — Master Swift, they call me. You've heard tell of Master Swift, the schoolmaster?"

Jan shrank back. He had heard of Master Swift as a man whose stick was more to be dreaded than Dame Datchett's strap, and of his school as a place where liberty was less than with the Dame.

" See thee!" said the old man, speaking broader and broader in his earnestness. " If thy father would send thee, — nay, what am I saying? — if I took thee for naught and gladly, thou 'dst sooner come to the old schoolmaster and his books than stay with pigs, even in a wood? Eh, laddie? Will ye come to school?"

But the tradition of Master Swift's severity was strong in Jan's mind, and the wood was pleasant to him, and he only shrank back farther, and said, " No." Children often give pain to their elders, of the intensity of which they have no measure; but, had Jan been older and wiser than he was, he might have been puzzled by the bitterness of the disappointment written on Master Swift's countenance.

An involuntary impulse made the old man break the blow by doing something. With trembling fingers he folded his spectacles, and crammed them into the shagreen case. But, when that was done, he still found nothing to say, and he turned his back and went away in silence.

In silence Jan watched him, half regretfully, and strained his ears to catch something that Master Swift began again to recite: —

> "Things sort not to my will,
> Even when my will doth study Thy renown:
> Thou turn'st the edge of all things on me still,
> Taking me up to throw me down."

Then, lifting a heavy bramble that had fallen across his path, the schoolmaster stooped under it, and passed from sight.

And a sudden gust of wind coming sharply down the way by which he went caught the fragments of Jan's picture, and whirled them broadcast through the wood.

CHAPTER XX.

SQUIRE AMMABY AND HIS DAUGHTER. — THE CHEAP JACK DOES BUSINESS ONCE MORE. — THE WHITE HORSE CHANGES MASTERS.

SQUIRE AMMABY was the most good-natured of men. He was very fond of his wife, though she was somewhat peevish, with weak health and nerves, and though she seemed daily less able to bear the rough and ready attentions of her husband, and to rely more and more on the advice and assistance of her mother, Lady Craikshaw. From this it came about that the Squire's affection for his wife took the shape of wishing Lady Louisa to have every thing that she wished for, and that the very joy of his heart was his little daughter Amabel.

Amabel was between three and four years old, and to some extent a prodigy. She was as tall as an average child of six or seven, and stout in proportion. The size of her shoes scandalized her grandmother, and once drew tears from Lady Louisa as she reflected on the probable size of Miss Ammaby's feet by the time she was "presented."

Lady Louisa was tall and weedy; the Squire was tall and robust. Amabel inherited height on both sides, but in face and in character she was more like her father than her mother. Indeed, Lady Louisa would close her eyes, and Lady Craikshaw would put up her gold glass at the child, and they would both cry, " Sadly coarse! *Quite an Ammaby!* " Amabel was not coarse, however; but she had a strength and originality of character that must have come from some bygone generation, if it was inherited. She had a pitying affection for her mother. With her grandmother she lived at daggers drawn. She kept up a pretty successful struggle for her own way in the nursery. She was devoted to her father, when she could get at him, and she poured an almost boundless wealth of affection on every animal that came in her way.

An uncle had just given her a Spanish saddle, and her father had promised to buy her a donkey. He had heard of one, and was going to drive to the town to see the owner. With great difficulty Amabel had got permission from her mother and grandmother to go with the Squire in the pony carriage. As she had faithfully promised to "be good," she submitted to be "well wrapped up," under her grandmother's direction, and staggered downstairs in coat, cape, gaiters, comforter, muffatees, and with a Shetland veil over her burning cheeks. She even displayed a needless zeal by carrying a big shawl in a lump in her arms, which she would give up to no one.

"No, no!" she cried, as the Squire tried to take it from her. " Lift me in, daddy, lift me in!"

The Squire laughed, and obeyed her, saying, "Why, bless my soul, Amaoel, I think you grow heavier every day."

Amabel came up crimson from some disposal of the shawl after her own ideas, and her eyes twinkled as he spoke, though her fat cheeks kept their gravity. It was not till they were far on their way that a voice from below the seat cried, "Yap!"

"Why, there's one of the dogs in the carriage," said the Squire.

On which, clinging to one of his arms and caressing him, Amabel confessed, "It's only the pug, dear daddy. I brought him in under the shawl. I did so want him to have a treat too. And grandmamma is so hard! She hardly thinks I ought to have treats, and she *never* thinks of treats for the dogs."

The Squire only laughed, and said she must take care of the dog when they got to the town; and Amabel was encouraged to ask if she might take off the Shetland veil. Hesitating between his fear of Amabel's catching cold, and a common-sense conviction that it was ludicrous to dress her according to her invalid mother's susceptibilities, the Squire was relieved from the responsibility of deciding by Amabel's promptly exposing her rosy cheeks to the breeze, and they drove on happily to the town. The Squire had business with the Justices, and Amabel was left at the Crown. When he came back, Amabel jumped down from the window and the black blind over which she was peeping into the yard, and ran up to her father with tears on her face.

"Oh, daddy!" she cried, "dear, good daddy! I don't want you to buy me a donkey, I want you to buy me a horse."

"That's modest!" said the Squire; "but what are you crying for?"

"Oh, it's such a poor horse! Such a very old, poor horse!" cried Amabel. And from the window Mr. Ammaby was able to confirm her statements. It was the

Cheap Jack's white horse, which he had been trying to persuade the landlord to buy as a cab-horse. More lean, more scarred, more drooping than ever, it was a pitiful sight, now and then raising its soft nose and intelligent eyes to the window, as if it knew what a benevolent little being was standing on a slippery chair, with her arms round the Squire's neck, pleading its cause.

"But when I buy horses," said the Squire, "I buy young, good ones, not very old and poor ones."

"Oh, but do buy it, daddy! Perhaps it's not had enough to eat, like that kitten I found in the ditch. And perhaps it'll get fat, like her; and mamma said we wanted an old horse to go in the cart for luggage, and I'm sure that one's very old. And that's such a horrid man, like hump-backed Richard. And when nobody's looking, he tugs it, and beats it. Oh, I wish I could beat him!" and Amabel danced dangerously upon the horsehair seat in her white gaiters with impotent indignation. The Squire was very weak when pressed by his daughter, but at horses, if at any thing, he looked with an eye to business. To buy such a creature would be ludicrous. Still, Amabel had made a strong point by what Lady Louisa had said. No one, too, knew better than the Squire what difference good and bad treatment can make in a horse, and this one had been good once, as his experienced eye told him. He said he "would see," and strolled into the yard.

Long practice had given the Cheap Jack a quickness in detecting a possible purchaser which almost amounted to an extra sense, and he at once began to assail the Squire. But a nearer view of the white horse had roused Mr. Ammaby's indignation.

"I wonder," he said, "that you're not ashamed to exhibit a poor beast that's been so ill-treated. For heaven's sake, take it to the knacker's, and put it out of its misery at once."

"Look ye, my lord," said the Cheap Jack, touching his cap. "The horse have been ill-treated, I knows. I'm an afflicted man, my lord, and the boy I've employed, he's treated him shameful; and when a man can't feed hisself, he can't keep his beast fat neither. That's why I wants to get rid on him, my lord. I can't keep him as I should, and I'd like to see him with a gentleman like yourself as'll do him justice. He comes of a good stock, my lord. Take him for fifteen pound," he added, waddling up to the Squire, "and when you've had him three months, you'll sell him for thirty."

This was too much. The Squire broke out in a furious rage.

"You unblushing scoundrel!" he cried. "D' ye think I'm a fool? Fifteen pounds for a horse you should be fined for keeping alive! Be off with it, and put it out of misery." And he turned indignantly into the inn, the Cheap Jack calling after him, "Say ten pound, my lord!" the bystanders giggling, and the ostler whistling dryly through the straw in his mouth, "Take it to the knacker's, Cheap John."

"Oh, daddy dear! have you got him?" cried Amabel, as the Squire re-entered the parlor.

"No, my dear; the poor beast isn't fit to draw carts, my darling. It's been so badly treated, the only kindness now is to kill it, and put it out of pain. And I've told the hunchback so."

It was a matter of course and humanity to the Squire, but it overwhelmed poor Amabel. She gasped, "Kill it!"

and then bursting into a flood of tears she danced on the floor, wringing her hands and crying, "Oh, oh, oh! don't, *please*, don't let him be killed! Oh! do, do buy him and let him die comfortably in the paddock. Oh, do, do, do!"

"Nonsense, Amabel, you mustn't dance like that. Remember, you promised to be good," said the Squire. The child gulped down her tears, and stood quite still, with her face pale from very misery.

"I don't want not to be good," said she. "But, oh dear, I do wish I had some money, that I might buy that poor old horse, and let him die comfortably at home."

It was not the money the Squire grudged; it was against all his instincts to buy a bad horse. But Amabel's wan face overcame him, and he went out again. He never lingered over disagreeable business, and, going straight up to the Cheap Jack, he said, "My little girl is so distressed about it, that I'll give you five pounds for the poor brute, to stop its sufferings."

"Say eight, my lord," said the Cheap Jack. Once more the Squire was turning away in wrath, when he caught sight of Amabel's face at the window. He turned back, and, biting his lip, said, "I'll give you five pounds if you'll take it now, and go. If you beat me down again, I'll offer you four. I'll take off a pound for every bate you utter; and, when I speak, I mean what I say. Do you think I don't know one horse from another?"

It is probable that the Cheap Jack would have made another effort to better his bargain, but his wife had come to seek him, and to her sharp eyes the Squire's resolution was beyond mistake.

"We'll take the five guineas, and thank you, sir," she said, courtesying. The Squire did not care to dispute the five shillings which she had dexterously added, and he paid the sum, and the worthy couple went away.

"Miles!" said the Squire. The servant he had brought with him in reference to the donkey appeared, and touched his hat.

"Miss Amabel has persuaded me to buy this poor brute, that it may die in peace in the paddock. Can you get it home, d' ye think?"

"I think I can, sir, this evening; after a feed and some rest."

The white horse had suddenly become a centre of interest in the inn-yard. Everybody, from the landlord to the stable-boy, felt its legs, and patted it, and suggested various lines of treatment.

Before he drove away, Mr. Ammaby overheard the landlord saying, "He be a sharp hand, is the Squire. I shouldn't wonder if he brought the beast round yet." Which, for his credit's sake, the Squire devoutly hoped he might. But, after all, he had his reward when Amabel, sobbing with joy, flung her arms round him, and cried, —

"Oh, you dear, darling, *good* daddy! How I love you and how the white horse loves you!"

CHAPTER XXI.

MASTER SWIFT AT HOME. — RUFUS. — THE EX-PIG-MINDER. — JAN AND THE SCHOOLMASTER.

IT was a lovely autumn evening the same year, when the school having broken up for the day, Master Swift returned to his home for tea. He lived in a tiny cottage on the opposite side of the water-meadows to that on which Dame Datchett dwelt, and farther down towards the water-mill. He had neither wife nor child, but a red dog with a plaintive face, and the name of Rufus, kept his house when he was absent, and kept him company when he was at home.

Rufus was a mongrel. He was not a red setter, though his coloring was similar. A politely disposed person would have called him a retriever, and his curly back and general appearance might have carried this off, but for his tail, which, instead of being straight and rat-like, was as plumy as the Prince of Wales's feathers, and curled unblushingly over his back, sideways, like a pug's. "It was a good one to wag," his master said, and, apart from the question of high breeding, it was handsome, and Rufus himself seemed proud of it.

Since half-past three had Rufus sat in the porch, blinking away positive sleep, with his pathetic face towards the road down which Master Swift must come. Unnecessarily pathetic, for there was every reason for his being the most jovial of dogs, and not one for that imposing melancholy which he wore. His large level eyelids shaded the pupils even when he was broad awake; an intellectual forehead, and a very long Vandykish nose, with the curly ears, which fell like a well-dressed peruke on each side of his face, gave him an air of disinherited royalty. But he was in truth a mongrel, living on the fat of the land; who, from the day that this wistful dignity had won the schoolmaster's heart, had never known a care, wanted a meal, or had any thing whatever demanded of him but to sit comfortably at home and watch with a broken-hearted countenance for the schoolmaster's return from the labors which supported them both. The sunshine made Rufus sleepy, but he kept valiantly watchful, propping himself against the garden-tools which stood in the corner. Flowers and vegetables for eating were curiously mixed in the little garden that lay about Master Swift's cottage. Not a corner was wasted in it, and a thick hedge of sweet-peas formed a fragrant fence from the outer world.

Rufus was nodding, when he heard a footstep. He pulled himself up, but he did not wag his tail, for the step was not the schoolmaster's. It was Jan's. Rufus growled slightly, and Jan stood outside, and called, "Master Swift!" He and Rufus both paused and listened, but the schoolmaster did not appear. Then Rufus came out and smelt Jan exhaustively, and excepting a slight flavor of being acquainted with cats, to whom Rufus objected, he smelt well. Rufus wagged his tail, Jan patted him, and they sat down to wait for the master.

The clock in the old square-towered church had struck a quarter-past four when Master Swift came down the lane, and Rufus rushed out to meet him. Though Rufus told him in so many barks that there was a stranger within, and that, as he smelt respectable, he had allowed him to wait, the schoolmaster was startled by the sight of Jan.

"Why, it's the little pig-minder!" said he. On which Jan's face crimsoned, and tears welled up in his black eyes.

"I bean't a pig-minder now, Master Swift," said he.

"And how's that? Has Master Salter turned ye off?"

"I gi'ed *him* notice!" said Jan, indignantly. "But I shan't mind pigs no more, Master Swift."

"And why not, Master Skymaker?"

"Don't 'ee laugh, sir," said Jan. "Master Salter he laughs. 'What's pigs for but to be killed?' says he. But I axed him not to kill the little black un with the white spot on his ear. It be such a nice pig, sir, such a very nice pig!" And the tears flowed copiously down Jan's cheeks, whilst Rufus looked abjectly depressed. "It would follow me anywhere, and come when I called," Jan continued. "I told Master Salter it be 'most as good as a dog, to keep the rest together. But a says 'tis the fattest, and 'ull be the first to kill. And then I telled him to find another boy to mind his pigs, for I couldn't look un in the face now, and know 'twas to be killed next month, not that one with the white spot on his ear. It do be such a *very* nice pig!"

Rufus licked up the tears as they fell over Jan's smock, and the schoolmaster took Jan in and comforted him. Jan dried his eyes at last, and helped to prepare for tea. The old man made some very good coffee in a shaving-pot, and put cold bacon and bread upon the table, and the three sat down to their meal. Jan and his host upon two rush-bottomed chairs, whilst Rufus scrambled into an armchair placed for his accommodation, from whence he gazed alternately at the schoolmaster and the victuals with sad, not to say reproachful, eyes.

"I thought that would be your chair," said Jan.

"Well, it used to be," said Master Swift, apologetically. "But the poor beast can't sit well on these, and I relish my meat better with a face on the other side of the table. He found that too slippery at first, till I bought yon bit of a patchwork-cushion for him at a sale."

Rufus sighed, and Master Swift gave him a piece of bread, which, having smelt, he allowed to lie before him on the table till his master, laughing, rubbed the bread against the bacon, with which additional flavor Rufus seemed content, and ate his supper.

"So you've come to the old schoolmaster, after all?" said Master Swift: "that's right, my lad, that's right."

"'Twas Abel sent me," said Jan; "he said I was to take to my books. So I come because Abel axed me. For I be main fond of Abel."

"Abel was right," said the old man. "Take to learning, my lad. Love your books,— friends that nobody can kill, or part ye from."

"I'd like to learn pieces like them you say," said Jan.

"So ye shall, so ye shall!" cried Master Swift. "It's a fine thing, is learning poetry. It strengthens the memory, and cultivates the higher faculties. Take some more bacon, my lad."

Which Jan did. At that moment he was not reflecting on his doomed friend, the spotted pig. Indeed, if we reflected about every thing, this present state of existence would become intolerable.

At much length did the schoolmaster speak on the joys of learning, and, pointing proudly to a few shelves filled by his savings, he formally made Jan " free of " his books. " When ye 've learnt to read them," he added. Jan thanked him for this, and for leave to visit him. But he looked out of the window instead of at the book-shelves.

Beyond Master Swift's gay flowers stretched the rich green of the water-meads, glowing yellow in the sunlight. The little river hardly seemed to move in its zig-zag path, though the evening breeze was strong enough to show the silver side of the willows that drooped over it. Jan wondered if he could match all these tints in the wood, and whether Master Swift would be willing to have leaf-pictures painted on that table in the window. Then he found that the old man was speaking, though he only heard the latter part of what he said. " — a celebrated inventor and mechanic, and that 's what you 'll be, maybe. Ay, ay, a Great Man, please the Lord ; and, when I 'm laid by in the churchyard yonder, folks 'll come to see the grave of old Swift, the great man's schoolmaster. Ye 'll be an inventor yet, lad, a benefactor to your kind, and an honor to your country. I 'm not raising false hopes in ye, without observing your qualities. You 've the quick eye, the slow patience, and the inventive spark. You can find your own tools and all, and don't stop where other folk leaves off: witness yon bluebells ye took to make skies with ! But, bless the lad, he 's not heeding me ! Is it the bit of garden you 're looking at ? Come out then." And, putting the biography back in the book-shelf, the kindly old man led Jan out of doors.

" Say what you said in the wood again," said Jan.

But Master Swift laughed, and, stretching his hand

towards the sweet-peas hedge began at another part of the poem: —

> "Here are sweet peas on tiptoe for a flight:
> With wings of gentle flush o'er delicate white,
> And taper fingers catching at all things
> To bind them all about with tiny rings."

Then, bending towards the river, he continued in a theatrical whisper: —

> "How silent comes the water round that bend!
> Not the minutest whisper does it send
> To the o'erhanging sallows" —

But here he stopped suddenly, though Jan's black eyes were at their roundest, and his attention almost breathless.

"There, there! I'm an old fool, and for making you as bad. Poetry's not your business, you understand: I'm giving ye no encouragement to dabble with the fine arts. Science is the ladder for a working-man to climb to fame. In addition to which, the poet Keats, though he certainly speaks the very language of Nature, was a bit of a heathen, I'm afraid, and the fascination of him might be injurious in tender youth. Never mind, child, if ye love poetry, I'll learn ye pieces by the poet Herbert. They're just true poetry, and manly, too; and they're a fountain of experimental religion. And, if this style is too sober for your fancy, Charles Wesley's hymns are touched with the very fire of religious passion."

"Are your folk religious, Jan?" he added, abruptly. And whilst Jan stood puzzling the question, he asked with an almost official air of authority, " Do ye any of ye come to church?"

"My father does on club-days," said Jan.

"And the rest of ye, — do ye attend any place of worship?" Jan shook his head.

"And I'll dare to say ye didn't know I was the clerk?" said Master Swift. "There's paganism for ye in a Christian parish! Well, well, you're coming to me, lad, and, apart from your secular studies, you'll be instructed in the Word of GOD, and in the Church Catechism on Fridays."

"Thank you, sir," said Jan. He felt this civility to be due, though of the schoolmaster's plans for his benefit he had a very confused notion. He then took leave. Rufus went with him to the gate, and returned to his master with a look which plainly said, "We could have done with him very well, if you had kept him."

When Jan had reached a bit of rising ground, from which the house he had just left was visible, he turned round to look at it again.

Master Swift was standing where he had left him, gazing out into the distance with painful intensity. The fast-sinking sun lit up his heavy face and figure with a transforming glow, and hung a golden mist above the meads, at which he stared like one spellbound. But when Jan turned to pursue his way to the windmill, the schoolmaster turned also, and went back into the cottage.

CHAPTER XXII.

THE PARISH CHURCH. — REMBRANDT. — THE SNOW SCENE. — MASTER SWIFT'S AUTOBIOGRAPHY.

IN most respects, Jan's conduct and progress were very satisfactory. He quickly learned to read, and his copy-books were models.

The good clerk developed another talent in him. Jan learned to sing, and to sing very well; and he was put into the choir-seats in the old church, where he sang with enthusiasm hymns which he had learned by heart from the schoolmaster.

No wild weather that ever blustered over the downs could keep Jan now from the services. The old church came to have a fascination for him, from the low, square tower without, round which the rooks wheeled, to the springing pillars, the solemn gray tints of the stone, and the round arches that so gratified the eye within. And did he not sit opposite to the one stained window the soldiers of the Commonwealth had spared to the parish! It was the only colored picture Jan knew, and he knew every line, every tint of it, and the separate expression on each of the wan, quaint faces of the figures. When the sun shone, they seemed to smile at him, and their ruby dresses glowed like garments dyed in blood. When the colors fell upon Abel's white head, Jan wished with all his heart that he could have gathered them as he gathered leaves, to make pictures with. Sometimes he day-dreamed that one of the figures came down out of the window, and brought the colors with him, and that he and Jan painted pictures in the other windows, filling them with gorgeous hues, and pale, devout faces. The fancy, empty as it was, pleased him, and he planned how every window should be done, and told Abel, to whom the ingenious fancy seemed as marvellous as if the work had been accomplished.

Abel was in the choir too, not so much because of his voice as of his great wish for it, and of the example of his good behavior. It was he who persuaded Mrs. Lake to come to church, and having once begun she came often. She tried to persuade her husband to go, and told him how sweetly the boys' voices sounded, led by Master Swift's fine bass, which he pitched from a key which he knocked upon his desk. But Master Lake had a proverb to excuse him. "The nearer the church, the further from GOD." Not that he pretended to maintain the converse of the proposition.

Jan learned plenty of poetry; hymns, which Abel learned again from him, some of Herbert's poems, and bits of Keats. But his favorites were martial poems by Mrs. Hemans, which he found in an old volume of collected verses, till the day he came upon "Marmion," and gave himself up to Sir Walter Scott. He spouted poetry to Abel in imitation of Master Swift, and they enjoyed all, and understood about half.

And yet Jan's progress was not altogether satisfactory to his teacher.

To learn long pieces of poetry was easy pastime to him, but he was dull or inattentive when the schoolmaster gave him some elementary lessons in mechanics. He wrote beautifully, but was no prodigy in arithmetic. He drew trees, windmills, and pigs on the desks, and admirable portraits of the schoolmaster, Rufus, and other local worthies, on the margins of the tables of weights and measures.

Much of his leisure was spent at Master Swift's cottage, and in reading his books. The schoolmaster had marked an old biographical dictionary at pages containing lives of "self-made" men, who had risen as inventors or improvers in mechanics or as discoverers of important facts of natural science. Jan had not hitherto studied their careers with the avidity Master Swift would have liked to see, but one day he found him reading the fat volume with deep interest.

"And whose life are ye at now, laddie?" he asked, with a smile.

Jan lifted his face, which was glowing. "'Tis Rembrandt the painter I be reading about. Eh, Master Swift, he lived in a windmill, and he was a miller's son!"

"Maybe he'd a miller's thumb," Jan added, stretching out his own, and smiling at the droll idea. "Do 'ee know what *etchings* be, then, Master Swift?"

"A kind of picture that's scratched on a piece of copper with needles, and costs a lot of money to print," said Master Swift, dryly; and he turned his broad back and went out.

It was one day in the second winter of Jan's learning under Master Swift that matters came to a climax. The schoolmaster loved punctuality, but Jan was not always punctual. He was generally better in this respect in winter than in summer, as there was less to distract his attention on the road to school. But one winter's day he loitered to make a sketch on his slate, and made matters worse by putting finishing touches to it after he was seated at the desk.

It was not a day to suggest sketching, but, turning round when he was about half way to the village, the view seemed to Jan to be exactly suitable for a slate sketch. The long slopes of the downs were white with snow; but it was a dull grayish white, for there was no sunshine, and the gray-white of the slate-pencil did it justice enough. In the middle distance rose the windmill, and a thatched cattle-shed and some palings made an admirable foreground. On the top and edges of these lay the snow, outlining them in white, which again the slate-pencil could imitate effectively. There only wanted something darker than the slate itself to do those parts of the foreground and the mill which looked darker than the sky, and for this Jan trusted to pen and ink when he reached his desk. The drawing was very successful, and Jan was so absorbed in admiring it that he did not notice the schoolmaster's approach, but feeling some one behind him, he fancied it was one of the boys, and held up the slate triumphantly, whispering, "Look 'ee here!"

It was Master Swift who looked, and snatching the slate he brought it down on the sharp corner of the desk, and broke it to pieces. Then he went back to his place, and spoke neither bad nor good to Jan for the rest of the school-time. Jan would much rather have been beaten. Once or twice he made essay to go up to Master Swift's desk, but the old man's stern countenance discouraged him, and he finally shrank into a corner and sat weeping bitterly. He sat there till every scholar but himself had gone, and still the schoolmaster did not speak. Jan slunk out, and when Master Swift turned homewards Jan followed silently in his footsteps through the snow. At the door of the cottage, the old man looked round with a relenting face.

"I suppose Rufus 'll insist on your coming in," said he; and Jan rushing in hid his face in Rufus's curls, and sobbed heavily.

"Tut, tut!" said the schoolmaster. "No more of that, child. There's bitters enough in life, without being so prodigal of your tears."

"Come and sit down with ye," he went on. "You're very young, lad, and maybe I'm foolish to be angry with ye that you're not wise. But yet ye've more sense than your years in some respects, and I'm thinking I'll try and make ye see things as I see 'em. I'm going to tell ye something about myself, if ye'd care to hear it."

"I'd be main pleased, Master Swift," said Jan, earnestly.

"I'd none of your advantages, lad," said the old man. "When I was your age, I knew more mischief than you need ever know, and uncommon little else. I'm a self-educated man, — I used to hope I should live to hear folk say a self-made Great Man. It's a bitter thing to have the ambition without the genius, to smoulder in the fire that great men shine by! However, it's something to have just the saving sense to know that ye've not got it, though it's taken a wasted lifetime to convince me, and I sometimes think the deceiving serpent is more scotched than killed yet. However, ye seem to me to be likelier to lack the ambition than the genius, so we may let that bide. But there's a snare of mine, Jan, that I mean your feet to be free of, and that's a mischosen vocation. I'm not a native of these parts, ye must know. I come from the north, and in those mining and manufacturing districts I've seen many a man that's got an education, and could keep himself sober, rise to own his house and his works, and have men under him, and bring up his children like the gentry. For mark ye, my lad. In such matters the experiences of the early part of an artisan's life are all so much to the good for him, for they're in the working of the trade, and the finest young gentleman has got it all to learn, if he wants to make money in that line. I got my education, and I was sober enough, but — Heaven help me — I must be a poet, and in *that* line a gentleman's son knows almost from the nursery many a thing that I had to teach myself with hard labor as a man. It was just a madness. But I read all the poetry I could lay my hands on, and I wrote as well."

"Did you write poetry, Master Swift?" said Jan.

"Ay, Jan, of a sort. At one time I worshipped Burns. And then I wrote verses in the dialect of my native place, which, ye must know, I can speak with any man when I've a mind," said Master Swift, unconscious that he spoke it always. "And then it was Wordsworth, for the love of nature is just a passion with me, and it's that that made the poet Keats a new world to me. Well, well, now I'm telling you how I came here. It was after my wife. She was lady's-maid to Squire Ammaby's mother, and the old Squire got me the school. Ah, those were happy days! I was a godless, rough sort of a fellow when she married me, but I became a converted man. And let me tell ye, lad, when a man and wife love GOD and each other, and live in the country, a bit of ground like this becomes a very garden of Eden."

"Did your wife like your poetry, sir?" said Jan, on whom the idea that the schoolmaster was a poet made a strong impression.

"Ay, ay, Jan. She was a good scholar. I wrote a bit about that time called Love and Ambition, in the style of the poet Wordsworth. It was as much as to say that Love had killed Ambition, ye understand? But it wasn't dead. It had only shifted to another object.

"We had a child. I remember the first day his blue eyes looked at me with what I may call sense in 'em. He was in his cradle, and there was no one but me with him. I went on like a fool. 'See thee, my son,' I said, 'thy father's been a bad 'un, but he'll keep thee as pure as thy mother. Thy father's a poor scholar, but he's not *that* dull but what he'll make *thee* as learned as the parson. Thy father's a needy man, a man in a small way, but he and thy mother'll stick here in this dull bit of a village, content, ay, my lad, right happy, so thou'rt a rich man, and can see the world!' I give ye my word, Jan, the child looked at me as if he understood it all. You're wondering, maybe, what made me hope he'd do different to what I'd done. But, ye see, his mother was just an angel, and I reckoned he'd be half like her. Then she'd lived with gentlefolks from a child, and knew manners and such like that I never learned. And for as little as I'd taught myself, he'd at any rate begin where his father left off. He was all we had. There seemed no fault in him. His mother dressed him like a little prince, and his manners were the same. Ah, we *were* happy! Then"—

"Well, Master Swift?" said Jan, for the schoolmaster had paused.

"Can't ye see the place is empty?" he answered

sharply. "Who takes bite or sup with me but Rufus? *She died.*

"I'd have gone mad but for the boy. All my thought was to make up her loss to him. A child learns a man to be unselfish, Jan. I used to think, 'GOD may well be the very fount of unselfish charity, when He has so many children, so helpless without Him!' I think He taught me how to do for that boy. I dressed him, I darned his socks: what work I couldn't do I put out, but I had no one in. When I came in from school, I cleaned myself, and changed my boots, to give him his meals. Rufus and I eat off the table now, but I give ye my word when *he* was alive we'd three clean cloths a week, and he'd a pinny every day; and there's a silver fork and spoon in yon drawer I saved up to buy him, and had his name put on. I taught him too. He loved poetry as well as his father. He could say most of Milton's 'Lycidas.' It was an unlucky thing to have learned him too! Eh, Jan! we're poor fools. I lay awake night after night reconciling my mind to troubles that were never to come, and never dreaming of what *was* before me. I thought to myself, 'John Swift, my lad, you're making yourself a bed of thorns. As sure as you make your son a gentleman, so sure he'll look down on his old father when he gets up. Can ye bear that, John Swift, and *her* dead, and him all that ye have?' I didn't ask myself twice, Jan. Of course I could bear it. Would any parent stop his child from being better than himself because he'd be looked down on? I never heard of one. 'I want him to think me rough and ignorant,' says I, 'for I want him to know what's better. And I shan't expect him to think on how I've slaved for him, till he's children of his own, and their mother a lady

But when I'm dead,' I says, 'and he stands by my grave, and I can't shame him no more with my common ways, he'll say, "The old man did his best for me," for he has his mother's feelings.' I tell ye, Jan, I cried like a child to think of him standing at my burying in a good black coat and a silk scarf like a gentleman, and I no more thought of standing at his than if he was bound to live for ever. And, mind ye, I did all I could to improve myself. I learned while I was teaching, and read all I could lay my hands on. Books of travels made me wild. I was young still, and I'd have given a deal to see the world. But I was saving every penny for him. 'He'll see it all,' says I, 'and that's enough,— Italy and Greece, and Egypt, and the Holy Land. And he'll see the sea (which I never saw but once, and that was at Cleethorpes), and he'll go to the tropics, and see flowers that 'ud just turn his old father's head, and he'll write and tell me of 'em, for he's got his mother's feelings.' . . . My GOD! He never passed the parish bounds, and he's lain alongside of her in yon churchyard for five and thirty years!"

Master Swift's head sank upon his breast, and he was silent, as if in a trance, but Jan dared not speak. The silence was broken by Rufus, who got up and stuffed his nose into the schoolmaster's hand.

"Poor lad!" said his master, patting him. "Thou'rt a good soul, too! Well, Jan, I'm here, ye see. It didn't kill me. I was off my head a bit, I believe, but they kept the school for me, and I got to work again. I'm rough pottery, lad, and take a deal of breaking. I've took up with dumb animals, too, a good deal. At least, they've took up with me. Most of 'em's come, like Rufus, of themselves. Mangy puppies no one would own, cats with kettles to their tails, and so on. I've always had a bit of company to my meals, and that's the main thing. Folks has said to me, 'Master Swift, I don't know how you can keep on schooling. I reckon you can hardly abide the sight of boys now you've lost your own.' But they're wrong, Jan: it seemed to give me a kind of love for every lad I lit upon.

"Are ye thinking ambition was dead in the old man at last? It came to life again, Jan. After a bit, I says to myself, 'In a dull place like this there's doubtless many a boy that might rise that never has the chance that I'd have given to mine. For what says the poet Gray? —

"But Knowledge to their eyes her ample page,
Rich with the spoils of Time, did ne'er unroll."'

"I think, Jan, sometimes, I'm like Rachel, who'd rather have taken to her servant's children than have had none. I thought, 'If there's a genius in obscurity here, I'll come across the boy, being schoolmaster, and I'll do for him as I'd have done for my own.' Jan, I've seen nigh on seven generations of lads pass through this school, but *he's never come!* Society's quit of that blame. There's been no 'mute, inglorious Miltons' here since I come to this place. There's been many a nice-tempered lad I've loved, for I'm fond of children, but never one that yearned to see places he'd never seen, or to know things he'd never heard of. There's no fool like an old one, and I think I've been more disappointed as time went on. I submitted myself to the Lord's will years ago; but I *have* prayed Him, on my knees, since He didn't see fit to raise me and mine, to let me have that satisfaction to help some other man's son to knowledge and to fame.

"Jan Lake," said Master Swift, "when I found you in yon wood, I found what I've looked for in vain for thirty-five years. Have I been schoolmaster so long, d' ye think, and don't know one boy's face from another? Lad! is it possible ye don't *care* to be a great man?"

Jan cared very much, but he was afraid of Master Swift; and it was by an effort that he summoned up courage to say, —

"Couldn't I be a great painter, Master Swift, don't 'ee think?"

The old man frowned impatiently. "What have I been telling ye? The Fine Arts are not the road to fame for working-men. Jan, Jan, be guided by me. Learn what I bid ye. And when ye've made name and fortune the way I show ye, ye can buy paints and paintings at your will, and paint away to please your leisure hours."

It did not need the gentle Abel's after-counsel to persuade Jan to submit himself to the schoolmaster's direction.

"I'll do as ye bid me, Master Swift; indeed, I will, sir," said he.

But, when the pleased old man rambled on of fame and fortune, it must be confessed that Jan but thought of them as the steps to those hours of wealthy leisure in which he could buy paints and indulge the irrepressible bent of his genius without blame.

CHAPTER XXIII.

THE WHITE HORSE IN CLOVER. — AMABEL AND HER GUARDIANS. — AMABEL IN THE WOOD. — BOGY.

THE white horse lived to see good days. He got safely home, and spent the winter in a comfortable stable, with no work but being exercised for the good of his health by the stable-boy. It was expensive, but expense was not a first consideration with the Squire, and when he had once decided a matter, he was not apt to worry himself with regrets. As to Amabel the very narrowness of the white horse's escape from death exalted him at once to the place of first favorite in her tender heart, even over the head (and ears) of the new donkey.

"Miss Amabel's" interest in the cart-horse offended her nurse's ideas of propriety, and met with no sympathy from her mother or grandmother. But she was apt to get her own way; and from time to time she appeared suddenly, like a fairy-imp, in the stable, where she majestically directed the groom to hold her up whilst she plied a currycomb on the old horse's back. This over, she would ask with dignity, "Do you take care of him, Miles?" And Miles, touching his cap, would reply, "Certainly, miss, the very greatest of care." And Amabel would add, "Does he get plenty to eat, do you think?" "Plenties to heat, miss," the groom would reply. And she generally closed the conversation with, "I'm very glad. You're a good man, Miles."

In spring the white horse was turned out into the paddock, where Amabel had begged that he might die comfortably. He lived comfortably instead; and Amabel visited him constantly, and being perfectly fearless would kiss his white nose as he drooped it into her little arms. Her visits to the stable had been discovered and forbidden, but the scandal was even greater when she was found in the paddock, standing on an inverted bucket, and grooming the white horse with Lady Louisa's tortoise-shell dressing-comb.

"They wouldn't let me have the currycomb," said Amabel, who was very hot, and perfectly self-satisfied. Lady Louisa was in despair, but the Squire laughed. The ladies of his family had been great horsewomen for generations.

In the early summer, some light carting being required by the gardener, he begged leave to employ "Miss Amabel's old horse," who came at last to trot soberly to the town with a light cart for parcels, when the landlord of the Crown would point him out in proof of the Squire's sagacity in horse-flesh.

But it was not by her attachment to the cart-horse alone that Amabel disturbed the composure of the head-nurse and of Louise the *bonne*. She was a very Will-o'-the-wisp for wandering. She grew rapidly, and the stronger she grew the more of a Tom-boy she became. Beyond the paddock lay another field, whose farthest wall was the boundary of a little wood, — the wood where Jan had herded pigs. Into this wood it had long been Amabel's desire to go. But nurses have a preference for the high road, and object to climbing walls, and she had not had her wish. She had often peeped through a hole in the wall, and had smelt honeysuckle. Once she had climbed half way up, and had fallen on her back in the ditch. Louise uttered a thousand and one exclamations when Amabel came home after this catastrophe; and Nurse, distrusting the success of any real penalties in her power, fell back upon imaginary ones.

"I'm sure it's a mercy you have got back, Miss Amabel," said she; "for Bogy lives in that wood; and, if you'd got in, it's ten to one he'd have carried you off."

"You *said* Bogy lived in the cellar," said Amabel.

Nurse was in a dilemma which deservedly besets people who tell untruths. She had to invent a second one to help out her first.

"That's at night," said she: "he lives in the wood in the daytime."

"Then I can go into the cellar in the day, and the wood at night," retorted Amabel; but in her heart she knew the latter was impossible.

For some days Nurse's fable availed. Amabel had suffered a good deal from Bogy; and, though the fear of him did not seem so terrible by daylight, she had no wish to meet him. But one lovely afternoon, wandering round the field for cowslips, Amabel came to the wall, and could not but peep over to see if there were any flowers to be seen. She was too short to do this without climbing, and it ended in her struggling successfully to the top. There were violets on the other side, and Amabel let down one big foot to a convenient hole, whence she hoped to be able to stoop and catch at the violets without actually treading in Bogy's domain. But once more she slipped and rolled over,— this time into the wood. Bogy lingered, and she got on to her feet; but the wall was deeper on this side than the other, and she saw with dismay that it was very doubtful if she could get back.

I think, as a rule, children are very brave. But a light heart goes a long way towards courage. At first Amabel made desperate and knee-grazing efforts to reclimb the wall, and, failing, burst into tears, and danced, and called aloud on all her protectors, from the Squire to Miles. No one coming, she restrained her tears, and by a real effort of that "pluck" for which the Ammaby race is famous began to run along the wall to find a lower point for climbing. In doing so, she startled a squirrel, and whizz!— away he went up a lanky tree. What a tail he had! Amabel forgot her terrors. There was at any rate some living thing in the wood besides Bogy; and she was now busy trying to coax the squirrel down again by such encouraging noises as she had found successful in winning the confidence of kittens and puppies. Amabel was the victim of that weakness for falling in love with every fussy, intelligent, or pitiable beast she met with, which besets some otherwise reasonable beings, leading to an inconvenient accumulation of pets in private life, though doubtless invaluable in the public services of people connected with the Zoölogical Gardens.

The squirrel sat under the shadow of his own tail, and winked. He had not the remotest intention of coming down. Amabel was calmer now, and she looked about her. The eglantine bushes were shoulder-high, but she had breasted underwood in the shrubberies, and was not afraid. Up, up, stretched the trees to where the sky shone blue. The wood itself sloped downwards; the spotted arums pushed boldly through last year's leaves, which almost hid the violets; there were tufts of primroses, which made Amabel cry out, and about them lay the exquisite mauve dog-violets in unplucked profusion. And hither and thither darted the little birds; red-breasts and sparrows, and yellow finches and blue finches, and blackbirds and thrushes, with their cheerful voices and soft waistcoats, and, indeed, every good quality but that of knowing how glad one would be to kiss them. In a few steps, Amabel came upon a path going zig-zag down the steep of the wood, and, nodding her hooded head determinedly, she said, " Amabel is going a walk. I don't mind Bogy," and followed her nose.

It is a pity that one's skirt, when held up, does not divide itself into compartments, like some vegetable dishes. One is so apt to get flowers first, and then lumps of moss, which spoil the flowers, and then more moss, which, earth downwards (as bread and butter falls), does no good to the rest. Amabel had on a nice, new dress, and it held things beautifully. But it did not hold enough, for at each step of the zig-zag path the moss grew lovelier. She had got some extinguisher-moss from the top of the wall, and this now lay under all the rest, which flattened the extinguishers. About half way down the dress was full, and some cushion-moss appeared that could not be passed by. Amabel sat down and reviewed her treasures. She could part with nothing, and she had just caught sight of some cup-moss lichen for dolls' wine-glasses. But, by good luck, she was provided with a white sun-bonnet, as clean and whole as her dress; and this she took off and filled. It was less fortunate that the scale-mosses and liverworts, growing nearer to the stream, came last, and, with the damp earth about them, lay a-top of every thing, flowers, dolls' wine-glasses, and all. It was a noble collection —

but heavy. Amabel's face flushed, and she was slightly overbalanced, but she staggered sturdily along the path, which was now level.

She had quite forgotten Nurse's warning, when she came suddenly upon a figure crouched in her path, and gazing at her with large, black eyes. Her fat cheeks turned pale, and with a cry of, "It's Bogy!" she let down the whole contents of her dress into one of Jan's leaf-pictures.

"Don't hurt me! Don't take me away! Please, please don't!" she cried, dancing wildly.

"I won't hurt you, Miss. I be going to help you to pick 'em up," said Jan. By the time he had returned her treasures to her skirt, Amabel had regained confidence, especially as she saw no signs of the black bag in which naughty children are supposed to be put.

"What are you doing, Bogy?" said she.

"I be making a picture, Miss," said Jan, pointing it out.

"Go on making it, please," said Amabel; and she sat down and watched him.

"Do you like this wood, Bogy?" she asked, softly, after a time.

"I do, Miss," said Jan.

"Why don't you sleep in it, then? I wouldn't sleep in a cellar, if I were you."

"I don't sleep in a cellar, Miss."

"Nurse *says* you do," said Amabel, nodding emphatically.

Jan was at a loss how to express the full inaccuracy of Nurse's statement in polite language, so he was silent; rapidly adding tint to tint from his heap of leaves, whilst the birds sang overhead, and Amabel sat with her two bundles watching him.

"I be making a picture, Miss," said Jan. — PAGE 184.

"I thought you were an old man!" she said, at length.

"Oh, no, Miss," said Jan, laughing.

"You don't look very bad," Amabel continued.

"I don't think I be very bad," said Jan, modestly.

Amabel's next questions came at short intervals, like dropping shots.

"Do you say your prayers, Bogy?"

"Yes, Miss."

"Do you go to church, Bogy?"

"Yes, Miss."

"Then where do you sit?"

"In the choir, Miss; the end next to Squire Ammaby's big pew."

"*Do you?*" said Amabel. She had been threatened with Bogy for misbehavior in church, and it was startling to find that he sat so near. She changed the subject, under a hasty remembrance of having once made a face at the parson through a hole in the bombazine curtains.

"Why don't you paint with paints, Bogy?" said she.

"I haven't got none, Miss," said Jan.

"I've got a paint-box," said Amabel. "And, if you like, I'll give it to you, Bogy."

The color rushed to Jan's face.

"Oh, thank you, Miss!" he cried.

"You must dip the paints in water, you know, and rub them on a plate; and don't let them lie in a puddle," said Amabel, who loved to dictate.

"Thank you, Miss," said Jan.

"And don't put your brush in your mouth," said Amabel.

"Oh, dear, no, Miss," said Jan. It had never struck

him that one could want to put a paint-brush in one's mouth.

At this point Amabel's overwrought energies suddenly failed her, and she burst out crying. "I don't know how I shall get over the wall," said she.

"Don't 'ee cry, Miss. I'll help you," said Jan.

"I can't walk any more," sobbed Amabel, who was, indeed, tired out.

"I'll take 'ee on my back," said Jan. "Don't 'ee cry."

With a good deal of difficulty, Amabel was hoisted up, and planted her big feet in Jan's hands. It was no light pilgrimage for poor Jan, as he climbed the winding path. Amabel was peevish with weariness; her bundles were sadly in the way, and at every step a cup-moss or *marchantia* dropped out, and Amabel insisted upon its being picked up. But they reached the wall at last, and Jan got her over, and made two or three expeditions after the missing mosses, before the little lady was finally content.

"Good-by, Bogy," she said, at last, holding up her face to be kissed. "And thank you very much. I'm not frightened of you, Bogy."

As Jan kissed her, he said, smiling, "What is your name, love?"

And she said, "Amabel."

To her parents and guardians, Amabel made the following statement: "I've seen Bogy. I like him. He doesn't sleep in the cellar, so Nurse told a story. And he didn't take me away, so that's another story. He says his prayers, and he goes to church, so he can't be the Bad Man. He makes pictures with leaves. He carried me on his back, but not in a bag" —

At this point the outraged feelings of Lady Craikshaw

exploded, and she rang the bell, and ordered Miss Amabel to be put to bed with a dose of rhubarb and magnesia (without sal-volatile), for telling stories.

" The eau-de-Cologne, mamma dear, please," said Lady Louisa, as the door closed on the struggling, screaming, and protesting Amabel. " Isn't it really dreadful? But Esmerelda Ammaby says Henry used to tell shocking stories when he was a little boy."

CHAPTER XXIV.

THE PAINT-BOX. — MASTER LINSEED'S SHOP. — THE NEW SIGN-BOARD. — MASTER SWIFT AS WILL SCARLET.

ON Sunday morning Jan took his place in church with unusual feelings. He looked here, there, and everywhere for the little damsel of the wood, but she was not to be seen. Meanwhile she had not sent the paint-box, and he feared it would never come. He fancied she must be the Squire's little daughter, but he was not sure, and she certainly was not in the big pew, where the back of the Squire's red head and Lady Louisa's aquiline nose were alone visible. She was a dear little soul, he thought. He wondered why she called him Bogy. Perhaps it was a way little ladies had of addressing their inferiors.

Jan did not happen to guess that, Amabel being very young, the morning services were too long for her. In the afternoon he had given her up, but she was there.

The old Rector had reached the third division of his sermon, and Lady Craikshaw was asleep, when Amabel, mounting the seat with her usual vigor, pushed her Sunday hood through the bombazine curtains, and said, —

"Bogy!"

Jan looked up, and then started to his feet as Amabel stuffed the paint-box into his hands. "I pushed it under my frock," she said in a stage whisper. "It made me so tight! But grandmamma is such" —

Jan heard and saw no more. Amabel's footing was apt to be insecure; she slipped upon the cushions and disappeared with a crash.

Jan trembled as he clasped the shallow old cedar-wood box. He wondered if the colors would prove as bright as those in the window. He fancied the wan, ascetic faces there rejoiced with him. When he got home, he sat under the shadow of the mill, and drew back the sliding lid of the box. Brushes, and twelve hard color cakes. They were Ackermann's, and very good. Cheap paint-boxes were not made then. He read the names on the back of them: Neutral Tint, Prussian Blue, Indian Red, Yellow Ochre, Brown Madder, Brown Pink, Burnt Umber, Vandyke Brown, Indigo, King's Yellow, Rose Madder, and Ivory Black.

It says much for Jan's uprightness of spirit, and for the sense of duty in which the schoolmaster was training him, that he did not neglect school for his new treasure. Happily for him the sun rose early, and Jan rose with it, and taking his paint-box to the little wood, on scraps of parcel paper and cap paper, on bits of wood and smooth white stones, he blotted-in studies of color, which he finished from memory at odd moments in the windmill.

In the summer holidays, Jan had more time for sketching. But the many occasions on which he could not take his paints with him led him to observe closely, and taught him to paint from memory with wonderful exactness. He was also obliged to reduce his outlines and condense his effects to a very small scale to economize paper.

About this time he heard that Master Chuter was going to have a new sign painted for the inn. Master Linseed was to paint it.

Master Linseed's shop had been a place of resort for Jan in some of his leisure time. At first the painter and decorator had been churlish enough to him, but, finding that Jan was skilful with a brush, he employed him again and again to do his work, for which he received instead of giving thanks. Jan went there less after he got a paint-box, and could produce effects with good materials of his own, instead of making imperfect experiments in color on bits of wood in the painter's shop.

But in this matter of the new sign-board he took the deepest interest. He had a design of his own for it, which he was most anxious the painter should adopt. "Look 'ee, Master Linseed," said he. "It be the Heart of Oak. Now I know a oak-tree with a big trunk and two arms. They stretches out one on each side, and the little branches closes in above till 'tis just like a heart. 'Twould be beautiful, Master Linseed, and I could bring 'ee leaves of the oak so that 'ee could match the yellows and greens. And then there 'd be trees beyond and beyond, smaller and smaller, and all like a blue mist between them, thee know. That blue in the paper 'ee 've got would just do, and with more white to it 'twould be beautiful for the sky. And " —

" And who 's to do all that for a few shillings? " broke in the painter, testily. " And Master Chuter wants it done and hung up for the Foresters' dinner."

Since the pressing nature of the commission was Master Linseed's excuse for not adopting his idea for the sign, it seemed strange to Jan that he did not set about it in some fashion. But he delayed and delayed, till Master Chuter was goaded to repeat the old rumor that real sign painting was beyond his powers.

It was within a week of the dinner that the little innkeeper burst indignantly into the painter's shop. Master Linseed was ill in bed, and the sign-board lay untouched in a corner.

"It be a kind of fever that's on him," said his wife.

"It be a kind of fiddlestick!" said the enraged Master Chuter; and turning round his eye fell on Jan, who was looking as disconsolate as himself. Day after day had he come in hopes of seeing Master Linseed at work, and now it seemed indefinitely postponed. But the innkeeper's face brightened, and, seizing Jan by the shoulder, he dragged him from the shop.

"Look 'ee here, Jan Lake," said he. "Do 'ee thenk *thee* could paint the sign? I dunno what I'd give 'ee if 'ee could, if 'twere only to spite that humbugging old hudmedud yonder."

Jan felt as if his brain were on fire. "If 'ee 'll get me the things, Master Chuter," he gasped, "and 'll let me paint it in your place, I'll do it for 'ee for nothin'."

The innkeeper was not insensible to this consideration, but his chief wish was to spite Master Linseed. He lost no time in making ready, and for the rest of the week Jan lived between the tallet (or hay-loft) of the inn and the wood where he had first studied trees. Master Chuter provided him with sheets of thick whitey-brown paper, on which he made water-color studies, from which he painted afterwards. By his desire no one was admitted to the tallet, though Master Chuter's delight increased with the progress of the picture till the secret was agony to him. Towards the end of the week they were disturbed by a scuffling on the tallet stairs, and Rufus bounced in, followed at a slower pace by the schoolmaster, crying, "Unearthed at last!"

"Come in, come in! That's right!" shouted Master Chuter. "Let Master Swift look, Jan. He be a scholar, and 'll tell us all about un."

But Jan shrank into the shadow. The schoolmaster stood in the light of the open shutter, towards which the painting was sloped, and Rufus sat by him on his haunches, and blinked with all the gravity of a critic; and in the half light between them and the stairs stood the fat little innkeeper, with his hands on his knees, crying, "There, Master Swift! Did 'ee ever see any thing to beat that? Artis' or ammytoor!"

Jan's very blood seemed to stand still. As Master Swift put on his spectacles, each fault in the painting sprang to the front and mocked him. It was indeed a wretched daub!

But Jan had been studying the scene under every lovely light of heaven from dawn to dusk for a week of summer days: Master Swift carried no such severe test in his brain. As he raised his head, the tears were in his eyes, and he held out his hand, saying, "My lad, it's just the spirit of the woods."

"But d' ye not think a figure or so would enliven it?" he continued. "One of Robin Hood's foresters 'chasing the flying roe'?"

"*Foresters!* To be sure!" said Master Chuter. "What did I say? Have the schoolmaster in, says I. He be a scholar, and knows what's what. Put 'em in, Jan, put 'em in! there's plenty of room."

What Jan had already suffered from the innkeeper's suggestions, only an artist can imagine, and his imagination will need no help!

"I'd be main glad to get a bit of red in there," said

Jan, in a low voice, to Master Swift; "but Robin Hood must be in green, sir, mustn't he?"

"There's Will Scarlet. Put Will in," said Master Swift, who, pleased to be appealed to, threw himself warmly into the matter. "He can have just drawn his bow at a deer out of sight." And with a charming simplicity the old schoolmaster flung his burly figure into an appropriate attitude.

"Stand so a minute!" cried Jan, and seizing a lump of charcoal, with which he had made his outlines, he rapidly sketched Master Swift's figure on the floor of the tallet. Thinned down to what he declared to have been his dimensions in youth, it was transferred to Jan's picture, and the touch of red was the culminating point of the innkeeper's satisfaction.

On the day of the dinner the new sign swung aloft. "It couldn't dry better anywhere," said Master Chuter.

Jan "found himself famous." The whole parish assembled to admire. The windmiller, in his amazement, could not even find a proverb for the occasion, whilst Abel hung about the door of the Heart of Oak, as if he had been the most confirmed toper, saying to all incomers, "Have 'ee seen the new sign, sir? 'Twas our Jan did un."

His fame would probably have spread more widely, but for a more overwhelming interest which came to distract the neighborhood, and which destroyed a neat little project of Master Chuter's for running up a few tables amongst his kidney-beans, as a kind of "tea garden" for folk from outlying villages, who, coming in on Sunday afternoons to service, should also want to see the work of the boy sign-painter.

It is a curious instance of the inaccuracy of popular impressions that, when Master Linseed died three days after the Foresters' dinner, it was universally believed that he had been killed by vexation at Jan's success. Nor was this tradition the less firmly fixed in the village annals, that the disease to which he had succumbed spread like flames in a gale. It produced a slight reaction of sentiment against Jan. And his achievement was absolutely forgotten in the shadow of the months that followed.

For it was that year long known in the **history of the district as the year of the Black Fever.**

CHAPTER XXV.

SANITARY INSPECTORS. — THE PESTILENCE. — THE PAR-
SON. — THE DOCTOR. — THE SQUIRE AND THE SCHOOL-
MASTER. — DESOLATION AT THE WINDMILL. — THE
SECOND ADVENT.

I REMEMBER a "cholera year" in a certain big village. The activity of the sanitary authorities (and many and vain had been the efforts to rouse them to activity *before*) was, for them, remarkable. A good many heads of households died with fearful suddenness and not less fearful suffering. Several nuisances were "seen to," some tar-barrels were burnt, and the scourge passed by. Not long ago a woman, whose home is in a court where some of the most flagrant nuisances existed, in talking to me, casually alluded to one of them. It had been ordered to be removed, she said, in the cholera year when the gentlemen were going round; but the cholera went away, and it remained among those things which were *not* "seen to," and for aught I know flourishes still. She was a sensible and affectionate person. Living away from her home at that time, she became anxious at once for the welfare of her relatives if they neglected to write to her. But she had never an anxiety on the subject of that unremedied abomination which was poisoning every breath they drew. That "the gentlemen who went round" felt it superfluous to have their orders carried out when strong men were no longer sickening and dying within two revolutions of the hands of the church clock will surprise no one who has had to do with local sanitary officers. They are like the children of Israel, and will only do their duty under the pressure of a plague. The people themselves are more like the Egyptians. Plagues won't convince them. A mother with all her own and her neighbors' children sickening about her would walk miles in a burst shoe to fetch the doctor or a big bottle of medicine, but she won't walk three yards farther than usual to draw her house-water from the well that the sewer doesn't leak into. That is a fact, not a fable; and, in the cases I am thinking of, all medical remonstrance was vain. Uneducated people will take any thing in from the doctor through their mouths, but little or nothing through their ears.

When such is the state of matters in busy, stirring districts, among shrewd artisans, and when our great seat of learning smells as it does smell under the noses of the professors, it is needless to say that the "black fever" found every household in the little village prepared to contribute to its support, and met with hardly an obstacle on its devastating path.

To comment on Master Salter's qualifications for the post of sanitary inspector would be to insult the reader's understanding. Of course he owned several of the picturesque little cottages where the refuse had to be pitched out at the back, and the slops chucked out in front, and where the general arrangements for health, comfort, and decency were such as one must forbear to speak of, since, on such matters, our ears — Heaven help us! — have all that delicacy which seems denied to our noses.

If the causes of the calamity were little understood, portents were plentifully noted. The previous winter had been mild. A thunderbolt fell in the autumn. There was a blight on the gooseberries, and Master Salter had a calf with two heads. As to the painter, a screech-owl had been heard to cry from his chimney-top, not three weeks before his death.

There was a pause of a day or so after Master Linseed died, and then victims fell thick and fast. Children playing happily with their mimic boats on the open drain that ran lazily under the noontide sun, by the footpath of the main street, were coffined for their hasty burial before the sun had next reached his meridian. The tears were hardly dry in their parents' eyes before these also were closed in their last sleep. The very aged seemed to linger on, but strong men sickened and died; and at the end of the week more than one woman was left sitting by an empty hearth, a worn-out creature whom Death seemed only to have forgotten to take away.

At first there was a reckless disregard of infection among the neighbors. But, after one or two of these family desolations, this was succeeded by a panic, and even the noble charity which the poor commonly show to each other's troubles failed, and no one could be got to nurse the sick or bury the dead.

Now the Rector was an old man. Most of the parish officers were aged, and patriarchs in white smock frocks were as plentiful as creepers at the cottage doors. The healthy breezes and the dull pace at which life passed in the district seemed to make men slow to wear out. If the Rector had profited by these features of the parish in health, it must be confessed that they had also had their influence on his career. He was a good man, and a learned one. He stuck close to his living, and he was benevolent. But he was not of those heroic natures who can resist the influence of the mental atmosphere around them; and in a dull parish, in a sleepy age, he had not been an active parson. Some men, however, who cannot make opportunities for themselves, can do nobly enough if the chance comes to them; and this chance came to the Rector in his sixty-ninth year, on the wings of the black fever. To quicken spiritual life in the soul of a Master Salter he had not the courage even to attempt; but a panic of physical cowardice had not a temptation for him. And so it came about that of four men who stayed the panic, by the example of their own courage, who went from house to house, and from sick-bed to sick-bed — who drew a cordon round the parish, and established kitchens and a temporary hospital, and nursed the sick, and encouraged the living, and buried the dead, — the most active was the old Rector.

The other three were the parish doctor, Squire Ammaby, and the schoolmaster.

On the very first rumor of the epidemic, Lady Louisa had carried off Amabel, and had gone with Lady Craikshaw to Brighton. Both the ladies were indignant with the Squire's obstinate resolve to remain amongst his tenants. In her alarm, Lady Louisa implored him to sell the property and buy one in Ireland, which was Lady Craikshaw's native country; and the list she contrived to run up of the drawbacks to the Ammaby estate would have driven a temper less stolid than her husband's to distraction.

When the fever broke out among the children, the schools were closed, and Master Swift devoted his whole time to laboring with the parson, the doctor, and the Squire.

No part of the Rector's devotion won more affectionate gratitude from his people than a single act of thoughtfulness, by which he preserved a record of the graves of their dead. He had held firmly on to a decent and reverent burial, and, foreseeing that the poor survivors would be quite unable to afford gravestones, he kept a strict list of the dead, and where they were buried, which was afterwards transferred to one large monument, which was bought by subscription. He cut the village off from all communication with the outer world, to prevent a spread of the disease; but he sent accounts of the calamity to the public papers, which brought abundant help in money for the needs of the parish. And in these matters the schoolmaster was his right-hand man.

The disease was most eccentric in its path. Having scourged one side only of the main street, it burst out with virulence in detached houses at a distance. Then it returned to the village, and after lulls and outbreaks it ceased as suddenly as it began.

It was about midway in its career that it fell with all its wrath upon Master Lake's windmill.

The mill stood in a healthy position, but the dwelling-room was ill-ventilated, and there were defective sanitary arrangements, which Master Swift had anxiously pointed out to the miller. The plague had begun in the village, and the schoolmaster trembled for Jan. But Master Lake was not to be interfered with, and, when the schoolmaster spoke of poison, thought himself witty as he replied, —

"It be a uncommon slow pison then, Master Swift."

It must also be allowed that such epidemics, once

started, do havoc in apparently clean houses and amongst well-fed people.

It was a little foster-sister of Jan's who sickened first. She died within two days. Her burial was hasty enough, but Mrs. Lake had no time to fret about that, for a second child was ill. Like many another householder, the poor windmiller was now ready enough to look to his drains, and so forth; but it may be doubted if the general stirring up of dirty places at this moment did not do as much harm as good. It was hot, — terribly hot. Day after day passed without a breeze to cool the burning skins of the sick, and yet it was not sunshiny. People did say that the pestilence hung like a murky vapor above the district, and hid the sun.

Trades were slack, corn-grinding amongst the rest, and Master Lake did the housework, helped by Jan and Abel. He was stunned by the suddenness and the weight of the calamity which had come to him. He was very kind to Mrs. Lake, but the poor woman was almost past any feeling but that which, as a sort of instinct or inspiration, guided a constant watching and waiting on her sick children. She never slept, and would not have eaten, but that Master Lake used his authority to force some food upon her. At this time Jan's chief occupations were cookery and dish-washing. His constant habit of observation made all the experiences of life an education for him; he had often watched his foster-mother prepare the family meals, and he prepared them now, for Abel and the windmiller could not, and she was with the sick children.

Before the second child died, two more fell ill on the same day. Only Abel and Jan were still "about." The mother moved like an automaton, and never spoke. Now and then a deep sigh or a low moan would escape her, and the miller would move tenderly to her side, and say, " Bear up, missus; bear up, my lass," and then go back to his pipe and his cherry-wood chair, where he seemed to grow gray as he sat.

Master Swift came from time to time to the mill. He was everywhere, helping, comforting, and exhorting. Some said his face shone with the light af another world, for which he was " marked." Others whispered that the strain was telling on him, and that it wore the look it had had in the brief insanity which followed his child's death. But all agreed that the very sight of him brought help and consolation. The windmiller grew to watch for him, and to lean on him in the helplessness of his despair. And he listened humbly to the old man's fervid religious counsels. His own little threads of philosophy were all blowing loose and useless in this storm of trouble.

The evening that Master Swift came up to arrange about the burial of the second child, he found the other two just dead. The first two had suffered much and been delirious, but these two had sunk painlessly in a few hours, and had fallen asleep for the last time in each other's arms.

It did not lessen the force of Master Swift's somewhat stern consolations that in all good faith he conveyed in them an expectation that the Last Day was at hand. Many people thought so, and it was, perhaps, not unnatural. In these days, which were long years of suffering, they were shut off from the rest of humanity, and the village was the world to them,— a world very near its end. With Death so busy, it seemed as if Judgment could hardly linger long.

It is true that this did not form a part of the Rector's religious exhortations. But some good people were shocked by the tea-party that he gave to the young people of the place, and the games that followed it in the Rectory meads, at the very height of the fever; though the doctor said it was better than a hogshead of medicine.

"To encourage low spirits in this panic is just to promote suicide, if ye like the responsibeelity of that," said the doctor to Master Swift, who had confided his doubts as to the seemliness of the entertainment. "I tell ye there's a lairge proportion of folk dies just because their neighbors have died before them, for the want of their attention being directed to something else. Away wi' ye, schoolmaster, and take your tuning-fork to ask the blessing wi'. What says the Scripture, man? 'The living, the living, he shall praise Thee!'"

The doctor was a Scotchman, and Master Swift always listened with sympathy to a North countryman. He was convinced, too, and took his tuning-fork to the meads, and led the grace.

Nor could his expectation of the speedy end of all things restrain his instinctive anxiety and watchfulness for Jan's health. On the evening of that visit to the mill, he used some little manœuvring to accomplish Jan's being sent back with him to the village, to arrange for the burial of the three children.

A glow of satisfaction suffused his rough face as he got Jan out of the tainted house into the fresh evening air, though it paled again before that other look which was now habitual to him, as, waving his hand towards the ripening corn-fields, he quoted from one of Mr. Herbert's loftiest hymns, —

"We talk of harvests, — there are no such things,
  But when we leave our corn and hay.
There is no fruitful year but that which brings
  The last and loved, though dreadful Day.
    Oh, show Thyself to me,
      Or take me up to Thee!"

CHAPTER XXVI.

THE BEASTS OF THE VILLAGE.— ABEL SICKENS.— THE GOOD SHEPHERD. — RUFUS PLAYS THE PHILANTHROPIST. — MASTER SWIFT SEES THE SUN RISE. — THE DEATH OF THE RIGHTEOUS.

AMID the havoc made by the fever amongst men, women, and children, the immunity of the beasts and birds had a sad strangeness.

There was a small herd of pigs which changed hands three times in ten days. The last purchaser hesitated, and was only induced by the cheapness of the bargain to suppress a feeling that they brought ill-luck. Cats mewed wistfully about desolated hearths. One dog moaned near the big grave in which his master lay, and others, with sad sagacious eyes, went to look for new friends and homes.

It was a day or two after the burial of the miller's three children, that, as Jan sat at dinner with Abel and his two parents, he was struck by the way in which the mill cats hung about Abel, purring and rubbing themselves against his legs.

"I do think they misses the others," he whispered to his foster-brother, and his tears fell thick and fast on to his plate.

Abel made no answer. He did not wish Jan to know that he had given all his food by bits to the cats, because he could not swallow it himself. But, later in the day, Jan found him in the round-house, lying on an empty sack, with his head against a full one.

"Don't 'ee tell mother," he said; "but I do feel bad."

And as Jan sat down, and put his arms about him, on the very spot where they had so often sat together, learning the alphabet and educating their thumbs, Abel laid his head on his foster-brother's shoulder, saying, —

"I do think, Janny dear, that Mary, she wants me, and the others too. I think I be going after them. But thee'll look to mother, Janny dear, eh?"

"But *I* want thee, too, Abel dear," sobbed Jan.

"I be thinking perhaps them that brought thee hither 'll fetch thee away some day, Jan. But thee'll see to mother?" repeated Abel, his eyes wandering restlessly with a look of pain.

Jan knew now that he was only an adopted child of the windmill, though he stoutly ignored the fact, being very fond of his foster-parents.

Abel's illness came with the force of a fresh blow. There had been a slight pause in the course of the fever at the mill, and it seemed as if these two boys were to be spared. Abel had been busy helping his father to burn the infected bedding, &c., that very morning, and at night he lay raving.

He raved of Jan's picture which swung unheeded above Master Chuter's door, and confused it with some church-window that he seemed to fancy Jan had painted; then of his dead brothers and sisters. And then from time to time he rambled about a great flock of sheep which he saw covering the vast plains about the windmill, and which he wearied himself in trying to count. And, as he tossed, he complained in piteous tones about some man who seemed to be the shepherd, and who would not do something that Abel wanted.

For the most part, he knew no one but Jan, and then only when Jan touched him. It seemed to give him pleasure. He understood nothing that was said to him, except in brief intervals. Once, after a short sleep, he opened his eyes and recognized the schoolmaster.

"Master Swift," said he, "do 'ee think that be our Lord among them sheep? With His hair falling on 's shoulders, and the light round His head, and the long frock?"

Master Swift's eyes turned involuntarily in the direction in which Abel's were gazing. He saw nothing but the dark corners of the dwelling-room; but he said,—

"Ay, ay, Abel, my lad."

"What be His frock all red for, then? Bright red, like blood. 'Tis like them figures in — in "—

Here Abel wandered again, and only muttered to himself. But when Jan crept near to him, and touching him said, "The figures in the window, Abel dear," he opened his eyes and said,—

"So it be, Janny. With the sun shining through 'em. Thee knows."

And then he wailed fretfully,—

"Why do He keep His back to me all along? I follows him up and down, all over, till I be tired. Why don't He turn His face?"

Jan was speechless from tears, but the old schoolmaster took Abel's hot hand in his, and said, with infinite tenderness,—

"He will, my lad. He'll turn His face to thee very soon. Wait for Him, Abel."

"Do 'ee think so?" said Abel. And after a while he muttered, "You be the schoolmaster, and ought to know."

And, seemingly satisfied, he dozed once more.

Master Swift hurried away. He had business in the village, and he wanted to catch the doctor, and ask his opinion of Abel's case.

"Will he get round, sir?" he asked.

The doctor shook his head, and Master Swift felt a double pang. He was sorry about Abel, but the real object of his anxiety was Jan. Once he had hoped the danger was past, but the pestilence seemed still in full strength at the windmill, and the agonizing conviction strengthened in his mind that once more his hopes were to be disappointed, and the desire of his eyes was to be snatched away. The doctor thought that he was grieving for Abel, and said, —

"I'm just as sorry as yourself. He's a fine lad, with something angelic about the face, when ye separate it from its surroundings. But they've no constitution in that family. It's just the want of strength in him, and not the strength of the fever, this time; for the virulence of the poison's abating. The cases are recovering now, except where other causes intervene."

Master Swift felt almost ashamed of the bound in his spirits. But the very words which shut out all hope of Abel's recovery opened a possible door of escape for Jan. He was not one of the family, and it was reasonable to hope that his constitution might be of sterner stuff. He turned with a lighter heart into his cottage, where he purposed to get some food and then return to the mill. There might be a lucid interval before the end, in which the pious Abel might find comfort from his lips; and if Jan sickened, he would nurse him night and day.

Rufus welcomed his master not merely with cordiality, but with fussiness. The partly apologetic character of his greeting was accounted for when a half starved looking dog emerged from beneath the table, and, not being immediately kicked, wagged the point of its tail feebly, keeping at a respectful distance, whilst Rufus introduced it.

"So ye're for playing the philanthropist, are ye?" said Master Swift. "Ye've picked up one of these poor houseless, masterless creatures? I'm not for undervaluing disinterested charity, Rufus, my man; but I wish ye'd had the luck to light on a better bred beast while ye were about it."

It is, perhaps, no disadvantage to what we call "dumb animals" if they understand the general drift of our remarks without minutely following every word. They have generally the sense, too, to leave well alone, and, without pressing the question of the new comer's adoption, the two dogs curled themselves round, put their noses into their pockets, and went to sleep with an air of its being unnecessary to pursue the topic farther.

Master Swift shared his meal with them, and left them to keep house when he returned to the mill.

His quick eye, doubly quickened by experience and by anxiety, saw that Jan's were full of fever, and his limbs languid. But he would not quit Abel's side, and Master Swift remained with the afflicted family.

Abel muttered deliriously all night, with short intervals of complete stupor. The fever, like a fire, consumed his strength, and the fancy that he was toiling over the downs seemed to weary him as if he had really been on foot. Just before sunrise, Master Swift left him asleep, and went to breathe some out-door air.

The fresh, tender light of early morning was over every thing. The windmill stood up against the red-barred sky with outlines softened by the clinging dew. The plains glistened, and across them, through the pure air, came the voice of Master Salter's chanticleer from the distant farm.

It was such a contrast to the scene within that Master Swift burst into tears. But even as he wept the sun leaped to the horizon, and, reflected from every dewdrop, and from the very tears upon the old man's cheeks, flooded the world about him with its inimitable glory.

The schoolmaster uncovered his head, and kneeling upon the short grass prayed passionately for the dying boy. But, as he knelt in the increasing sunshine, his prayers for the peace of the departing soul unconsciously passed almost into thanksgiving that so soon, and so little stained, it should exchange the dingy sick-room — not for these sweet summer days, which lose their sweetness! — but to taste, in peace which passeth understanding, what GOD has prepared for them that love Him.

It was whilst the schoolmaster still knelt outside the windmill that Abel awoke, and raised his eyes to Jan's with a smile.

"Thee must go out a bit soon, Janny dear," he whispered, "it be such a lovely day."

Jan was too much pleased to hear him speak to wonder how he knew what kind of a day it was, and Abel lay with his head in Jan's arms, breathing painfully and gazing before him. Suddenly he raised himself, and cried, — so loudly that the old man outside heard the cry, —

"Janny dear! He 've turned his face to me. He be coming right to me. Oh! He" —

But HE had come.

CHAPTER XXVII.

JAN HAS THE FEVER. — CONVALESCENCE IN MASTER SWIFT'S COTTAGE. — THE SQUIRE ON DEMORALIZATION.

JAN took the fever. He was very ill, too, partly from grief at Abel's death. He had also a not unnatural conviction that he would die, which was unfavorable to his recovery.

The day on which he gave Master Swift his old etching as a last bequest, he fairly infected him also with this belief, and during a necessary visit to the village the schoolmaster hung up the little picture in his cottage with a breaking heart.

But the next time Rufus saw him, he came to prepare for a visitor. Jan was recovering, and Master Swift had persuaded the windmiller to let him come to the cottage for a few days, the rather that Mrs. Lake was going to stay with a relative whilst the windmill was thoroughly cleansed and disinfected. The weather was delightful now, and, feeble as he had become, Jan soon grew strong again. If he had not done so, it would have been from no lack of care on Master Swift's part. The old schoolmaster was a thrifty man, and had some money laid by, or he would have been somewhat pinched at this time. As it was, he drew freely upon his savings for Jan's benefit, and made many expeditions to the town to buy such delicacies as he thought might tempt his appetite. Nor was this all. The morning when Jan came languidly into the kitchen from the little inner room, where he and the schoolmaster slept, he saw his precious paint-box on the table, to fetch which Master Swift had been to the windmill. And by it lay a square book with the word *Sketch-book* in ornamental characters on the binding, a couple of Cumberland lead drawing pencils, and a three-penny chunk of bottle India-rubber, delicious to smell.

If the schoolmaster had had any twinges of regret as he bought these things, in defiance of his principles for Jan's education, they melted utterly away in view of his delight, and the glow that pleasure brought into his pale cheeks. Master Swift was regarded, too, by a colored sketch of Rufus sitting at table in his arm-chair, with his more mongrel friend on the floor beside him. It was the best sketch that Jan had yet accomplished. But most people are familiar with the curious fact that one often makes an unaccountable stride in an art after it has been laid aside for a time.

It must not be supposed that Master Swift had neglected his duties in the village, or left the Parson, the Squire, and the doctor to struggle on alone, during the illness of Abel and of Jan. Even now he was away from the cottage for the greater part of the day, and Jan was left to keep house with the dogs. His presence gave great contentment to Rufus, if it scarcely lessened the melancholy dignity of his countenance; for dogs who live with human beings never like being left long alone. And Jan, for his own part, could have wished for nothing better than to sit at the table where he had once hoped to make leaf-pictures, and paint away with materials that Rembrandt himself would not have disdained.

The pestilence had passed away. But the labors of the Rector and his staff rather increased than diminished at this particular point. To say nothing of those vile wretches who seem to spring out of such calamities as putrid matter breeds vermin, and who use them as opportunities for plunder, there were a good many people to be dealt with of a lighter shade of demoralization, — people who had really suffered, and whose daily work had been unavoidably stopped, but to whom idleness was so pleasant, and the fame of their misfortunes so gratifying, that they preferred to scramble on in dismantled homes, on the alms extracted by their woes, to setting about such labor as would place them in comfort. Then that large class — the shiftless — was now doubly large, and there were widows and orphans in abundance, and there was hardly a bed or a blanket in the place.

"I have come," said Mr. Ammaby, joining the Rector as he sat at breakfast, "to beg you, in the interests of the village, to check the flow of that fount of benevolence which springs eternal in the clerical pocket. You will ruin us with your shillings and half crowns."

"Bless my soul, Ammaby," said the Rector, pausing with an eggshell transfixed upon his spoon, "shillings and half crowns don't go far in the present condition of our households. There are not ten families whose beds are not burnt. What do you propose to do?"

"I'll tell you, when I have first confessed that my ideas are not entirely original. I have been studying political economy under that hard-headed Sandy, our friend the doctor. In the first place, from to-morrow, we must cease to *give* any thing whatever, and both announce that determination and stick to it."

"And *then*, my dear sir?" said the Rector, smiling, and nursing his black gaiter.

"And *then*, my dear sir," said Mr. Ammaby, "I shall be able to get some men to do some work about my place, and those people at a distance who have widows here will relieve them (at least the widows will look up their well-to-do relatives), and the Church, in your person, will not be charged. And some of the widows will consent to scrub for payment, instead of sitting weeping in your kitchen — also for payment. They will, furthermore, compel their interesting sons to mind pigs, or scare birds, instead of hanging about the Heart of Oak, begging of the visitors who now begin to invade us. Do you know that the very boys won't settle to work, that the children are taking to gutter-life and begging, that the women won't even tidy up their houses, and that the men are retailing the horrors of the fever in every alehouse in the county, instead of getting in the crops? I give you my word, I had to go down to the inn yesterday, and a lad of eleven or twelve, who didn't recognize me in Chuter's dark kitchen, came up and began to beg with a whine that would have done credit to a professional mendicant. I stood in the shadow and let him tell his whole story, of a widowed mother and three brothers and sisters living, and six dead; and when he'd finished, and two visitors were fumbling in their pockets, I took him by the collar and lifted him clean through the kitchen and down the yard into the street. I nearly knocked Swift over, or rather I nearly fell myself, from concussion with his burly person, but he was the very man I wanted. I said, 'Mr. Swift, may I ask you to do me a favor? This boy — whose father was a respectable man — has been begging — *begging!* in a public room. His excuse is that his mother is starving. Will you kindly take him to the Hall, and put him in charge of the gardener, with my strict orders that he is to do a good afternoon's work at weeding in the shrubbery. And that the gardener is to see that he comes every day at nine o'clock in the morning, and works there till four in the afternoon, till the day you reopen school, meal-times and Sundays excepted. I will pay his mother five shillings a week, and, if he is a good boy, I'll give him some old clothes. And if ever you see or hear of his disgracing himself and his friends by begging again, if you don't thrash him within an inch of his life, I shall.' I promise you, the widow might starve for the want of that five shillings if the young gentleman could slip out of his bargain. His face was a study. But less so than the schoolmaster's. The job exactly suited him, and I suspect he knew the lad of old."

"From what I've heard Swift say, I fancy he sympathizes with your theories," said the Rector.

"I fear he sympathizes with my temper as well as my theories!" laughed the Squire. "As I felt the flush on my own cheek-bone, I caught the fire in his eye. But now, my dear sir, you will consent to some strong measures to prevent the village becoming a mere nest of *lazzaroni?* Let us try the system at any rate. I propose that we do not shut up the soup kitchen yet, but charge a small sum for the soup towards its expenses. And I want to beg you to write another of those graphic and persuasive letters, in which you have appealed to the sympathy of the public with our misfortune."

"But, bless me!" said the Rector, "I thought you were a foe to assisting the people, even out of their own parson's pocket."

"Well, I taunted the doctor myself with inconsistency, but we do not propose to make a sixpenny dole of the fund. You know there are certain things they can't do, and some help they seem fairly entitled to receive. We've made them burn their bedding, in the interests of the public safety, and it's only fair they should be helped to replace it. Then there is a lot of sanitary work which can only be done by a fund for the purpose; and, if we get the money, we can employ idlers. The women will tidy their houses when they see new blankets, and the sooner the churchyard is made nice, and that monument of yours erected, and we all get into orderly, respectable ways again, the better."

"Enough, enough, my dear Ammaby!" cried the Rector; "I put myself in your hands, and I will see to the public appeal at once; though I may mention that the credit of those compositions chiefly belongs to old Swift. He knows the *data* minutely, and he delights in the putting together. I think he regards it as a species of literary work. I hope you hear good news of Lady Louisa and little Amabel?"

"They are quite well, thank you," said the Squire; "they are in town just now with Lady Craikshaw, who has gone up to consult her London doctor."

"Well, farewell, Ammaby, for the present. Tell the doctor I'll give his plan a trial, and we'll get the place into working order as fast as we can."

"He will be charmed," said the Squire. "He says, as we are going on now, we are breeding two worse pests than the fever, — contentment under remediable discomfort, and a dislike to work."

CHAPTER XXVIII.

MR. FORD'S CLIENT. — THE HISTORY OF JAN'S FATHER. — AMABEL AND BOGY THE SECOND.

AMONG the many sounds blended into that one which roared for ever round Mr. Ford's offices in the city was the cry of the newsboys.

"Horful p'ticklers of the plague in a village in —— shire!" they screamed under the windows. Not that Mr. Ford heard them. But in five minutes the noiseless door opened, and a clerk laid the morning paper on the table, and withdrew in silence. Mr. Ford cut it leisurely with a large ivory knife, and skimmed the news. His eye happened to fall upon the Rector's letter, which, after a short summary of the history of the fever, pointed out the objects for which help was immediately required. There was a postscript. To give some idea of the ravages of the epidemic, and as a proof that the calamity was not exaggerated, a list of some of the worst cases was given, with names and particulars. It was gloomy enough. "Mary Smith, lost her husband (a laborer) and six children between the second and the ninth of the month. George Harness, a blacksmith, lost his wife and four children Master Abel Lake, windmiller of the Tower Mill, lost all his children, five in number, between the fifth and the fifteenth of the month. His wife's health is completely broken up"—

At this point Mr. Ford dropped the paper, and, unlocking a drawer beside him, referred to some memoranda, after which he cut out the Rector's letter with a large pair of office scissors, and enclosed it in one which he wrote before proceeding to any other business. He had underlined one name in the doleful list, — *Abel Lake, windmiller.*

Some hours later the silent clerk ushered in a visitor, one of Mr. Ford's clients. He was a gentleman of middle height and middle age, — the younger half of middle age, though his dark hair was prematurely gray. His eyes were black and restless, and his manner at once haughty and nervous.

"I am very glad to see you, my dear sir," said Mr. Ford, suavely; "I had just written you a note, the subject of which I can now speak about." And, as he spoke, Mr. Ford tore open the letter which lay beside him, whilst his client was saying, "We are only passing through town on our way to Scotland. I shall be here two nights."

"You remember instructing me that it was your wish to economize as much as possible during the minority of your son?" said Mr. Ford. His client nodded.

"I think," continued the man of business, "there is a quarterly payment we have been in the habit of making on your account, which is now at an end." And, as he spoke, he pushed the Rector's letter across the table, with his fingers upon the name *Abel Lake, windmiller.* His client always spoke stiffly, which made the effort with which he now spoke less noticed by the lawyer. "I should like to be certain," he said. "I mean, that there is no exaggeration or mistake."

"You have never communicated with the man, or given him any chance of pestering you," said Mr. Ford. "I should hardly do so now, I think."

"I certainly kept the power of reopening communication in my own hands, knowing nothing of the man; but I should be sorry to discontinue the allowance under a — a mistake of any kind."

Mr. Ford meditated. It may be said here that he by no means knew all that the reader knows of Jan's history; but he saw that his client was anxious not to withhold the money if the child were alive.

"I think I have it, my dear sir," he said suddenly. "Allow me to write, in my own name, to this worthy clergyman. I must ask you to subscribe to his fund, in my name, which will form an excuse for the letter, and I will contrive to ask him if the list of cases has been printed accurately, and has his sanction. If there has been any error, we shall hear of it. The object of the subscription is — let me see — is — a monument to those who have died of the fever and "—

But the dark gentleman had started up abruptly.

"Thank you, thank you, Mr. Ford," he said; "your plan is, as usual, excellent. Pray oblige me by sending ten guineas in your own name, and you will let me know if — if there *is* any mistake. I will call in to-morrow about other matters."

And before Mr. Ford could reply his client was gone.

The peculiar solitude to be found in the crowded heart of London was grateful to his present mood. To have been alone with his thoughts in the country would have been intolerable. The fields smack of innocence, and alone with them the past is apt to take the simple tints of right and wrong in the memory. But in that seething mass, which represents ten thousand heartaches and anxieties, doubtful shifts, and open sins, as bad or worse than a man's own, there is a silent sympathy and no reproach. Mr. Ford's client did not lean back, the tension of his mind was too great. He sat stiffly, and gazed vacantly before him, half seeing and half transforming into other visions whatever lay before the hansom, as it wound its way through the streets. Now for a moment a four-wheeled cab, loaded with schoolboy luggage, occupied the field of view, and idle memories of his own boyhood flitted over it. Then, crawling behind a dray, some strange associations built up the barrels into an old weather-stained wooden house in Holland, and for a while an intense realization of past scenes which love had made happy put present anxieties to sleep. But they woke again with a horrible pang, as a grim, hideous funeral car drove slowly past, nodding like a nightmare.

As the traffic became less dense, and the cab went faster, the man's thoughts went faster too. He strove to do what he had not often tried, to review his life. He had unconsciously gained the will to do it, because a reparation which conscience might hitherto have pressed on him was now impossible, and because the plague that had desolated Abel Lake's home had swept the skeleton out of his own cupboard, and he could repent of the past and do his duty in the future. His conscience was stronger than his courage. He had long wished to repent, though he had not found strength to repair.

On one point he did not delude himself as he looked back over his life. He had no sentimental regrets for the careless happiness of youth. Is any period of human life so tormented with cares as a self-indulgent youth? He had been a slave to expensive habits, to social traditions, to past follies, ever since he could remember. He had been in debt, in pocket or in conscience, from his schoolboy days to this hour. His tradesmen were paid long since, and, if death had cancelled what else he owed, how easy virtue would henceforth be!

It had not been easy at the date of his first marriage. He was deeply in debt, and out of favor with his father. It was on both accounts that he went abroad for some months. In Holland he married. His wife was Jan's mother, and Jan was their only child.

Her people were of middle rank, leading quiet though cultivated lives. Her mother was dead, and she was her old father's only child. It would be doing injustice to the kind of love with which she inspired her husband to dwell much upon her beauty, though it was of that high type which takes possession of the memory for ever. She was very intensely, brilliantly fair, so that in a crowd her face shone out like a star. Time never dimmed one golden thread in her hair; and Death, who had done so much for Mr. Ford's client, could not wash that face from his brain. It blotted the traffic out of the streets, and in their place Dutch pastures, whose rich green levels were unbroken by hedge or wall, stretched flatly to the horizon. It bent over a drawing on his knee as he and she sat sketching together in an old-world orchard, where the trees bore more moss than fruit. The din of London was absolutely unheard by Mr. Ford's client, but he heard her voice, saying, "You must learn to paint cattle, if you mean to make any thing of Dutch scenery. And also, where the earth gives so little variety, one must study the sky. We have no mountains, but we have clouds." It was in the orchard, under the apple-tree, across the sketch-book, that they had plighted their troth — ten years ago.

They were married. Had he ever denied himself a single gratification, because it would add another knot to the tangle of his career? He had pacified creditors by incurring fresh debts, and had evaded catastrophes by involving himself in new complications all his life. His marriage was accomplished at the expense of a train of falsehoods, but his father-in-law was an unworldly old man, not difficult to deceive. He spent most of the next ten months in Holland, and, apart from his anxieties, it was the purest, happiest time he had ever known. Then his father recalled him peremptorily to England.

When Mr. Ford's client obeyed his father's summons, the climax of his difficulties seemed at hand. The old man was anxious for a reconciliation, but resolved that his son should "settle in life;" and he had found a wife for him, the daughter of a Scotch nobleman, young, handsome, and with a good fortune. He gave him a fortnight for consideration. If he complied, the old man promised to pay his debts, to make him a liberal allowance, and to be in every way indulgent. If he thwarted his plans, he threatened to allow him nothing during his lifetime, and to leave him nothing that he could avoid bequeathing at his death.

It was at this juncture that Jan's mother followed her husband to England. Her anxieties were not silenced by excuses which satisfied her father. The crisis could hardly have been worse. Mr. Ford's client felt that confession was now inevitable; and that he could confess more easily by letter when he reached London. But before the letter was written, his wife died.

Weak men, harassed by personal anxieties, become hard in proportion to their selfish fears. It is like the cruelty that comes of terror. He had loved his wife; but he was terribly pressed, and there came a sense of relief even with the bitterness of the knowledge that he was free. He took the body to Holland, to be buried under the shadow of the little wooden church where they were married; and to the desolate old father he promised to bring his grandson — Jan. But just after the death of the old nurse, in whose care he had placed his child, another crisis came to Mr. Ford's client. On the same day he got letters from his father and from his father-in-law. From the first, to press his instant return home; from the second, to say that, if he could not at once bring Jan, the old man would make the effort of a voyage to England to fetch him. Jan's father almost hated him. That the child should have lived when the beloved mother died was in itself an offence. But that that freedom, and peace, and prosperity, which were so dearly purchased by her death, should be risked afresh by him, was irritating to a degree. He was frantic. It was impossible to fail that very peremptory old gentleman, his father. It was out of the question to allow his father-in-law to come to England. He could not throw away all his prospects. And the more he thought of it, the more certain it seemed that Jan's existence would for ever tie him to Holland; that for his grandson's sake the old man would investigate his affairs, and that the truth would come out sooner or later. The very devil suggested to him that if the child had died with its mother he would have been quite free, and intercourse with Holland would have died away naturally. He wished to forget. To a nature of his type, when even such a love as he had been privileged to enjoy had become a memory involving pain, it was instinctively evaded like any other unpleasant thing. He resolved, at last, to let nothing stand between him and reconciliation with his father. Once more he must desperately mortgage the future for present emergencies. He wrote to the old father-in-law to say that the child was dead. He excused this to himself on the ground of Jan's welfare. If the truth became fully known, and his father threw him off, he would be a poor embarrassed man, and could do little for his child. But with his father's fortune, and, perhaps, the Scotch lady's fortune, it would be in his power to give Jan a brilliant future, *even if* he never fully acknowledged him. As yet he hardly recognized such an unnatural possibility. He said to himself, that when he was free, all would be well, and the Dutch grandfather would forgive the lie in the joy of discovering that Jan was alive, and would be so well provided for.

Mr. Ford's client was reconciled to his father. He married Lady Adelaide, and announced the marriage to his father-in-law. After which, his intercourse with Holland died out.

It was a curious result of a marriage so made that it was a very happy one. Still more curious was the likeness, both physical and mental, between the second wife and the first. Lady Adelaide was half Scotch and half English, a blonde of the most brilliant type, and of an intellectual order of beauty. But fair women are common enough. It was stranger still that the best affections of two women of so high a moral and intellectual standard should have been devoted to the same and to such a husband. Not quite in vain. Indeed, but for that grievous sin towards his eldest son, Mr. Ford's client would probably have become an utterly different man. But there is no rising far in the moral atmosphere with a wilful, unrepented sin as a clog.

It was a miserable result of the weakness of his character that he could not see that the very nobleness of Lady Adelaide's should have encouraged him to confess to her what he dared not trust to his father's imperious, petulant affection. But he was afraid of her. It had been the same with his first wife. He had dreaded that she should discover his falsehoods far more than he had feared his father-in-law. And years of happy companionship made it even less tolerable to him to think of lowering himself in Lady Adélaide's regard.

But there was a far more overwhelming consideration which had been gathering strength for eight years between him and the idea of recognizing Jan as his eldest son, and his heir. He had another son, Lady Adelaide's only child. If he had hesitated when the boy was only a baby to tell her that her darling was not his only son, it was less and less easy to him to think of bringing Jan — of whom he knew nothing — from the rough life of the mill to supplant Lady Adelaide's child, when the boy grew more charming as every year went by. Clever, sweet-tempered, of aristocratic appearance, idolized by the relatives of both his parents, he seemed made by Providence to do credit to the position to which he was believed to have been born.

Mr. Ford's client had almost made the resolve against which that fair face that was not Lady Adelaide's for ever rose up in judgment: he was just deciding to put Jan to school, and to give up all idea of taking him home, when death seemed once more to have solved his difficulties. An unwonted ease came into his heart. Surely Heaven, knowing how sincerely he wished to be good, was making goodness easy to him, — was permitting him to settle with his conscience on cheaper terms than those of repentance and restitution. (And indeed, if amendment, of the weak as well as of the strong, be GOD'S great purpose for us, who shall say that the ruggedness of the narrow road is not often smoothed for stumbling feet?) The fever seemed quite providential, and Mr. Ford's client felt quite pious about it. He was conscious of no mockery in dwelling to himself on the thought that Jan was " better off " in Paradise with his mother. And he himself was safe — for the first time since he could remember, — free at last to become worthier, with no black shadow at his heels. Very touching was his resolve that he would be a better father to his son than his own father had been to him. If he could not train him in high principles and self-restraint, he would at least be indulgent to the consequences of his own indulgence, and never drive him to those fearful straits. "But he'll be a very different young man from what I was," was his final thought. "Thanks to his good mother."

His mind was full of Lady Adelaide's goodness as he entered his house, and she met him in the hall.

"Ah, Edward!" she cried, "I am so glad you've come home. I want you to see that quaint child I was telling you about."

"I don't remember, my dear," said Mr. Ford's client.

"You're looking very tired," said Lady Adelaide, gently; "but about the child. It is Lady Louisa Ammaby's little girl. You know I met her just before we left Brighton. I only saw the child once, but it is the quaintest, most original little being! So unlike its mother! She and her mother are in town, and they were going out to luncheon to-day I found, so I asked the child here to dine with D'Arcy. Her *bonne* is taking off her things, and I must go and bring her down."

As Lady Adelaide went out, her son came in, and rushed up to his father. If Mr. Ford's client had failed in natural affection for one son, his love for the other had a double intensity. He put his arm tenderly round him, whilst the boy told some long childish story, which was not finished when Lady Adelaide returned, leading Amabel by the hand. Amabel was a good deal taller. Her large feet were adorned with ornamental thread socks, and leathern shoes buttoned round the ankle. Her hair was cropped, because Lady Craikshaw said this made it grow. She wore a big pinafore by the same authority, in spite of which she carried herself with an admirable dignity. The same candor, good sense, and resolution shone from her clear eyes and fat cheeks as of old. Mr. Ford's client was alarming to children, but Amabel shook hands courageously with him.

She was accustomed to exercise courage in her behavior. From her earliest days a standard of manners had been expected of her beyond her age. It was a consequence of her growth. "You're quite a big girl now," was a nursery reproach addressed to her at least two years before the time, and she tried valiantly to live up to her inches.

But when Amabel saw D'Arcy, she started and stopped short. "Won't you shake hands with my boy, Amabel?" said Lady Adelaide. "Oh, you must make friends with him, and he'll give you a ride on the rocking-horse after dinner. Surely such a big girl can't be shy?"

Goaded by the old reproach, Amabel made an effort, and, advancing by herself, held out her hand, and said, "How do you do, Bogy?"

D'Arcy's black eyes twinkled with merriment. "How do you do, Mother Bunch?" said he.

"My *dear* D'Arcy!" said Lady Adelaide, reproachfully.

"Mamma, I am not rude. I am only joking. She calls me Bogy, so I call her Mother Bunch."

"But I'm *not* Mother Bunch," said Amabel.

"And I'm not Bogy," retorted D'Arcy.

"Yes, you are," said Amabel. "Only you had very old clothes on in the wood."

Lady Craikshaw had cruelly warned Lady Adelaide that Amabel sometimes told stories, and, thinking that the child was romancing, Lady Adelaide tried to change the subject. But D'Arcy cried, "Oh, do let her talk, mamma. I do so like her. She is such fun!"

"You oughtn't to laugh at me," said poor Amabel, as D'Arcy took her into the dining-room, "I gave you my paint-box."

The boy's stare of amazement awoke a doubt in Amabel's mind of his identity with the Bogy of the woods. Between constantly peeping at him, and her anxiety to conduct herself conformably to her size in the etiquette of the dinner-table, she did not eat much. When dinner was over, and D'Arcy led her away to the rocking-horse, he asked, "Do you still think I'm Bogy?"

"N—no," said Amabel, "I think perhaps you're not. But you're very like him, though you talk differently. Do you make pictures?"

D'Arcy shook his head.

"Not even of leaves?" said Amabel.

When she was going away, D'Arcy asked, "Which do you like best, me or Bogy?"

Amabel pondered. "I like you very much. You made the rocking-horse go so fast; but I liked Bogy. He carried me all up the hill, and he picked up my moss. I wasn't afraid of him. I gave him a kiss."

"Well, give me a kiss," said D'Arcy. But there was a tone of raillery in his voice which put Amabel on her dignity, and she shook her head, and began to go down the steps of the house, one leg at a time.

"If I'm Bogy, you know, you *have* kissed me *once*," shouted D'Arcy. But Amabel's wits were as well developed as her feet.

"Once is enough for bogies," said she, and went sturdily away.

CHAPTER XXIX.

JAN FULFILS ABEL'S CHARGE. — SON OF THE MILL. — THE LARGE-MOUTHED WOMAN.

BY the time Jan went back to the windmill he was quite well.

"Ye'll be fit for the walk by I open school," said Master Swift.

Jan promised himself that he would redouble his pains in class, from gratitude to the good schoolmaster. But it was not to be.

The day before the school opened, Jan came to the cottage. "Master Swift," said he, "I be come to tell ye that I be afraid I can't come to school."

"And how's that?" said Master Swift.

"Well, Master Swift, I do think I be wanted at home. My father's not got Abel now; but it's my mother that mostly wants me. I be bothered about mother, somehow," said Jan, with an anxious look. "She do forget things so, and be so queer. She left the beer-tap running yesterday, and near two gallons of ale ran out; and this morning she put the kettle on, and no water in it. And she do cry terrible," Jan added, breaking down himself. "But Abel says to me the day he was took ill, 'Janny,' he says, 'look to mother.' And so I will."

"You're a good lad, Jan," said the schoolmaster. "Sit

ye down and get your tea, and I'll come back with ye to the mill. A bit of company does folk good that's beside themselves with fretting."

But the windmiller's wife was beyond such simple cure. The overtasked brain was giving way, and though there were from time to time such capricious changes in her condition as led Jan to hope she was better, she became more and more imbecile to the end of her life.

To say that he was a devoted son is to give a very vague idea of his life at this time to those for whom filial duty takes the shape of compliance rather than of action, or to those who have no experience of domestic attendance on the infirm both of body and of mind.

It was not in moments of tender feeling, or at his prayers, or by Abel's grave, that Jan recalled his foster-brother's dying charge; but as he emptied slops, cleaned grates, or fastened Mrs. Lake's black dress behind. Nor did gratitude flatter his zeal. "Boys do be so ackered with hooks and eyes," the poor woman grumbled in her fretfulness, and then she sat down to bemoan herself that she had not a daughter left. She had got a trick of stopping short half way through her dressing, and giving herself up to tears, which led to Jan's assisting at her toilette. He was soon expert enough with hooks and eyes, the more tedious matter was getting up her courage, which invariably failed her at the stage of her linsey-woolsey petticoat. But when Jan had hooked her up, and tied her apron on, and put a little shawl about her shoulders, and got her close-fitting cap set straight, — a matter about as easy as putting another man's spectacles on his nose, — and seated her by the fire, the worst was over. Mrs. Lake always cheered up after breakfast, and Jan always to the very end hoped that this was the beginning of her getting better.

Even after a niece of the windmiller's came to live at the mill, and to wait on Mrs. Lake, the poor woman was never really content without Jan. As time went on, she wept less, but her faculties became more clouded. She had some brighter hours, and the company of the schoolmaster gave her pleasure, and seemed to do her good. When the Rector visited her, his very sympathy made him delicate about dwelling on her bereavement. When the poor woman sobbed, he changed the subject in haste, and his condolences were of a very general character. But Master Swift had no such scruples; and as he sat by her chair, with a kindly hand on hers, he spoke both plainly and loudly. The latter because Mrs. Lake's hearing had become dull. Nor did he cease to speak because tears dropped perpetually from the eyes which were turned to him, and which seemed day by day to lose color from the pupils, and to grow redder round the lids from weeping.

"Them that sleep in Jesus shall GOD bring with Him. Ah! Mrs. Lake, ma'am, they're grand words for you and me. The Lord has dealt hardly with us, but there are folk that lose their children when it's worse. There's many a Christian parent has lived to see them grow up to wickedness, and has lost 'em in their sins, and has had to carry *that* weight in his heart besides their loss, that the Lord's counsels for them were dark to him. But for yours and mine, woman, that have gone home in their innocence, what have we to say to the Almighty, except to pray of Him to make us fitter to take them when He brings them back?"

Through the cloud that hung over the poor woman's

spirit, Master Swift's plain consolations made their way. The ruling thought of his mind became the one idea to which her unhinged intellect clung, — the second coming of the Lord. For this she watched — not merely in the sense of a readiness for judgment, but — out of the upper windows of the windmill, from which could be seen a vast extent of that heaven in which the sign of the Son of Man should be, before He came.

Sky-gazing was an old habit with Jan, and his active imagination was not slow to follow his foster-mother's fancies. The niece did all the house-work, for the freakish state of Mrs. Lake's memory made her help too uncertain to be trusted to. But, with a restlessness which was perhaps part of her disease, she wandered from story to story of the windmill, guided by Jan, and the windmiller made no objection.

The country folk who brought grist to the mill would strain their ears with a sense of awe to catch Mrs. Lake's mutterings as she glided hither and thither with that mysterious shadow on her spirit, and the miller himself paid a respect to her intellect now it was shattered which he had not paid whilst it was whole. Indeed he was very kind to her, and every Sunday he led her tenderly to church, where the music soothed her as it soothed Saul of old. As the brain failed, she became happier, but her sorrow was like a pain numbed by narcotics; it awoke again from time to time. She would fancy the children were with her, and then suddenly arouse to the fact that they were not, and moan that she had lost all.

"Thee've got one left, mother dear," Jan would cry, and his caresses comforted her. But at times she was troubled by an imperfect remembrance of Jan's history, and, with some echo of her old reluctance to adopt him, she would wail that she "didn't want a stranger child." It cut Jan to the heart. Ever since he had known that he was not a miller's son, he had protested against the knowledge. He loved the windmill and the windmiller's trade. He loved his foster-parents, and desired no others. He had a miller's thumb, and he flattened it with double pains now that his right to it was disputed. He would press Mrs. Lake's thin fingers against it in proof that he belonged to her, and the simple wile was successful, for she would smile and say, "Ay, ay, love! Thee's a miller's boy, for thee've got the miller's thumb."

Two or three causes combined to strengthen Jan's love for his home. His revolt from the fact that he was no windmiller born gave the energy of contradiction. Then to fulfil Abel's behests, and to take his place in the mill, was now Jan's chief ambition. And whence could be seen such glorious views as from the windows of a windmill?

Master Lake was very glad of his help. The quarterly payment had now been due for some weeks, but, in telling the schoolmaster, he only said, "I'd be as well pleased if they forgot un altogether, now. I don't want him took away, no time. And now I've lost Abel, Jan'll have the mill after me. He's a good son is Jan."

And, as he echoed Jan's praises, it never dawned on Master Swift that he was the cause of the allowance having stopped. Jan was jealous of his title as Master Lake's son, but the schoolmaster dwelt much in his own mind on the fact that Jan was no real child of the district; partly in his ambition for him, and partly out of a dim hope that he would himself be some day allowed to adopt him. In stating that the windmiller had lost all his children by the fever, he had stated the bare fact in all good faith; and as neither he nor the Rector guessed the real drift of Mr. Ford's letter, the mistake was never corrected.

Jan was useful in the mill. He swept the round-house, coupled the sacks, received grist from the grist-bringers, and took payment for the grinding in money or in kind, according to custom. The old women who toddled in with their bags of gleaned corn looked very kindly on him, and would say, "Thee be a good bwoy, sartinly, Jan, and the Lard 'll reward thee." If the windmiller came towards one of these dames, she would say, "Aal right, Master Lake, I be in no manners of hurry, Jan 'll do for me." And, when Jan came, his business-like method justified her confidence. "Good day, mother," he would say. "Will ye pay, or toll it?" "Bless ye, dear love, how should I pay?" the old woman would reply. "I'll toll it, Jan, and thank ye kindly." On which Jan would dip the wooden bowl or tolling-dish into the sack, and the corn it brought up was the established rate of payment for grinding the rest.

But, though he constantly assured the schoolmaster that he meant to be a windmiller, Jan did not neglect his special gift. He got up with many a dawn to paint the sunrise. In still summer afternoons, when the mill-sails were idle, and Mrs. Lake was dozing from the heat, he betook himself to the water-meads to sketch. In the mill itself he made countless studies. Not only of the ever-changing heavens, and of the monotonous sweeps of the great plains, whose aspect is more changeable than one might think, but studies on the various floors of the mill, and in the round-house, where old meal-bins and swollen sacks looked picturesque in the dim light falling from above, in which also the circular stones, the shaft, and the very hoppers, became effective subjects for the Cumberland lead-pencils.

Towards the end of the summer following the fever, Mrs. Lake failed rapidly. She sat out of doors most of the day, the miller moving her chair from one side to another of the mill to get the shade. Master Swift brought her big nosegays from his garden, at which she would smell for hours, as if the scent soothed her. She spoke very little, but she watched the sky constantly.

One evening there was a gorgeous sunset. In all its splendor, with a countless multitude of little clouds about it bright with its light, the glory of the sun seemed little less than that of the Lord Himself, coming with ten thousand of His saints, and the poor woman gazed as if her withered, wistful eyes could see her children among the radiant host. "I do think the Lord be coming to-night, Master Swift," she said. "And He'll bring them with Him."

She gazed on after all the glory had faded, and lingered till it grew dark, and the schoolmaster had gone home. It was not till her dress was quite wet with dew that Jan insisted upon her going indoors.

They were coming round the mill in the dusk, when a cry broke from Mrs. Lake's lips, which was only an echo of a louder one from Jan. A woman creeping round the mill in the opposite direction had just craned her neck forward so that Jan and his foster-mother saw her face for an instant before it disappeared. Why Jan was so terrified, he would have been puzzled to say, for the woman was not hideous, though she had an ugly mouth. But he was terrified, and none the less so from a conviction that she was looking intently and intentionally at him. When he got his foster-mother indoors, the miller was disposed to think the affair was a fancy; but, as if the shock had given a spur to her feeble senses, Mrs. Lake said in a loud clear voice, "Measter, it be the woman that brought our Jan hither!"

But when the miller ran out, no one was to be seen.

CHAPTER XXX.

JAN'S PROSPECTS AND MASTER SWIFT'S PLANS. — TEA AND MILTON. — NEW PARENTS. — PARTING WITH RUFUS. — JAN IS KIDNAPPED.

THIS shock seemed to give a last jar to the frail state of Mrs. Lake's health, and the sleep into which she fell that night passed into a state of insensibility in which her sorely tried spirit was released without pain.

It was said that the windmiller looked twice his age from trouble. But his wan appearance may have been partly due to the inroads of a lung disease, which comes to millers from constantly inhaling the flour-dust. His cheeks grew hollow, and his wasted hands displayed the windmiller's coat of arms* with painful distinctness. The schoolmaster spent most of his evenings at the mill; but sometimes Jan went to tea with him, and by Master Lake's own desire he went to school once more.

Master Swift thought none the less of Jan's prospects that it was useless to discuss them with Master Lake. All his plans were founded on the belief that he himself would live to train the boy to be a windmiller, whilst Master Swift's had reference to the conviction that "miller's consumption" would deprive Jan of his foster-father long be-

* The blue marks on the hands of a miller who "sets" his own stones are called in the trade the "miller's coat of arms."

fore he was old enough to succeed him. And had the miller made his will? Master Swift made his, and left his few savings to Jan. He could not help hoping for some turn of Fortune's wheel which should give the lad to him for his own.

Jan was not likely to lack friends. The Squire had heard with amazement that Master Chuter's new sign was the work of a child, and he offered to place him under proper instruction to be trained as an artist. But, at the time that this offer came, Jan was waiting on his foster-mother, and he refused to betray Abel's trust. The Rector also wished to provide for him, but he was even more easily convinced that Jan's present duty lay at home. Master Swift too urged this in all good faith, but his personal love for Jan, and the dread of parting with him, had an influence of which he was hardly conscious.

One evening, a few weeks after Mrs. Lake's death, Jan had tea, followed by poetry, with the schoolmaster. Master Swift often recited at the windmill. The miller liked to hear hymns his wife had liked, and a few patriotic and romantic verses; but he yawned over Milton, and fell asleep under Keats, so the schoolmaster reserved his favorites for Jan's ear alone.

When tea was over, Jan sat on the rush-bottomed chair, with his feet on Rufus, on that side of the hearth which faced the window, and on the other side sat Master Swift, with the mongrel lying by him, and he spouted from Milton. Jan, familiar with many a sunrise, listened with parted lips of pleasure, as the old man trolled forth, —

"Right against the eastern gate,
Where the great sun begins his state,
Robed in flames and amber light,"

and with even more sympathy to the latter part of 'Il Penseroso;' and, as when this was ended he begged for yet more, the old man began 'Lycidas.' He knew most of it by heart, and waving his hand, with his eyes fixed expressively on Jan, he cried, —

> "Fame is the spur that the clear spirit doth raise
> (That last infirmity of noble minds)
> To scorn delights, and live laborious days."

And tears filled his eyes, and made his voice husky, as he went on, —

> "But the fair guerdon when we hope to find,
> And think to burst out into sudden blaze,
> Comes the blind Fury with the abhorred shears"—

Master Swift stopped suddenly. Rufus was growling, and Jan was white and rigid, with his eyes fixed on the window.

As in most North countrymen, there was in the schoolmaster an ineradicable touch of superstition. He cursed the "unlucky" poem, and flinging the book from him ran to his favorite. As soon as Jan could speak, he gasped, "The woman that brought me to the mill!" But when Master Swift went to search the garden he could find no one.

Remembering the former alarm, and that no one was to be seen then, Master Swift came to the conclusion that in each case it was a delusion.

"Ye're a dear good lad, Jan," said he, "but ye've fagged yourself out. Take the dog with ye to-morrow for company, and your sketch-book, and amuse yourself. I'll not expect ye at school. And get away to your bed now. I told Master Lake I shouldn't let ye away to-night."

Jan went to bed, and next morning was up with the lark, and with Rufus at his heels went off to a distant place, where from a mound, where a smaller road crossed the highway to London, there was a view which he wished to sketch under an early light. As he drew near, he saw a small cart, at one side of which the horse was feeding, and at the foot of the mound sat a woman with a pedler's basket.

When Jan recognized her, it was too late to run away. And whither could he have run? The four white roads gleamed unsheltered over the plains; there was no place to hide in, and not a soul in sight.

When the large-mouthed woman seized Jan in her arms, and kissing him cried aloud, "Here he is at last! My child, my long lost child!" the despair which sank into the poor boy's heart made him speechless. Was it possible that this woman was his mother? His foster-mother's words tolled like a knell in his ears, — "The woman that brought our Jan hither." At the sound of Sal's voice the hunchback appeared from behind the cart, and his wife dragged Jan towards him, crying, "Here's our dear son! our pretty, clever little son."

"I bean't your son!" cried poor Jan, desperately. "My mother's dead." For a moment the Cheap Jack's wife seemed staggered; but unluckily Jan added, "She died last month," and it was evident that he knew nothing of his real history.

"Oh, them mill people, them false wretches!" screamed the woman. "Have I been a paying 'em for my precious child, all this time, for 'em to teach him to deny his own mother! The brutes!"

Jan's face and eyes blazed with passion. "How dare you

abuse my good father and mother!" he cried. "*You* be the wretch, and"—

But at this, and the same moment, the Cheap Jack seized Jan furiously by the throat, and Rufus sprang upon the hunchback. The hunchback was in the greater danger, from which only his wife's presence of mind saved him. She shrieked to him to let Jan go, that he might call off the dog, which the vindictive little Cheap Jack was loath to do. And when Jan had got Rufus off, and was holding him by the collar, the hunchback seized a hatchet with which he had been cutting stakes, and rushed upon the dog. Jan put himself between them, crying incoherently, "Let him alone! He's not mine—he won't hurt you—I'll send him home—I'll let un loose if ye don't;" and Sal held back her husband, and said, "If you'll behave civil, Jan, my dear, and as you should do to your poor mother, you may send the dog home. And well for him too, for John's a man that's not very particular what he does to them that puts him out in a place like this where there's no one to tell tales. He'd chop him limb from limb, as soon as not."

Jan shuddered. There was no choice but to save Rufus. He clung round the curly brown neck in one agonized embrace, and then steadied his voice for an authoritative, "Home, Rufus!" as he let him go. Rufus hesitated, and looked dangerously at the hunchback, who lifted the hatchet. Jan shouted angrily, "Home, Rufus!" and Rufus obeyed. Twenty times, as his familiar figure, with the plumy tail curled sideways, lessened along the road, was Jan tempted to call him back to his destruction; but he did not. Only when the brown speck was fairly lost to sight, his utter friendlessness overwhelmed him, and falling on his knees he besought the woman with tears to let him go,—at least to tell Master Lake all about it.

The hunchback began to reply with angry oaths, but Sal made signs to him to be silent, and said, "It comes very hard to me, Jan, to be treated this way by my only son, but, if you'll be a good boy, I'm willing to oblige you, and we'll drive round by the mill to let you see your friends, though it's out of the way too."

Jan was profuse of thanks, and by the woman's desire he sat down to share their breakfast. The hunchback examined his sketch-book, and, as he laid it down again, he asked, "Did you ever make picters on stone, eh?"

"Before I could get paper, I did, sir," said Jan.

"But could you now? Could you make 'em on a flat stone, like a paving-stone?"

"If I'd any thing to draw with, I could," said Jan. "I could draw on any thing, if I had something in my hand to draw with."

The Cheap Jack's face became brighter, and in a mollified tone he said to his wife, "He's a prime card for such a young un. It's a rum thing, too! A man I knowed was grand at screeving, but he said himself he was nowheres on paper. He made fifteen to eighteen shillin' a week on a average," the hunchback continued. "I've knowed him take two pound."

"Did you ever draw fish, my dear?" he inquired.

"No, sir," said Jan. "But I've drawn pigs and dogs, and I be mostly able to draw any thing I sees, I think."

The Cheap Jack whistled. "Profiles pays well," he murmured; "but the tip is the Young Prodigy."

"We're so pleased to see what a clever boy you are, Jan," said Sal; "that's all, my dear. Put the bridle on the horse, John, for we've got to go round by the mill."

Whilst the Cheap Jack obeyed her, Sal poked in the cart, from which she returned with three tumblers on a plate. She gave one to her husband, took one herself, and gave the third to Jan.

"Here's to your health, love," said she; "drink to mine, Jan, and I'll be a good mother to you." Jan tasted, and put his glass down again, choking. "It's so strong!" he said.

The Cheap Jack looked furious. "Nice manners they've taught this brat of yours!" he cried to Sal. "Do ye think I'm going to take my 'oss a mile out of the road to take him to see his friends, when he won't so much as drink our good healths?"

"Oh! I will, indeed I will, sir," cried Jan. He had taken a good deal of medicine during his illness, and he had learned the art of gulping. He emptied the little tumbler into his mouth, and swallowed the contents at a gulp.

They choked him, but that was nothing. Then he felt as if something seized him in the inside of every limb. After he lost the power of moving, he could hear, and he heard the Cheap Jack say, "I'd go in for the Young Prodigy, genteel from the first; only, if we goes among the nobs, he may be recognized. He's a rum-looking beggar."

"If you don't go a drinking every penny he earns," said Sal, pointedly, "we'll soon get enough in a common line to take us to Ameriky, and he'll be safe enough there."

On this Jan thought that he made a most desperate struggle and remonstrance. But in reality his lips never moved from their rigidity, and he only rolled his head upon his shoulder. After which he remembered no more.

CHAPTER XXXI.

SCREEVING. — AN OLD SONG. — MR. FORD'S CLIENT. — THE PENNY GAFF. — JAN RUNS AWAY.

THERE was a large crowd, but large crowds gather quickly in London from small causes. It was in an out-of-the-way spot too, and the police had not yet tried to disperse it.

The crowd was gathered round a street-artist who was "screeving," or drawing pictures on the pavement in colored chalks. A good many men have followed the trade in London with some success, but this artist was a wan, meagre-looking child. It was Jan. He drew with extraordinary rapidity; not with the rapidity of slovenliness, but with the rapidity of a genius in the choice of what Ruskin calls "fateful lines." At his back stood the hunchback, who "pattered" in description of the drawings as glibly as he used to "puff" his own wares as a Cheap Jack.

"Cats on the roof of a 'ouse. Look at 'em, ladies and gentlemen; and from their harched backs to their tails and whiskers, and the moon a-shining in the sky, you'll say they're as natteral as life. Ob-serve the fierceness in the eye of that black Tom. The one that's a-coming round the chimney-pot is a Sandy; yellow ochre in the body, and the markings in red. There isn't a hartist living could do 'em better, though I says it that's the lad's father."

"What's your name, boy?" — PAGE 247.

The cats were very popular, and so were the Prize Pig, Playful Porkers, Sow and her Little Ones, as exhibited by the Cheap Jack. But the prime favorite was "The Faithful Friend," consisting of sketches of Rufus in various attitudes, including a last sleep on the grave of a supposititious master, which Jan drew with a heart that ached as if it must break.

It was growing dark, but the exhibition had been so successful that day, and the crowd was still so large, that the hunchback was loath to desist. At a sign from him, Jan put his colored chalks into a little pouch in front of him, and drew in powerful chiaroscuro with soft black chalk and whitening. These sketches were visible for some time, and the interest of the crowd did not abate.

Suddenly a flush came over Jan's wan cheeks. A baker who had paused for a moment to look, and then passed on, was singing as he went, and the song and the man's accent were both familiar to Jan.

> "The swallow twitters on the barn,
> The rook is cawing on the tree,
> And in the wood the ring-dove cooes"—

"What's your name, boy?"

The peremptory tone of the question turned Jan's attention from the song, which died away down the street, and looking up he met a pair of eyes as black as his own, and Mr. Ford's client repeated his question. On seeing that a "swell" had paused to look, the Cheap Jack hurried to Jan's side, and was in time to answer.

"John Smith's his name, sir. He's slow of speech, my lord, though very quick with his pencil. There's not many artists can beat him, though I says it that shouldn't, being his father."

"*You* his father?" said the gentleman. "He is not much like you."

"He favors his mother more, my lord," said the Cheap Jack; "and that's where he gets his talents too."

"No one ever thought he got 'em from you, old humpy!" said one of the spectators, and there was a roar of laughter from the bystanders.

Mr. Ford's client still lingered, though the staring and pushing of the rude crowd were annoying to him.

"Do you really belong to this man?" he asked of Jan, and Jan replied, trembling, "Yes, sir."

"Your son doesn't look as if you treated him very well," said the gentleman, turning to the Cheap Jack. "Take that, and give him a good supper this evening. He deserves it."

As the Cheap Jack stooped for the halfcrown thrown to him, Mr. Ford's client gave Jan some pence, saying, "You can keep these yourself." Jan's face, with a look of gratitude upon it, seemed to startle him afresh, but it was getting dark, and the crowd was closing round him. Jan had just entertained a wild thought of asking his protection, when he was gone.

What the strange gentleman had said about his unlikeness to the Cheap Jack, and also the thoughts awakened by hearing the old song, gave new energy to a resolve to which Jan had previously come. He had resolved to run away.

Since he awoke from the stupor of the draught which Sal had given him at the cross-roads, and found himself utterly in the power of the unscrupulous couple who pretended to be his parents, his life had been miserable enough. They had never intended to take him back to the mill, and, since they came to London and he was quite at their mercy, they had made no pretence of kindness. That they kept him constantly at work could hardly be counted an evil, for his working hours were the only ones with happiness in them, except when he dreamed of home. Not the cold pavement chilling him through his ragged clothes, not the strange staring and jesting of the rough crowds, not even the hideous sense of the hunchback's vigilant oversight of him, could destroy his pleasure in the sense of the daily increasing powers of his fingers, in which genius seemed to tremble to create. In the few weeks of his apprenticeship to screeving, Jan had improved more quickly than he might have done under such teaching as the Squire had been willing to procure for the village genius. At the peril of floggings from the Cheap Jack, too many of which had already scarred his thin shoulders, he ransacked his brains for telling subjects, and forced from his memory the lines which told most, and told most quickly, of the pathetic look on Rufus's face, the anger, pleasure, or playfulness of the mill cats. Perhaps none of us know what might be forced, against our natural indolence, from the fallow ground of our capabilities in many lines. The spirit of a popular subject in the fewest possible strokes was what Jan had to aim at for his daily bread, under peril of bodily harm hour after hour, for day after day, and his hand gained a cunning it might never otherwise have learned, and could never unlearn now.

In other respects, his learning was altogether of evil. Perhaps because they wished to reconcile him to his life, perhaps because his innocent face and uncorrupted character were an annoyance and reproach to the wicked couple, they encouraged Jan to associate with the boys of their own and the neighboring courts.

Many people are sorry to believe that there are a great many wicked and depraved grown-up people in all large towns, whose habits of vice are so firm, and whose moral natures are so loose, that their reformation is practically almost hopeless. But much fewer people realize the fact that thousands of little children are actively, hideously vicious and degraded. And yet it is better that this should be remembered than that, since, though it is more painful, it is more hopeful. It is hard to reform vicious children, but it is easier than to reform vicious men and women.

Little boys and little girls of eight or nine or ten years old, who are also drunkards, swearers, thieves, gamblers, liars, and vicious, made Jan a laughing-stock, because of his simple childlike ways. They called him " green ;" but, when he made friends with them by drawing pictures for them, they tried to teach him their own terrible lore. Once the Cheap Jack gave Jan a penny to go with some other boys to a penny theatre, or "gaff." The depravity of the entertainment was a light matter to the depravity of the children by whom the place was crowded, and who had not so much lost as never found shame. Jan was standing amongst them, when he caught sight of a boy with a white head leaning over the gallery, whose face had a curious accidental likeness to Abel's. The expression was quite different, for this one was partly imbecile, but there was just likeness enough to recall the past with an unutterable pang. What would Abel have said to see him there? Jan could not breathe in the place. The others were engaged, and he fought his way out.

What he had heard and seen rang in his ears and danced before his eyes after he crept to bed, as the dawn broke over the streets. But as if Abel himself had watched by his bedside as he used to do, and kept evil visions away, it did not trouble his dreams. He dreamed of the windmill, and of his foster-mother; of the little wood, and of Master Swift and Rufus.

After that night Jan had resolved that, whether Sal were his mother or not, he would run away In the strength of his foster-brother's pious memory he would escape from this evil life. He would beg his way back to the village, and to the upright, godly old schoolmaster, or at least die in the country on the road thither. He had not associated with the ragamuffins of the court without learning a little of their cunning; and he had waited impatiently for a chance of eluding the watchfulness of the Cheap Jack.

But the sound of that song and the meeting with Mr. Ford's client determined him to wait no longer, but to make a desperate effort for freedom then and there. The Cheap Jack was collecting the pence, and Jan had made a few bold black strokes as a beginning of a new sketch, when he ran up to the Cheap Jack and whispered, "Get me a ha'perth of whitening, father, as fast as you can. There's an oil-shop yonder."

"All right, Jan," said the hunchback. "Keep 'em together, my dear, meanwhile. We're doing prime, and you shall have a sausage for supper."

As the Cheap Jack waddled away for the whitening, Jan

said to the lookers-on, " Keep your places, ladies and gentlemen, till I return, and keep your eyes on the drawing, which is the last of the series," and ran off down a narrow street, at right angles to the oil-shop.

The crowd waited patiently for some moments. Then the Cheap Jack hurried back with the whitening. But Jan returned no more.

CHAPTER XXXII.

THE BAKER. — ON AND ON. — THE CHURCH BELL. — A DIGRESSION. — A FAMILIAR HYMN. — THE BOYS' HOME.

JAN stopped at last from lack of breath to go on. His feet had been winged by terror, and he looked back even now with fear to see the Cheap Jack's misshapen figure in pursuit. He had had no food for hours, but the pence the dark gentleman had given him were in his chalk pouch, and he turned into the first baker's shop he came to to buy a penny loaf. It was a small shop, served by a pleasant-faced man, who went up and down, humming, whistling, and singing, —

> "Like tiny pipe of wheaten straw,
> The wren his little note doth swell,
> And every living thing that flies" —

"A penny loaf, please," said Jan, laying down the money, and the man turned and said, "Why, you be the boy that draws on the pavement!"

For a moment Jan was silent. It presented itself to him as a new difficulty, that he was likely to be recognized. There was a flour barrel by the counter, and as he pondered he began mechanically to sift the flour through his finger and thumb.

"You be used to flour seemingly," said the baker, smiling. "Was 'ee ever in a mill? 'ee seems to have a miller's thumb."

In a few minutes Jan had told his story, and had learned, with amazement and delight, that the baker had not only been a windmiller's man, but had worked in Master Lake's tower mill. He was, in fact, the man who had helped George the very night that Jan arrived. But he confirmed the fact that it was Sal who brought Jan, by his account of her, and he seemed to think that she was probably his mother. He was very kind. He refused to take payment for the loaf, and went, humming, whistling, and singing, away to get Jan some bacon to eat with it.

When he was alone, Jan's hand went back to the flour, and he sifted and thought. The baker was kind, but he had said that "it was an ackerd thing for a boy to quarrel with 's parents." Jan felt that he expected him to go home. Perhaps at this moment the baker had gone, with the best intentions, to fetch the Cheap Jack, and bring about a family reunion. Terror had become an abiding state of Jan's mind, and it seized him afresh, like a palsy. He left the penny on the counter, and shook the flour-dust from his fingers, and, stealing with side glances of dread into the street, he sped away once more.

He had no knowledge of localities. He ran "on and on," as people do in fairy tales. Sometimes he rested on a doorstep, sometimes he hid in a shutter box or under an archway. He had learned to avoid the police, and he moved quickly from one dark corner to another with a hunted look in his black eyes. Late in the night he found a heap of straw near a warehouse, on which he lay down and fell asleep. At eight o'clock the next morning he was awakened by the clanging of a bell, and he jumped up in time to avoid a porter who was coming to the warehouse, and ran " on and on."

It was a bright morning, and the sun was shining; but Jan's feet were sore, and his bones ached from cold and weariness. Yesterday the struggle to escape the Cheap Jack had kept him up, but now he could only feel his utter loneliness and misery. There was not a friendly sound in all the noises of the great city, — the street cries of food he could not buy, the quarrelling, the laughter with which he had no concern, the tramp of strange feet, the roar of traffic and prosperity in which he had no part.

He was so lonely, so desolate, that when a sound came to him which was familiar and pleasant, and full of old and good and happy associations, it seemed to bring his sad life to a climax,to give just one strain too much to his powers of endurance. Like the white lights he put to his black sketches, it seemed to bring the darkness of his life into relief, and he felt as if he could bear no more, and would like to sit down and die. The sound came through the porch of a church. It was the singing of a hymn, — one of Charles Wesley's hymns, of which Master Swift was so fond.

The sooty iron gates were open, and so was the door. Jan crept in to peep, and he caught sight of a stained window full of pale faces, which seemed to beckon him, and he went into the church and no one molested him.

There is a very popular bit of what I venture to think a partly false philosophy which comes up again and again in magazines and story books in the shape of satirical contrasts between the words of the General Confession, or the Litany, and the particular materials in which the worshippers, the intercessors, and the confessing sinners happen to be clothed. But, since broadcloth has never yet been made stout enough to keep temptation from the soul, and silk has proved no protection against sorrow, I confess that I never could see any thing more incongruous in the confessions and petitions of handsomely dressed people than of ragged ones. That any sinner can be "miserable" in satin, seems impossible, or at least offensive, to some minds; perhaps to those who know least of the reckless, callous light-heartedness of the most ragged reprobates.

This has nothing to do, it seems to me, with the fact that a certain degree of outlay on dress is criminal, on several grave accounts; nor even with the incongruous spectacle of a becoming bonnet arranged during the Litany by the tightly gloved fingers of a worshipper, who would probably not be any the more devout for being uncomfortably conscious of bad clothes. An old friend of my childhood used to tell me that she always thought a good deal of her dress before going to church, that she might quite forget it when there.

Surely, dress has absolutely nothing to do with devotion. And the impertinent patronage of worshippers in "fustian" is at least as offensive as the older-fashioned vulgarity of pride in congregations who "come in their own carriages." And I do protest against the flippant inference that good clothes for the body must lower the assumptions of the spirit, or make repentance insincere; which I no more believe than that the worship of a clean Christian is less acceptable than that of a brother who cannot afford or does not value the use of soap.

I am perhaps anxious to defend this congregation, on which Jan stumbled in the pale light of early morning in the city, from any imputation on the sincerity of its worship, because it was mostly very comfortably clad. The men were chiefly business men, with a good deal of the obnoxious "broadcloth" about them, and with well-brushed hats beneath their seats. One of the stoutest and most comfortable-looking, with an intelligent face and a fair clean complexion which spoke of good food, stood near the door. He wore a new great-coat with a velvet collar, but his gray eyes (they had seen middle age, and did not shine with any flash of youthful enthusiasm) were fixed upon the window, and he sang very heartily, and by heart, —

> "Other Refuge have I none!
> Hangs my helpless soul on Thee;
> Leave, ah! leave me not alone,
> Still support and comfort me."

The tears flowed down Jan's cheeks. It had been a favorite hymn of his foster-mother, and he had often sung it to her. Master Swift used to "give the note," and then sink himself into the bass part, and these quaint duets had been common at the mill. How delightful such simple pleasures seem to those who look back on them from the dark places of the earth, full of misery and wickedness!

In spite of his tears, Jan was fain to join as the hymn went on, and he sang like a bird, —

> "All my trust on Thee is stayed,
> All my help from Thee I bring;
> Cover my defenceless head
> With the shadow of Thy wing."

It was the hymn after the third collect, and when it was ended the comfortable-looking gentleman motioned Jan into a seat, and he knelt down.

When the service was over, the same gentleman took him by the arm, and asked, "What's the matter with you, my boy?"

A rapid survey of his woes led Jan to reply, "I've no home, sir."

The congregation had dispersed quickly, for the men were going to business.

This gentleman walked fast, and he hurried Jan along with him.

"Who are your parents?" he asked. The service had recalled Jan's highest associations, and he was anxious to tell the strict truth.

"I don't rightly know, sir," said he.

"Are you hungry?"

"Yes, sir," sobbed poor Jan.

They were stopping before a large house, and the gentleman said, "Look here, my boy. If you had a good home, and good food, and clothes, would you work? Would you try to be a good lad, and learn an honest trade?"

"I'd be glad, sir," said Jan.

"Have you ever worked? What can you do?" asked the gentleman.

"I can mind pigs; but I do think 'twould be best for I to be in a mill, and I've got a miller's thumb." Jan said this because the idea had struck him that if he could only get home again he might hire himself out at a mop to Master Lake. A traditional belief in the force of the law of hiring made him think that this would protect him against any claim of the Cheap Jack. Before the gentleman could reply, the house-door was opened by a boy some years older than Jan, who was despatched to fetch "the master." Jan felt sure that it must be a school, though he was puzzled by the contents of the room in which they waited. It was filled with pretty specimens of joiner's and cabinet-maker's work, some quite and some partly finished. There were also brushes of various kinds, so that, if there had been a suitable window, Jan would have concluded that it was a shop. In two or three moments the master's step sounded in the passage.

Jan had pleasant associations with the word "master," and he looked up with some vague fancy of seeing a second Master Swift. Not that Master Swift, or any one else in the slow-going little village, ever walked with this sharp, hasty tread, as if one hoped to overtake time! With such a step the gentleman himself went away, when he had said to Jan, "Be a good boy, my lad, and attend to your master, and he'll be a good friend to you."

He was not in the least like Master Swift. He was young, and youthfully dressed. A schoolmaster with neither spectacles nor a black coat was a new idea to Jan; but he seemed to be kind, for, with a sharp look at Jan's pinched face, he said, "You'll be glad of some breakfast, my lad, I fancy; and breakfast's only just over. Come along." And away he went at double quick time down the passage, and Jan ran after him.

On their way to the kitchen, they crossed an open court where boys were playing, and round which ran mottoes in large letters.

"You can read?" said the master, quickly, as he caught Jan's eyes following the texts. "Have you ever been to school?"

"Yes, sir," said Jan.

"Can you write? What else have you learned?"

Jan pondered his stock of accomplishments. "I can

write, sir, and cipher. And I've learned geography and history, and Master Swift gave I lessons in mechanics, and I be very fond of poetry and painting, and "—

The master was painfully familiar with the inventive and boastful powers of street boys. He pushed Jan before him into the kitchen, saying smartly, but good-humoredly, "There, there! Don't make up stories, my boy. You must learn to speak the truth, if you come into the Home. We don't expect poets and painters," he added, smiling. "If you can chop wood, and learn what you're taught, you'll do for us."

A smile stole over the face of a shrewd-looking lad who was washing dishes at the table. Jan saw that he was not believed, and his tears fell into the mug of cocoa, and on to the bread which formed his breakfast.

CHAPTER XXXIII.

THE BUSINESS MAN AND THE PAINTER. — PICTURES AND POT BOILERS. — CIMABUE AND GIOTTO. — THE SALMON-COLORED OMNIBUS.

THE business men were half way to their business when the shadow of the sooty church still fell upon one or two of the congregation who dispersed more slowly; a few aged poor who lingered from infirmity as well as leisure; and a man neither very old nor very poor, whose strong limbs did not bear him away at a much quicker pace. His enjoyment of the peculiar pleasures of an early walk was deliberate as well as full, and bustle formed no necessary part of his trade. He was a painter.

The business gentleman hurrying out of the Boys' Home stumbled against the painter, whom he knew, but whom just now he would not have been sorry to avoid. The very next salmon-colored omnibus that passed the end of the street would only just enable him to be punctual if he could catch it; and the painter, in his opinion, had "no sense of the value of time." The painter, on the other hand, held as strong a conviction that his friend's sense of the monetary value of time was so exaggerated as to hinder his sense of many higher things in this beautiful world. But they were fast friends nevertheless, and with equal charity pitied each other respectively for a slovenly and a slavish way of life.

"My dear friend!" cried the artist, seizing the other by the elbow, "you are just coming from where I was thinking of going."

"By all means, my dear fellow," said Jan's friend, shaking hands to release his elbow, "the master will be delighted, and — my time is not my own, you know."

"I know well," said the artist, with a little humorous malice. "It belongs to others. That is your benevolence. So " —

"Come, come!" laughed the other. "I'm not a man of leisure like you. I must catch the next salmon-colored omnibus."

"I'll walk with you to it, and talk as we go. You can't propose to run at your time of life, and with your position in the city! Now tell me, my good friend, the boys in your Home are the offscouring of the streets, aren't they?"

"They are mostly destitute lads, but they have never been convicted of crime any more than yourself. It is the fundamental distinction between our Home and other industrial schools. Our effort is to save boys whom destitution has *all but* made criminal. It is not a reformatory."

"I beg your pardon, I know. But I was speaking of their bodily condition only. I want a model, and should be glad to get it without the nuisance of sketching in the slums. Such a ragged, pinched, eager, and yet stupid child as might sit homeless between the black walls of Newgate and the churchyard of St. Sepulchre, — a waif of the richest and most benevolent society in Christendom, for whom the alternative of the churchyard would be the better."

"Not the only one, I trust," said the business gentleman,

almost passionately. "I trust in GOD, not the only alternative. If I have a hope, it is that of greater and more effective efforts than hitherto to rescue the children of London from crime."

In the warmth of this outburst, he had permitted a salmon-colored omnibus to escape him, but, being much too good a man of business to waste time in regrets, he placed himself at a convenient point for catching the next, and went on speaking.

"I am glad to hear you have another picture in hand.'

"Not a *picture* — a *pot boiler*," said the artist, testily. "Low art — domestic sentiment — cheap pathos. My *picture* no one would look at, even if it were finished, and if I could bring myself to part with it."

"Mind, you give me the first refusal."

"Of my *picture*?"

"Yes, that is, I mean your street boy. It is just in my line. I delight in your things. But don't make it too pathetic, or my wife won't be able to bear it in the drawing-room. Your things always make her cry."

"That's the pot boiler," said the artist; "I really wish you'd look at my picture, unfinished as it is. I should like you to have it. Anybody'll take the pot boiler. I want a model for the picture too, and, oddly enough, a boy; but one *you* can't provide me with."

"No? The subject you say is" — said the man of business, dreamily, as he strove at the same time to make out if a distant omnibus were yellow or salmon-colored.

"Cimabue finding the boy Giotto drawing on the sand. Ah! my friend, can one realize that meeting? Can one picture the generous glow with which the mature and courtly artist recognized unconscious genius struggling under the form of a shepherd lad, — yearning out of his great Italian eyes over that glowing landscape whose beauties could not be written in the sand? Will the golden age of the arts ever return? We are hardly moving towards it, I fear. For I have found a model for my Cimabue, — an artist too, and a true one; but no boy Giotto! Still I should like you to see it. I flatter myself the coloring " —

"Salmon," said the man of business, briskly. "I thought it was yellow. My dear fellow — *Hi!* — take as many boys as you like — *To the City!*"

The conductor of the salmon-colored omnibus touched his bell, and the painter was left alone.

CHAPTER XXXIV.

A CHOICE OF VOCATIONS. — RECREATION HOUR. — THE BOW-LEGGED BOY. — DRAWING BY HEART. — GIOTTO.

JAN found favor with his new friends. The master's sharp eyes noted that the prescribed ablutions seemed both pleasant and familiar to the new boy, and the superintendent of the wood-chopping department expressed his opinion that Jan's intelligence and dexterity were wasted among the fagots, and that his vocation was to be a brush-maker at least, if not a joiner.

Of such trades as were open to him in the Home Jan inclined to cabinet-making. It must be amusing to dab little bunches of bristles so deftly into little holes with hot pitch as to produce a hearth-brush, but as a life-work it does not satisfy ambition. For boot-making he felt no fancy, and the tailor's shop had a dash of corduroy and closeness in the atmosphere not grateful to nostrils so long refreshed by the breezes of the plains. But, when an elder boy led him into the airy room of the cabinet-maker, Jan found a subject of interest. The man was making a piece of furniture to order; the boys had done the rough work, and he was finishing it. It was a combination of shelves and cupboard, and was something like an old oak cabinet which stood in Master Chuter's parlor, and which, in Jan's opinion, was both handsomer and more convenient than this. When the joiner, amused by the keen gaze of Jan's black eyes, asked him good-naturedly "how he liked it," Jan expressed his opinion, to illustrate which he involuntarily took up the fat pencil lying on the bench, and made a sketch of Master Chuter's cabinet upon a bit of wood.

News spreads with mysterious swiftness in all communities, large and small. Before dinner-time, it was known throughout the Home that the master-joiner had applied for the new boy as a pupil, and that he could draw with a black-lead pencil, and set his betters to rights.

The master had passed through several phases of feeling over Jan during that morning. His first impression had been dispelled by Jan's orderly ways, and the absence of any vagrant restlessness about him. The joiner's report awoke a hope that he would become a star of the institution, but as his acquirements came to the light, and he proved not merely to have a good voice, but to have been in a choir, the master's generous hopes received a check, and as the day passed on he became more and more convinced that it was a case to be "restored to his friends."

When two o'clock came, and the boys were all out for "recreation," Jan had to endure some chaff on the subject of his accomplishments. But the banter of London street boys was familiar to him, and he took it in good part. When they found him good-tempered, he was soon popular, and they asked his history with friendly curiosity.

"And vot sort of a mansion did you hang out in ven

you wos at home?" inquired a little lad, whose rosy cheeks and dancing eyes would have qualified him to sit as a model for the hero of some little tale of rustic life and simplicity, but who had graduated in the lowest lore of the streets so much before he was properly able to walk that he was bandy-legged in consequence. There must have been some blood in him that was domestic and not vagrant in its currents, for he was as a rule one of the steadiest and best-behaved boys in the establishment. Only from time to time he burst out into street slang of the strongest description, apparently as a relief to his feelings. Happily for the cause it had at heart, the Boys' Home was guided by large-minded counsels, and if the eyes of the master were as the eyes of Argus, they could also wink on occasion. "Hout with it!" said the bow-legged boy, straddling before Jan. "If it wos Buckingham Palace as you resided in, make a clean breast of it, and hease your mind."

"Thee knows more of palaces than the likes of me. Thee manners be so fine," said Jan; and the repartee drew a roar of laughter, in which the bandy-legged boy joined. "But I've lived in a windmill," Jan added, "and that be more than thee've done, I fancy."

Some of the boys had seen windmills, and some had not; and there was a strong tendency among the boys who had to give exaggerated, not to say totally fictitious, descriptions of those buildings to the boys who had not. There was a quick, prevailing impression, however, that Jan's word could be trusted, and he was appealed to. "Take it off in a picter," said the bandy-legged boy. "We heered as you took off a *sweet of furnitur* in the Master's face. Take off the windmill, if you lived in it."

There was a bit of chalk in Jan's pocket, and the courtyard was paved. He knelt down, and the boys gathered round him. They were sharp enough to be sympathetic, and when he begged them to be quiet they kept a breathless silence, which was broken only by the distant roar of London outside, and by the Master's voice speaking in an adjoining passage.

"I can hardly say, sir, that I *fear*, but I think you'll find most of them look too hearty and comfortable for your purpose."

About Jan the silence was breathless. The bow-legged boy literally laid his hand upon his mouth, and he had better have laid it over his eyes, for they seemed in danger of falling out of their sockets.

Jan covered his for a moment, and then looked upwards. Back upon his sensitive memory rolled the past, like a returning tide which sweeps every thing before it. Much clearer than those roofs and chimney-stacks the windmill stood against the sky, with arms outstretched as if to recall its truant son. If he had needed it to draw from, it was there, plain enough. But how should he need to see it, on whose heart every line of it was written? He could have laid his hand in the dark upon the bricks that were weather-stained into fanciful landscapes upon its walls, and planted his feet on the spot where the grass was most worn down about its base.

He drew with such power and rapidity that only some awe of the look upon his face could have kept silence in the little crowd whom he had forgotten. And when the last scrap of chalk had crumbled, and he dragged his blackened finger over the foreground till it bled, the voice which broke the silence was the voice of a stranger, who stood with the master on the threshold of the court-yard.

Never perhaps was more conveyed in one word than in that which he spoke, though its meaning was known to himself alone, —

"GIOTTO!"

CHAPTER XXXV.

"WITHOUT CHARACTER?"—THE WIDOW.—THE BOW-LEGGED BOY TAKES SERVICE.—STUDIOS AND PAINTERS.

"MANAGE it as you like," the artist had said to the master of the Boys' Home. "Lend him, sell him, apprentice him, give him to me,—whichever you prefer. Say I want a boot-black—a clothes-brusher—a palette-setter—a bound slave—or an adopted son, as you please. The boy I must have: in what capacity I get him is nothing to me."

"I am bound to remind you, sir," said the master, "that he was picked up in the streets, and has had no training, and earned no outfit from us. He comes to you without clothes, without character"—

"Without character?" cried the artist. "Heavens and earth! Did you ever study physiognomy? Do you know any thing of faces?"

"It is part of my duty to know something of them, sir," began the master, who was slightly nettled.

"Then don't talk nonsense, my friend, but send me the boy, as soon as is consistent with your rules and regulations."

The boy was Jan. The man of business gave his consent, but he implored his "impulsive friend," as he termed the artist, not to ruin the lad by indulgence, but to keep him in his proper place, and give him plenty to do. In conformity with this sensible advice, Jan's first duties in his new home were to clean the painter's boots when he could find them, shake his velveteen coat when the pockets were empty, sweep the studio, clean brushes, and go errands. The artist was an old bachelor, infamously cheated by the rheumatic widow he had paid to perform the domestic work of his rooms; and when this afflicted lady gave warning on being asked for hot water at a later hour than usual, Jan persuaded the artist to enforce her departure, and took her place. So heavy is the iron weight of custom — when it takes the form of an elderly and widowed domestic to a single gentleman — that even Jan's growing influence would not have secured her dismissal, had not the artist had a particular reason for wishing the boy's practical talents to be displayed. He suspected his business friend of distrusting them because of Jan's artistic genius, and he was proud to boast that he had never known the comfort of clean rooms and well-cooked food till "the boy Giotto" became his housekeeper.

The work was play to Jan after his slavery to the hunchback, and on his happiness in living with a painter it is needless to dwell. For a week or two, the artist was busy with his "pot boiler," and did not pay much attention to his new apprentice, and Jan watched without disturbing him; so that when he offered to set the painter's palette, his master regarded his success as an inspiration of genius, rather than as a result of habits of observation.

The painter, though clever and ambitious, and with a very pure and very elegant taste, was no mighty genius himself. The average of public taste in art is low enough, but in refusing his "high art" pictures, and buying his domestic ones, the public was not far wrong. It must be confessed that he had also a vein of indolence in his nature, and Jan soon painted most of the pot boilers. Another of his duties was to sit as a model for the picture. The painter sketched him again and again, and was never quite satisfied. What the vision of the windmill had lit up in the depth of his black eyes could not be recalled to order in the painter's studio.

"I tell you what it is," said the artist one day; "domestic servitude is taking the poetry out of you. You're getting fat, Giotto! Understand that from henceforth I forbid you to black boots or grates, to brush, dust, wash, cook, or whatever disturbs the peace or hinders the growth of the soul. I must get the widow back!" and the painter heaved a deep sigh.

But Jan was resolute against the widow. He effected a compromise. The bandy-legged boy from the Home was taken into the painter's service, and Jan made himself responsible for his good conduct. He began by warning his vivacious friend that no freemasonry of common street-boyhood could hinder the duty he owed to his master of protecting his property and insuring his comfort, and that he must sooner tell tales of his friend than have the painter wronged. To this homily the bandy-legged boy listened with his red cheeks artificially distended, and occasional murmurs of "Crikey!" but he took service on these terms, and did Jan no discredit. He was incorruptibly honest, and when from time to time the street fever seized him, and he left his work to play at post-leaping outside, Jan would quietly take his place, and did not betray him. This kindness invariably drew tears of penitence from the soft-hearted young vagrant, his freaks grew rarer and rarer, and he finally became as steady as he was quick-witted.

Jan's duties were now confined to the painting-room, and he soon became familiar with the studios of other artists, where his intelligent admiration of paintings which took his fancy, his modesty, his willing good-nature, and his precocious talent made him a general favorite.

He went regularly with his master to the early service in the sooty little church, in the choir of which he was finally enrolled. And the man of business kept a friendly eye on him, and gave him many a piece of sensible and very practical advice, to balance the evils of an artistic career.

With the Bohemianism of artist-life Jan was soon as familiar as with the Bohemianism of the streets. A certain old-fashioned gravity, which had always been amongst his characteristics, helped him to preserve both his dignity and modesty in a manner which gave the man of business great satisfaction. He might easily have been spoiled, but he was not. He answered respectfully to about a dozen names which the vagrant fancy of the young painters bestowed upon him: Jan-of-all-work — Jan Steen — The Flying Dutchman — Crimson Lake — Madder Lake — and Miller's Thumb.

But his master called him GIOTTO.

He was very happy, but the old home haunted him, and he longed bitterly for some news of his foster-father and the schoolmaster. Whilst the terror of the Cheap Jack was still oppressing him, he had feared to open any communication with the past, for fear the wretched couple who were supposed to be his parents should discover and reclaim him. But as his nerves recovered their tone, as the horrors of his life as a screever faded into softer tints, as that boon of poor humanity — forgetfulness — healed his wounds, and he began to go about the streets without thinking of the hunchback at every corner, he felt more and more inclined to risk any thing to know how his old friends fared. There also grew upon him a conviction that the Cheap Jack's story was false. He knew enough of art now, and of the value of his own powers, and of the struggle for livelihoods in London, to see that it had been a very good speculation to kidnap him. He had serious doubts whether the cart had been driven round by the mill, and whether Master Lake had refused to let him be awakened from his sleep, and had said it was, "All right, and he hoped the lad would do his duty to his good parents." He remembered, too, the hunchback's words when he lay speechless from the drugged liquor, and these raised a puzzling question: Why should "the nobs" recognize him? He had learned what *nobs* are. Spelt without a "k," they are grand people, and what had grand people to do with Sal's son?

One cannot live without sympathy, and Jan confided the complexities of his history to the bow-legged boy, and the interest they awakened in this young gentleman could not but be gratifying to his friend. He kept one eye closed during the story, as if he saw the whole thing (*too clearly*) at a glance. He broke the thread of Jan's narrative by comments which had no obvious bearing on the facts, and, when it was ended, he gave it as his opinion that certain penny romances which he named were a joke to it.

"Oh, my! what a pity we can't employ a detective!"

he said. "Whoever knowed a young projidy find his noble relations without a detective? But never mind, Jan. I knows their ways. I'm up to their dodges. Fust of all, you makes up your mind deep down in your inside, and then you says nothing to nobody, but follows it up. Fol-lows it up!"

"I don't know what to follow," said Jan; "and how can I make up my mind, when I know nothing?"

"That's just where it is," said his friend; "if you knowed every thing, wot 'ud be the use of coming the detective tip, and making it up in your inside?"

The bow-legged boy had made it up in his. He had decided that Jan was a nobleman in disguise, and that his father was a duke, or a "jook," as he called him. Jan's active imagination could not quite resist the influence of this romance, and he lay awake at night patching together the hunchback's reference to the nobs, and the incredulous glance of the dark-eyed gentleman who had given him the half pence, and who was certainly a nob himself. And never did he leave the house on an errand for the painter that the bow-legged boy did not burst forth, dish-cloth or dirty boots in hand, from some unexpected quarter, and adjure him to "look out for the jook."

It was a lovely afternoon when, by his friend's advice, Jan betook himself to the Park, that the nobs might have that opportunity of recognizing him which the wide-mouthed woman had feared. He had washed his face very clean, and brushed his old jacket with trembling hands, and the bow-legged boy had tied a spotted scarf, that had been given to himself by a stableman in the mews opposite, round Jan's neck in what he called "a gent's knot," and the poor child went to seek his fate with a beating heart.

There were nobs enough. Round and round they came, in all the monotony of a not very exhilarating amusement. The crowd was so great that the carriages crawled rather than drove, and Jan could see the people well. Many a lovely face, set in a soft frame of delicate hue, caught his artistic eye, and he watched for and recognized it again. But only a passing glance of languid curiosity met his eager gaze in return. Not a nob recognized him. But a policeman looked at him as if he did, and Jan crept away.

When he got home, he found household matters at a standstill, for the bow-legged boy had been tearfully employed in thinking how Jan would despise his old friends when the "jook" had acknowledged him, and he had become a nob. And as Jan set matters to rights, he resolved that he would not go to the Park again to look for relatives.

CHAPTER XXXVI.

THE MILLER'S LETTER. — A NEW POT BOILER SOLD.

JAN was very happy, and the brief dream of the "jook" was over, but his heart clung to his old home. If love and care, if tenderness in sickness and teaching in health, are parental qualities, why should he seek another parent than Master Swift? And had he not a foster-father to whom he was bound by all those filial ties of up-bringing from infancy, and of a common life, a common trade, and common joys and sorrows in the past, such as could bind him to no other father?

He begged a bit of paper from the painter, and wrote a letter to Master Lake, which would have done more credit to the schoolmaster's instructions had it been less blotted with tears. He besought his foster-father not to betray him to the Cheap Jack, and he inquired tenderly after the schoolmaster and Rufus.

The windmiller was no great scholar, as was shown by his reply: —

"MY DEAR JAN,

"Your welcome letter to hand, and I do hope, my dear Jan, It finds you well as it leave me at present. I be mortal bad with a cough, and your friends as searched everywhere, and dragged every place for you, encluding the plains for twenty mile round and down by the watermill. That Cheap John be no more your vather nor mine, an e'd better not show his dirty vace yearabouts after all he stole. but your poor mother, she was allus took in by him, but she said with her own mouth, that woman be no more the child's mother, and never wos a mother, and your mother knowed wots wot, poor zowl! And I'm glad, my dear Jan, you be doing well in a genteel line, though I did hope you'd take to the mill; but work is slack, and I'm not wot I wos, and I do miss Master Swift. He had a stroke after you left, and confined to the house, so I will conclude, my dear Jan, and go down and rejoice his heart to hear you be alive. I'd main like to see you, Jan, my dear, and so for sartin would he and all enquiring friends; and I am till deth your loving vather, or as good, and I shan't grudge you if so be you finds a better.

"Abel Lake."

"P. S. I'd main like to see your vace again, Jan, my dear."

Jan sobbed so bitterly in reading the postscript that, after vain attempts to console him by chaff, the bow-legged boy wept from sympathy.

As to the painter, the whole letter so caught his capricious fancy that he was for ever questioning Jan as to the details of his life in that out-of-the-world district where the purest breath of heaven turned the sails of the windmill, and where the miller took payment for his work "in kind."

"It must be a wonderful spot, Giotto," said he; "and, if I were richer, just now we'd go down together, and paint sunsets, and see your friends." And he walked up and down the studio, revolving his new caprice, whilst Jan tried to think if any thing were likely to bring money into his master's pocket before long. Suddenly the artist seized a sketch that was lying near, and, turning it over, began one on the other side, questioning Jan as he drew. "What do old country wives dress in down yonder? — What did you wear in the mill? — Where does the light come from in a round-house," &c.

Presently he flung it to Jan, and, in answer to the boy's cry of admiration, growled, "Ay, ay. You must do what *you* can now, for every after-touch of mine will spoil it. There are hundreds of men, Giotto, whose sketches are good, and their paintings daubs. But it is only the sketches of great men that sell. The public likes canvas and linseed oil for its money, where small reputations are concerned."

The sketch was of a peep into the round-house. Jan, toll-dish in hand, with a quaint business gravity, was met by a dame who was just raising her old back after letting down her sack of gleanings, with garrulous good-humor in her blinking eyes and withered face.

"Chiaroscuro good," dictated the painter; "execution sketchy; coloring quiet, to be in keeping with the place and subject, but pure. You know the scene better than I, so work away, Giotto. Motto — 'Will ye pay or toll it, mother?' Price twenty-five guineas. Take it to What's-his-name's, and if it sells we'll go to Arcadia, Giotto mio! The very thought of those breezes is as quinine to my languid faculties!"

Jan worked hard at the new "pot boiler." The artist painted the boy's figure himself, and Jan did most of the rest. The bow-legged boy stooped in a petticoat as a model for the old woman, murmuring at intervals, "Oh, my, here *is* a game!" and, when the painter had left the room, his grave speculations as to whether the withered face of the dame were a good likeness of his own chubby cheeks made Jan laugh till he could hardly hold his palette. It was done at last, and Jan took it to the picture-dealer's.

The poor boy could hardly keep out of the street where the picture-dealer lived. One afternoon, as he was hanging about the window, the business gentleman came by and asked kindly after his welfare. Jan was half ashamed of the hope with which he told the tale of the pot boiler.

"And you did some of it?" said the business gentleman, peering in through his spectacles.

"Only the painting, sir, not the design," said Jan.

"And you want very much to go and see your old home?"

"I do, sir," said Jan.

The business gentleman put his gold spectacles into their case, and laid his hand on Jan's shoulder. "I am not much of a judge of genius," said he, "but if you have it, and if you live to make a fortune by it, remember, my boy, that there is no luxury which money puts in a man's power like the luxury of helping others." With which he stepped briskly into the picture-dealer's.

And half an hour afterwards Jan burst into the painter's studio, crying, "It's sold, sir!"

"Sold!" shouted the painter, in boyish glee. "Hooray! Where's that rascal Bob? Oh, I know! I sent him for the beer. Giotto, my dear fellow, I have some shooting-boots somewhere, if you can find them, and a tourist's knapsack, and " —

But Jan had started to find the boots, and the bow-legged boy, who had overheard the news as he left the house, rushed up the street, with his head down, crying, "It's sold! it's sold!" and, as he ran, he jostled against a man in a white apron, carrying a pot of green paint to some area railings.

"Wot's sold?" said he, testily, as he recovered his balance.

"You a painter, and don't know?" said the rosy-cheeked boy. "Oh, my! Wot's sold? Why, I'm sold, and *it's* sold. That walable picter I wos about to purchase for my mansion in Piccadilly." And, feigning to burst into a torrent of tears, he darted round the corner and into the public-house.

CHAPTER XXXVII.

SUNSHINE AFTER STORM.

IT had been a wet morning. The heavy rain-clouds rolled over the plains, hanging on this side above the horizon as if in an instant they must fall and crush the solid earth, and passing away on that side in dark, slanting veils of shower; giving to the vast monotony of the wide field of view that strange interchange of light and shadow, gleam and gloom, which makes the poetry of the plains.

The rain had passed. The gray mud of the chalk roads dried up into white dust almost beneath the travellers' feet as they came out again after temporary shelter; and that brightest, tenderest smile with which, on such days, the sun makes evening atonement for his absence, shone and sparkled, danced and glowed from the windmill to the water-meads. It reopened the flowers, and drew fragrant answer from the meadow-sweet and the bay-leaved willow. It made the birds sing, and the ploughboy whistle, and the old folk toddle into their gardens to smell the herbs. It cherished silent satisfaction on the bronze face of Rufus resting on his paws, and lay over Master Swift's wan brow like the aureole of some austere saint canonized just on this side the gates of Paradise.

The simile is not inapt, for the coarse and vigorous features of the schoolmaster had been refined to that peculiar nobleness which, perhaps, the sharp tool of suffering —

used to its highest ends — can alone produce. And the smile of patience, like a victor's wreath, lay now where hot passions and imperious temper had once struggled and been overcome.

The schoolmaster was paralyzed in his lower limbs, and he sat in a wheel-chair of his own devising, which he could propel with his own hands. The agonizing anxiety and suspense which followed Jan's disappearance had broken him down, and this was the end. Rufus was still his only housekeeper, but a woman from the village came in to give him necessary help.

"And it be 'most like waiting upon a angel," said she.

This woman had gone for the night, and Master Swift sat in his invalid chair in the little porch, where he could touch the convolvulus bells with his hand, and see what some old pupil of his had done towards "righting up" the garden. It was an instance of that hardly earned grace of patience in him that he did not vex himself to see how sorely the garden suffered by his helplessness.

Not without cause was the evening smile of sunlight reflected on Master Swift's lips. Between the fingers of a hand lying on his lap lay Jan's letter to announce that he and the artist were coming to the cottage, and in intervals of reading and re-reading it the schoolmaster spouted poetry, and Rufus wagged a sedately sympathetic tail.

> "How fresh, O Lord, how sweet and clean
>   Are Thy returns! even as the flowers in spring;
>   To which, besides their own demean,
>   The late past frosts tributes of pleasure bring.
>   Grief melts away
>   Like snow in May,
>   As if there were no such cold thing."

And, waving his hand after the old manner towards the glowing water-meadows, he went on with increasing emphasis:—

"Who would have thought my shrivelled heart
 Could have recovered greennesse?"

Perhaps Rufus felt himself bound to answer what had a tone of appeal in it, or perhaps some strange sympathy, not with Master Swift, began already to disturb him. He rose and knocked up the hand in which the letter lay with his long nose, and wandered restlessly about, and then settled down again with his eyes towards the garden-gate.

The old man sat still. The evening breeze stirred his white hair, and he drank in the scents drawn freshly from field and flowers after the rain, and they were like balm to him. As he sat up, his voice seemed to recover its old power, and he clasped his hands together over Jan's letter, and went on:—

"And now in age I bud again,
 After so many deaths I live and write;
I once more smell the dew and rain,
 And relish versing: O my only Light!
  It cannot be
  That I am he
 On whom Thy tempests fell all night!"

So far Mr. George Herbert; but the poem was never finished, for Rufus jumped up with a cry, and after standing for a moment with stiffened limbs, and muffled whines, as if he could not believe his own glaring yellow eyes, he burst away with tenfold impetus, and dragged, and tore, and pulled, and all but carried Jan to the schoolmaster's feet.

And the painter walked away down the garden, and stood looking long over the water-meadows.

CHAPTER XXXVIII.

A PAINTER'S EDUCATION. — MASTER CHUTER'S PORT — A FAREWELL FEAST. — THE SLEEP OF THE JUST.

"I HOPE, Jan," said Master Swift, "that the gentleman will overlook my want of respect towards himself, in consideration of what it was to me to see your face again."

"Don't distress me by speaking of it, Mr. Swift," said the painter, taking his hand, and sitting down beside him in the porch.

As he returned the artist's friendly grasp, the schoolmaster scanned his face with some of the old sharpness. "Sir," said he, "I beg you to forgive my freedom. I'm a rough man with a rough tongue, which I could never teach to speak the feelings of my heart; but I humbly thank you, sir, for your goodness to this boy."

"It's a very selfish kind of goodness at present, Mr. Swift, and I fancy some day the obligation of the acquaintance will be on my side."

"Jan," said the schoolmaster, "take Rufus wi' ye, and run that errand I telled ye. Rufus 'll carry your basket." When they had gone, he turned earnestly to the painter.

"Sir, I'm speaking to ye out of my ignorance and my anxiety. Ye want the lad to be a painter. Will he be a great painter? I'm reminding you of what ye'll know better than me (though not by yourself, for Jan tells me you're a grand artist), that a man may have the ambition and the love, and some talent for an art, and yet be just without that divine spark which the gods withhold. Sir, GOD forbid that I should undervalue the pure pleasure of even that little gift; but it's ill for a lad when he has just that much of an art to keep him from a thrifty trade — and *no more.*"

The painter replied as earnestly as Master Swift had spoken, —

"Jan's estimate of me is weaker than his judgment in art is wont to be. I speak to understanding ears, and you will know that I have some true feeling for my art, when I tell you that I know enough to know that I shall never be a great painter; and it will help you to put confidence in my assurance that, if he lives, *Jan will.*"

Deep emotion kept the old man silent. It was a mixed feeling, — first, intense pride and pleasure, and then a pang of disappointment. Had he not been the first to see genius in the child? Had he not built upon him one more ambition for himself, — the ambition of training the future great man? And now another had taken his office.

"You look disappointed," said the artist.

"It is the vile selfishness in me, sir. I had hoped the boy's gifts would have been what I could have trained at my own hearth. It is only one more wilful fancy, once more thwarted."

"Selfish I am sure it is not!" said the painter, hotly; "and as to such benevolence being thwarted as a sort of punishment for I don't know what, I believe nothing of the kind."

"You don't know, sir," said the old man, firmly. "Not that I'm speaking of the Lord's general dealings. There are tender, gentle souls, I know well, who seem only to grow the purer and better for having the desire of their eyes granted to them; but there are others whom, for their own good, the Father of all sees needful to chasten to the end."

"My experience lies in another direction," said the painter, impetuously. "With what awe do you suppose indolent men, whose easy years of self-indulgent life have been broken by no real calamity, look upon others on whose heads blow falls after blow, though their existence is an hourly struggle towards perfection? There are some stagnant pools whose peace the Angel never disturbs. Does GOD, who takes pleasure in perfecting the saint and pardoning the sinner, forget some of us because we are not worth remembering?"

"He forgets none of us, my dear sir," said the schoolmaster, "and He draws us to Himself at different times, and by different roads. I wanted to be the child's teacher, but He has chosen you, and will bless ye in the work."

The painter drove his hands through his bushy hair, and spoke more vehemently than before.

"*I* his teacher, and not you? My good friend, I at least am the better judge of what makes a painter's education. Is the man who shows a Giotto how to use this brush, or mix that paint, to be called his teacher? No, not for teaching him, forsooth, what he would have learned of anybody, everybody, nobody, somehow, anyhow, or done just as well without. But the man who taught him to work as a matter of principle, and apart from inclination (a lesson which not all geniuses learn); the man who fostered the love of Nature in him, and the spirit of poetry, — qualities without which draughtsmanship and painting had better not be the man who by example and precept led him to find satisfaction in duty done, and happiness in simple pleasures and domestic affections; the man who so fixed these high and pure lessons in his mind, at its most susceptible age, that the foulest dens of London could not corrupt him; the man whose beloved and reverenced face would rise up in judgment against him if he could ever hereafter degrade his art to be a pander of vice, or a mere trick of the workshop; — this man, Master Swift, has been the painter's schoolmaster!"

Master Swift was not accustomed to betray emotion, but his nerves were less strong than they had been, and self-control was more difficult, and with his horny hands he hid the cheeks down which tears of gratified pride would force their way.

He had not found voice to speak, when Rufus appeared at the gate with one basket, followed by Jan and the little innkeeper with another. Why Master Chuter had come, and why Jan was looking so particularly well satisfied, must be explained.

Whilst the painter was still gazing across the watermeadows, Master Swift, who was the soul of hospitality, had told Jan where to find a few shillings in a certain drawer, and had commissioned him to lay these out in the wherewithal for an evening meal. Jan had had some anxiety in connection with the duty intrusted to him. Firstly, he well knew that the few shillings were what the schoolmaster must depend on for that week's living. Secondly, though it was his old friend's all, it was a sum very inadequate to provide such a meal as Jan would have liked to set before the painter. At his age, children are very sensitive on behalf of their grown-up friends, and like to maintain the credit of home. The provoking point was that Jan had plenty of pocket-money, with which he could have supplied deficiencies, had he dared; for the painter, besides buying him an outfit for the journey, had liberally rewarded him for his work at the pot boiler. But Jan knew the pride of Master Swift's heart too well to venture to add a half penny to his money, or to spend a half penny less than all.

It was whilst he was going with an anxious countenance towards the village shop that Master Chuter met him with open arms. The little innkeeper was genuinely delighted to see him; and the news of his arrival having spread, several old friends (including "Willum" Smith) were waiting for him, about the yardway of the Heart of Oak. When the innkeeper discovered Jan's errand, he insisted on packing up a prime cut of bacon, some new-laid eggs, and a bottle of "crusty" old port, such as the squires drank at election dinners, to take to the schoolmaster. Jan was far too glad of this seasonable addition to the feast to suggest doubts of its acceptance; indeed, he ventured on a hint about a possible lack of wine-glasses, which Master Chuter quickly took, and soon filled up his basket with ancient glasses on bloated legs, a clean table-cloth, and so forth.

"We needn't say any thing about the glasses," suggested Jan, as they drew near the cottage.

Master Chuter winked the little eye buried in his fat left cheek.

"I knows the schoolmaster, Jan. He be mortal proud; and I wouldn't offend he, sartinly not, Jan. But Master Swift and me have seen a deal of each other since you left, and he've tasted this port before, when he were so bad, and he'll not take it amiss from an old friend."

Master Chuter was right. The schoolmaster only thanked him heartily, and pressed him to remain. But the little innkeeper, bustling round the table with professional solicitude, declined the invitation.

"I be obliged to 'ee all the same, Master Swift. But I hope I knows better manners than to intrude on you and Jan just now, let alone a gentleman on whom I shall have pleasure in waiting at the Heart of Oak. There be beds, sir, at your service and Jan's, and well aired they be. And I'll be proud to show you the sign, sir, painted by that boy when he were an infant, as I may say. But I knowed what was in un. Master Swift can bear me witness. 'Mark my words,' says I, 'the boy Jan 'll be 'most as good as a sign-painter yet.' And I do think a will. But you knows best, sir."

"I feel quite convinced that he will," said the painter, gravely.

Whilst Master Chuter and the artist thus settled Jan's career, he cooked the eggs and bacon; and when Master Swift had propelled himself to the table, and the others (including Rufus) had taken their seats, the innkeeper drew cork, dusted the bottle-mouth, and filled the fat-legged wine-glasses; then, throwing a parting glance over the arrangements of the table, he withdrew.

Jan's fears for the credit of his home, his anxieties as to the effect of the frugal living of his old friends upon the more luxurious taste of his new patron, were very needless. The artist was delighted with every thing, and when he said that he had never tasted food so good as the eggs and bacon, or relished any wine like that from the cellar of the Heart of Oak, he quite believed what he said. In truth, none should be so easily pleased as the artistic, when they wish to be so, since if "we receive but what we give," and our happiness in any thing is according to the mind we bring to it, imaginative people must have an advantage in being able to put so much rose color into their spectacles.

Warmed by the good cheer, Master Swift discoursed as vigorously as of old. With a graphic power of narration, commoner in his class than in a higher one, he entertained the artist with stories of Jan's childhood, and gave a vivid picture of his own first sight of him in the wood. He did not fail to describe the long blue coat, the pig-switch, and the slate, nor did he omit to quote the lines which so well described the scene which the child-genius was painting in leaves.

"Well have I named him Giotto!" said the artist; "the shepherd boy drawing on the sand."

"If ye'd seen the swineherd painting with nature's own tints," said Master Swift, with a pertinacious adherence to his own view of things, which had always been characteristic of him, "I reckon you'd have thought he beat the shepherd boy. Not that I could pretend to be a judge of the painting myself, sir; what took *my* mind was the inventive energy of the child. For maybe fifty men in a hundred do a thing, if you find them the tools, and show them the way, but not five can make their own materials and find a way for themselves."

"Necessity's the mother of invention," said the painter, smiling.

"So they say, sir," said the schoolmaster, smartly; "though, from my own experience of the shiftlessness of necessitous folk, I've been tempted to doubt the truth of the proverb."

The painter laughed, and thought of the widow, as Master Swift added, " Necessity may be the *mother* of invention, sir, but the father must have had a good head on his shoulders."

The sun had set, the moon had risen, and the dew mixed with kindred rain-drops on the schoolmaster's flowers, when Jan and the painter bade him good-by. For half an hour past it had seemed to the painter that he was exhausted, and spoke languidly.

"Don't get up till I come in the morning, Master Swift," said Jan; "I'll come early and dress you."

Rufus walked with them to the gate, and waved his tail as Jan kissed his soft nose and brow, but then he went back to Master Swift and lay down at his feet. The old man had refused to have the door shut, and he propelled his chair to the porch again, and lay looking at the stars. The moon set, and the night grew cold, so that Rufus tucked his nose deeper into his fur, but Master Swift did not close the door.

The sun was shining brightly when Jan came back in the morning. It was very early. The convolvulus bells were open, but Rufus and the schoolmaster still slept. Jan's footsteps roused Rufus, who stretched himself and yawned, but Master Swift did not move, nor answer to Jan's passionate call upon his name. And in the very peace and beauty of his countenance Jan saw that he was dead.

But at what hour the silent messenger had come — whether at midnight, or at cock-crow, or in the morning — there was none to tell.

CHAPTER XXXIX.

GEORGE AGAIN. — THE PAINTER'S ADVICE. — "HOME BREWED" AT THE HEART OF OAK. — JAN CHANGES THE PAINTER'S MIND.

MASTER SWIFT'S death was a great shock to the windmiller, who was himself in frail health; and Jan gave as much time as he could to cheering his foster-father.

He had been spending an afternoon at the windmill, and the painter had been sketching the old church from the water-meadows, when they met on the little bridge near Dame Datchett's, and strolled together to the Heart of Oak. Master Chuter met them at the door.

"There be a letter for you, Jan," said he. "'Twas brought by a young varment I knows well. He belongs to them that keeps a low public at the foot of the hill, and he do be for all the world like a hudmedud, without the usefulness of un." The letter was dirty and ill-written enough to correspond to the innkeeper's account of its origin. Misspellings omitted, it ran thus: —

"MASTER JAN FORD,

"Sir, — If so be you wants to know where you come from, and where to look for them as belongs to you, come to the public at the foot of the hill this evening, with a few pounds in your pocket to open the lips of them as knows.

But fair play, mind. Gearge bean't such a vool as a looks, and cart-horses won't draw it out of un, if you sets on the police. Don't you be took in by that cusnashun old rascal Cheap John. You may hold your head as high as the Squire yet, if you makes it worth the while of *One who knows*. I always was fond of you, Jan, my dear. Keep it dark."

The painter decided to accept the invitation; but when George Sannel's face loomed out of the smoke of the dingy little kitchen, all the terrors of his childhood seemed to awake again in Jan. The face looked worn and hungry, and alarmed; but it was the face of the miller's man. In truth, he had deserted from his regiment, and was in hiding; but of this Jan and his master knew nothing.

If George's face bore some tokens of change, he seemed otherwise the same as of old. Cunning and stupidity, distrust and obstinacy, joined with unscrupulous greed, still marked his loutish attempts to overreach. Indeed, his surly temper would have brought the conference to an abrupt end but for the interference of the girl at the inn. She had written the letter for him, and seemed to take an interest in his fate which it is hardly likely that he deserved. She acted as mediator, and the artist was all the more disposed to credit her assurance that " Gearge did know a deal about the young gentleman, and should tell it all," because her appearance was so very picturesque. She did good service, when George began to pursue his old policy of mixing some lies with the truth he told, by calling him to account. Nor was she daunted by his threatening glances. "It be no manners of use thee looking at me like that, Gearge Sannel," said she, folding her arms in a defiant attitude, which the painter hastily committed to memory. "Haven't I give my word to the gentleman that he should hear a straight tale? And it be all to your advantage to tell it. You wants money, and the gentleman wants the truth. It be no mortal use to you to make up a tale, beyond annying the gentleman."

Under pressure, therefore, George told all that he knew himself, and what he had learned from the Cheap Jack's wife, and part of the purchase-money of the pot boiler was his reward.

Master Lake confirmed his account of Jan's first coming to the mill. He took the liveliest interest in his foster-son's fate, but he thought, with the artist, that there was little "satisfaction" to be got out of trying to trace Jan's real parentage. It was the painter's deliberate opinion, and he impressed it upon Jan, as they sat together in Master Chuter's parlor.

"My dear Giotto, I do hope you are not building much on hopes of a new home and new relatives. If all we have heard is true, your mother is dead; and, if your father is not dead too, he has basely deserted you. You have to make a name, not to seek one; to confer credit, not to ask for it. And I don't say this, Giotto, to make you vain, but to recall your responsibilities, and to dispel useless dreams. Believe me, my boy, your true mother, the tender nurse of your infancy, sleeps in the sacred shadow of this dear old church. It is your part to make her name, and the name of your respectable foster-father, famous as your own; to render your windmill as highly celebrated as Rembrandt's, and to hang late laurels of fame on the grave of your grand old schoolmaster. Ah! my child, I know well that the ductile artistic nature takes shape very early. The coloring of childhood stains every painter's canvas who paints from the heart. You can never call any other place home, Giotto, but this idyllic corner of the world!"

It will be seen that the painter's rose-colored spectacles were still on his nose. Every thing delighted him. He was never weary of sketching garrulous patriarchs in snowy smocks under rickety porches. He said that in an age of criticism it was quite delightful to hear Daddy Angel say, "Ay, ay," to every thing; and he waxed eloquent on the luxury of having only one post a day, and that one uncertain. But his highest flights of approbation were given to the home-brewed ale. That pure, refreshing beverage, sound and strong as a heart of oak should be, which quenched the thirst with a certain stringency which might hint at sourness to the vulgar palate, had — so he said — destroyed for ever his contentment with any other malt liquor. He spoke of Bass and Allsopp as "palatable tonics" and "non-poisonous medicinal compounds." And when, with a flourish of hyperbole, he told Master Chuter's guests that nothing to eat or drink was to be got in London, they took his word for it; and it was without suspicion of satire that Daddy Angel said, "The gen'leman do look pretty middlin' hearty too — con-sid'rin'."

It was evident that the painter had no intention of going away till the pot boiler fund was exhausted, and Jan was willing enough to abide, especially as Master Lake had caught cold at the schoolmaster's funeral, and was grateful for his foster-son's company and care. Jan was busy in many ways. He was Master Swift's heir; but the old man's illness had nearly swallowed up his savings, and Jan's legacy consisted of the books, the furniture, the gardening tools, and Rufus, who attached himself to his new master with a wistful affection which seemed to say "You belong to the good old times, and I know you loved him."

Jan moved the schoolmaster's few chattels to the windmill, and packed the books to take to London. With them he packed the little old etching that had been bought from the Cheap Jack. "It's a very good one," said the painter. "It's by an old Dutch artist. You can see a copy in the British Museum." But it was not in the Museum that Jan first saw a duplicate of his old favorite.

He was nailing up this box one afternoon, and humming as he did so, —

> "But I alone am left to pine,
> And sit beneath the withy tree,
> For truth and honesty be gone" —

when the painter came in behind him.

"Stop that doleful strain, Giotto, I beg; you've been painfully sentimental the last day or two."

"It's an old song they sing about here, sir," said Jan.

"Never mind the song, you've been doleful yourself, Giotto! I believe you're dissatisfied that we do not push the search for your father. Is it money you want, child? Believe me, riches enough lie between your fingers and your miller's thumb. Or do you want a more fashionable protector than the old artist?"

"No, no, sir!" cried Jan. "I never want to leave you; and it's not money I want, but" —

"Well, my boy? Don't be afraid."

"It's my mother, sir," said Jan, with flushed cheeks. "My real mother, I mean. She didn't desert me, sir; she died — when I was born. I doubt nobody sees to her grave, sir. Perhaps there's nobody but me who would. I can't do any thing for her now, sir, I know; but it seems as if I hardly did my duty in not knowing where she lies."

The painter's hands were already deep in his loose pockets, from which, jumbled up with chalk, india-rubber, bits of wash-leather, cakes of color, reed pens, a penknife, and some drawing-pins, he brought the balance of his loose cash, and became absorbed in calculations. "Is that box ready?" he asked. "We start to-morrow, mind. You are right, and I was wrong; but my wish was to spare you possible pain. I now think it is your duty to risk the possible pain. If those rascally creatures who stole you are in London, the police will find them. Be content, Giotto; you shall stand by your mother's grave!"

CHAPTER XL.

D'ARCY SEES BOGY. — THE ACADEMY. — THE PAINTER'S PICTURE.

THE Ammabys were in London. Amabel preferred the country; but she bore the town as she bore with many other things that were not quite to her taste, including painfully short petticoats, and Mademoiselle, the French governess. She was in the garden of the square one morning, when D'Arcy ran in.

"O Amabel!" he cried, "I'm so glad you're alone! Whom do you think I've seen? The boy you called Bogy. It must be he; I've looked in the glass, and oh, he *is* like me!"

"Where did you see him?" asked Amabel.

"Well, you know I've told you I get up very early just now?"

"I wish you wouldn't tell me," interrupted Amabel, "when you know Mademoiselle won't let me get up till half-past eight. Oh, I wish we were going home this week!"

"I'm very sorry, Amabel, but do listen. I was down by the river, and there he was sketching; and oh, so beautifully! I shall burn all my copies; I can never draw like him. Amabel, he is *awfully* like me, and just my age. He's like what people's twin-brothers are, you know. I wish he were my twin-brother!"

"He couldn't be your twin-brother," said Amabel, gravely; "he's not a gentleman."

"Well, he's not exactly not a gentleman," said D'Arcy. "However, I asked him if he sent his pictures to the Academy, and he said no, but his master does, the artist he lives with. And he told me his master's name, and the number of his pictures; and I've brought you a catalogue, and the numbers are 401, 402, and 403. And we are going to the Academy this afternoon, and I've asked mamma to ask Lady Louisa to let you come with us. But don't say any thing about me and the boy, for I don't want it to be known I have been out early."

At this moment Mademoiselle, who had been looking into the garden from an upper window, hastened to fetch Amabel indoors.

It was between three and four o'clock in the afternoon, and the Academy was crowded. The crush was so oppressive that Lady Adelaide wanted to go away, but D'Arcy had expressed a wish to see No. 401, and D'Arcy's wishes were law to his father, so he struggled in search of the picture, and the others followed him. And when a small crowd that was round it had dispersed, they saw it quite clearly.

It was the painter's *picture*. As the other spectators passed, they spoke of the coloring and the draughtsmanship; of the mellow glow of sunshine, which, faithful to the richness of southern summers, carried also a poetical hint of the air of glory in which genius lives alone. To some the graceful figure of Cimabue was familiar, but the new group round the picture saw only the shepherd lad. And if, as the spectators said, his eyes haunted them about the room, what ghosts must they not have summoned to haunt Mr. Ford's client as he gazed?

"Mais c'est Monsieur D'Arcy!" screamed the French governess. And Amabel said, "It's Bogy; but he's got no leaves." Lady Adelaide was quite composed. The likeness was very striking, but her maternal eyes saw a thousand points of difference between the Giotto of the painting and her son. "How very odd!" she said. "I wonder who sat for the Giotto? If he really were the boy Amabel thinks she saw in the wood, I think her Bogy and the model must both be the same as a wonderful child Mr. Ammaby was telling me about, who painted the sign of the inn in his village; but his father was a windmiller called Lake, and" —

"Mamma! mamma!" cried D'Arcy, "papa is ill."

The sound of his son's voice recalled Mr. Ford's client to consciousness; but it was a very partial and confused consciousness. He heard voices speaking of the heat, the crush, &c., as in a dream. He was not sure whether he was being carried or led along. The painting was no longer before him, but it mattered little. The shepherd boy's eyes were as dark as his own; but that look in their upward gaze, which stirred every heart, pierced his as it had moved it years ago from eyes the color of a summer sky. To others their pathos spoke of yearning genius at war with fortune; but for Mr. Ford's client they brought back, out of the past, words which rang more clearly in his ears than the condolences of the crowd, —

"You'll remember your promise, D'Arcy? You will be quite sure to take me home to bury me? And you will call my child after my father, — JAN?"

CHAPTER XLI.

THE DETECTIVE. — THE "JOOK." — JAN STANDS BY HIS MOTHER'S GRAVE. — HIS AFTER HISTORY.

AS he had resolved, the painter secured the help of the police in tracing Jan's pedigree. He did not take the bow-legged boy into his confidence, but that young gentleman recognized the detective officer when he opened the door for him; and he laid his finger by his snub nose, with a wink of intense satisfaction.

On hearing the story, the detective expressed his opinion (founded on acquaintance with Sal) that George's pocket had been picked by his companions, and not by chance thieves in the fair; and he finally proved his sagacity in the guess by bringing the pocket-book and the letter to the artist.

With his mother's letter (it had been written at Moerdyk, on her way to England) before them, Jan and the artist were sitting, when Mr. Ford's client was announced, and Jan stood face to face with his father.

The gentle reader will willingly leave a veil over that meeting, which the artist felt a generous shame to witness. With less delicacy, the bow-legged boy had lingered outside the door, but when the studio rang with a passionate cry, — "My son! my son!" — he threw his green baize apron over his head, and crying, "The jook!" plunged downwards into the basement, and shed tears of sympathy amongst the boots and bottles.

To say that Lady Adelaide forgave the past, and received her husband's son with kindness, is to do scant justice to the generous affection which he received from her. With pity for her husband mingled painful astonishment that he should have trusted her so little; but if the blow could never be quite repaired, love rarely meets with its exact equivalent in faith or tenderness, and she did not suffer alone. She went with Jan and his father to visit Master Lake, and her gracious thanks to the windmiller for his care of her step-son gave additional bitterness to her husband's memories of the windmill.

It was she who first urged that they should go to Holland. Jan's grandfather was dead, — Mr. Ford's client could make no reparation there, — but the cousin to whom the old wooden house now belonged gave Jan many things which had been his mother's. Amongst these was a book of sketches by herself, and a collection of etchings by her great-grandfather, a Dutch artist; and in this collection Jan found the favorite of his childhood. Did the genius in him really take its rise in the old artist who etched those willows which he had once struggled to rival with slate-pencil?

His mother's sketches were far inferior to his own; but with the loving and faithful study of nature which they showed, perhaps, too, with the fact that they were chiefly gathered from homely and homelike scenes, from level horizons and gray skies, Jan felt a sympathy which stirred him to the heart. His delight in them touched Lady Adelaide even more than it moved his father. But then no personal inconvenience in the past, no long habits of suffering and selfishness, blunted her sense of the grievous wrong that had been done to her husband's gifted son. Nor to him alone! It was with her husband's dead wife that Lady Adelaide's sympathies were keenest, — the mother, like herself, of an only child.

Mr. Ford's client went almost unwillingly to his wife's grave, by the side of which her old father's bones now rested. But Jan and Lady Adelaide hastened thither, hand in hand, and the painter's pledge was redeemed. Since the old man died, it had been little tended, and weeds grew rank where flowers had once been planted. Jan threw himself on the neglected grave. "My poor mother!" he cried, almost bitterly. For a moment the full sense of their common wrong seemed to overwhelm him, and he shrank even from Lady Adelaide. But when, kneeling beside him, she bent her face as if the wind that sighed among the grass stalks could carry her words to ears long dulled in death, — "My *poor* child! *I* will be a mother to your son!" — Jan's heart turned back with a gush of gratitude to his good stepmother.

He had much reason to be grateful: then, and through many succeeding years, when her training fitted him to take his place without awkwardness in society, and her tender care atoned (so she hoped) for the hardships of the past.

The brotherly love between Jan and D'Arcy was a source of great comfort to her. Once only was it threatened with estrangement. It was when they had grown up into young men, and each believed that he was in love with Amabel. Jan had just prepared to sacrifice himself (and Amabel) with enthusiasm to his brother, when D'Arcy luckily discovered that he and the playmate of his childhood were not really suited to each other. It was the case. The conventionalities of English society in his own rank were part of D'Arcy's very life, but to Amabel they had been made so distasteful in the hands of Lady Craikshaw that her energetic, straightforward spirit was in continual revolt; and it was not the least of Jan's merits in her eyes that his life had been what it was, that he was so different from the rest of the people amongst whom she lived, and that the interests and pleasures which they had in common were such as the world of fashion could neither give nor take away.

Withheld from sacrificing his affections to his brother, Jan joined with his father to cut off the entail of his property. "D'Arcy is your heir, sir," he said. "I hope to live well by my art, and GOD forbid that I should disinherit Lady Adelaide's son."

His great gift did indeed bring fortune as well as fame to our hero.

The Boys' Home knows this. It has some generous patrons (it should have many!), and first amongst them must rank the great painter who sometimes presides at its annual festival, and is wont on such occasions pleasantly to speak of himself as "an old boy."

More accurately entitled to that character is the bow-legged man-servant of another artist, — Jan's old master. These two live on together, and each would find it difficult to say whether pride and pleasure in the good luck of their old companion, or the never healed pain of his loss, is the stronger feeling in their kindly hearts.

Amabel was her father's heir, and in process of time Jan became the Squire, and went back to spend his life under the skies which inspired his childhood. But his wife is wont to say that she believes his true vocation was to be a miller, so strong is the love of windmills in him, and so proud is he of his Miller's Thumb.

At one time Mr. Ammaby wished him to take his name and arms, but Jan decided to keep his own. And it is by this name that Fame writes him in her roll of painters, and not by that of the old Squires of Ammaby, nor by the name he bore when he was a Child of the Windmill.

CHAPTER XLII.

CONCLUSION.

A SOUTH-WEST wind is blowing over the plains It drives the "messengers" over the sky, and the sails of the windmill, and makes the dead leaves dance upon the graves. It does much to dispel the evil effects of the foul smells and noxious gases, which are commoner yet in the little village than one might suppose. (But it is a long time, you see, since the fever was here.) It shows the silver lining of the willow leaves by the little river, and bends the flowers which grow in one glowing mass — like some gorgeous Eastern carpet — on Master Swift's grave. It rocks Jan's sign in mid-air above the Heart of Oak, where Master Chuter is waiting upon a newly arrived guest.

It is the man of business. Long has he promised to try the breezes of the plains for what he calls dyspepsia, and the artist calls "money-grubbing-on-the-brain," but he never could find leisure, until a serious attack obliged him to do so. But at that moment the painter could not leave London, and he is here alone. He has not said that he knows Jan, for it amuses him to hear the little innkeeper ramble on with anecdotes of the great painter's childhood.

"This ale is fine," says the man of business. "I never can touch beer at home. The painter is married, you say?"

"He 've been married these two year," Master Chuter replies. "And they do say Miss Amabel have been partial to him from a child. He come down here, sir, soon after his father took to him, and he draad out Miss Amabel's old white horse for her; and the butler have told me, sir, that it hangs in the library now. It be more fit for an inn sign, sartinly, it be, but the gentry has their whims, sir, and Miss Amabel was a fine young lady. The Squire's moral image she be; affable and free, quite different to her ladyship. Coffee, sir? No, sir? Dined, sir? It be a fine evening, sir, if you 'd like to see the church. I 'd be glad to show it you, myself, sir. Old Solomon have got the key."

In the main street of the village even the man of business strolls. There is no hurrying in this atmosphere. It is a matter of time to find Old Solomon, and of more time to make him hear when he is found, and of most time for him to find the key when he hears. But time is not money to the merchant just now, and he watches the western sky patiently, and is made sleepy by the breeze. When at last they saunter under the shadow of the gray church tower, his eye is caught by the mass of color, out of which springs a high cross of white marble, whose top is just flushed by the setting sun. It is of fine design and workmanship, and marks the grave where the great man's schoolmaster sleeps near his wife and child. Hard by, Master Chuter shows the "fever monument," and the names of Master Lake's children. And then, as Daddy Solomon has fumbled the door open, they pass into the church. The east end has been restored, the innkeeper says, by the Squire, under the advice of his son-in-law.

And then they turn to look at the west window,— the

new window, the boast of the parish, — at which even old Solomon strains his withered eyes with a sense of pride. The man of business stands where Jan used to sit. The unchanged faces look down on him from the old window. But it is not the old window that he looks at, it is the new one. The glory of the setting sun illumines it, and throws crimson lights from the vesture of the principal figure — like stains of blood — upon the pavement.

"It be the Good Shepherd," Master Chuter explains; but his guest is silent. The pale-faced, white-haired angels in the upper lights seem all ablaze, and Old Solomon cannot look at them.

"Them sheep be beautiful," whispers the innkeeper; but the stranger heeds him not. He is reading the inscription : —

To the Glory of GOD,
And the pious memory of Abel, my dear foster-brother:
I, who designed this window,
Dedicate it.

HE shall gather the lambs into His arms.